BLOOD TIES AND THE NA

NEW ANTHROPOLOGIES OF EUROPE

Michael Herzfeld, Melissa L. Caldwell,
and Deborah Reed-Danahay, *editors*

BLOOD TIES AND THE NATIVE SON

Poetics of Patronage in Kyrgyzstan

Aksana Ismailbekova

Indiana University Press

This book is a publication of

Indiana University Press
Office of Scholarly Publishing
Herman B Wells Library 350
1320 East 10th Street
Bloomington, Indiana 47405 USA

iupress.indiana.edu

♾ The paper used in this publication meets the minimum
requirements of the American National Standard for Information
Sciences—Permanence of Paper for Printed Library Materials,
ANSI Z39.48-1992.

Manufactured in the United States of America

Cataloging information is available from the Library of Congress.

ISBN 978-0-253-02528-9 (cloth)
ISBN 978-0-253-02539-5 (paperback)
ISBN 978-0-253-02577-7 (ebook)

1 2 3 4 5   22 21 20 19 18 17

Contents

Foreword: On Native Sons, Fake Brothers, and Big Men / Peter Finke *vii*

Acknowledgments *xiii*

Note on Transliteration *xvii*

List of Acronyms *xix*

Introduction: The Native Son and Blood Ties *1*

1 Kinship and Patronage in Kyrgyz History 22

2 Scales of Rahim's Kinship: Zooming In and Zooming Out 42

3 "Renewing the Bone": Kinship Categories, Practices, and
   Patronage Networks in Bulak Village 67

4 The Irony of the Circle of Trust: The Dynamics and Mechanisms
   of Patronage on the Private Farm 89

5 Patronage and Poetics of Democracy 112

6 The Return of the Native Son: The Symbolic Construction
   of the Election Day 134

7 Rahim's Victory Feast: Political Patronage and Kinship in Solidarity 155

Concluding Words: Native Son, Democratization, and Poetics
   of Patronage 181

Glossary of Local Terms 191

Bibliography 197

Index 211

Foreword

On Native Sons, Fake Brothers, and Big Men

IF I WERE to summarize this book in one sentence, I would probably proceed with something along the lines of "Aksana Ismailbekova has provided us with a wonderful and theoretically inspired ethnography on kinship and patronage in post-socialist Kyrgyzstan." If I were to add a second sentence, this would go on to elaborate on the impact of both institutions on local economics and on national politics. That is to say, one key argument of Ismailbekova is that in local understanding there is no contradiction between patronage and democracy, as most of the political science literature would want us to believe, but that both are intricately entangled and, to a certain degree, mutually supportive. And for the very same reason, neither kinship nor patronage necessarily disappear with the appearance of "modernity."

There would be nothing wrong with such a statement, but it would provide only a glimpse of what the author has to offer to the interested reader. All in all, this is what the book is all about, and it undoubtedly succeeds in making this point. In contrast to much of the recent scholarship, Ismailbekova shows us that patronage is neither an alternative path nor necessarily a contradiction to kinship but in the Kyrgyz case both institutions must be considered as closely interwoven and overlapping categories. This also implies that membership in either category is open to manipulative strategies to make things look neat and tight. Thus, definitions of kinship are stretched to include those linked in patron-client relationships, yet the latter are framed in a more hierarchical and reciprocal way than they actually are in order to correspond to social expectations of kin relations.

As such, one merit of this book is that it sets an important counterargument against scholarly as well as popular accounts of tribalism and clan politics in contemporary Central Asia. These all too often take a rather simplistic, and sometimes plainly wrong, concept of kinship and of local political processes as their starting point. And often they do not efficiently support their claims with, admittedly difficultly obtainable, data. Ismailbekova clearly shows, as have others before in less thorough ways, that on-the-ground patterns and motives for alliances are far more complex and flexible. This is not to say that nepotism and corruption do not exist. But they come in a variety of forms that might more aptly be labeled as networks or cliques, thus stripping them of their putatively archaic nature and also highlighting their similarity to phenomena well known also in Western societies.

What Ismailbekova also demonstrates is that patronage in Kyrgyzstan in its current form is neither a traditional nor a new institution but one that underwent several metamorphoses in the course of its history. In particular, it thoroughly survived the socialist period, during which it achieved new meanings within the command chains of a planned economy and came out alive and well. It then proved even more to be a very valuable institution—though not for everyone in equal shares—in the period thereafter. Today, possibly more than ever, patronage should be seen, so Ismailbekova, as a coping mechanism that provides guideline and support in times of economic shortage and social instability.

The "native son" is thus a superb ethnography of the transformation period in Kyrgyzstan. It touches in particular on the economic and political aspects of this process that has so fundamentally changed the lives of millions of people in the former Soviet Union. With mass unemployment and increasing poverty after independence, people have faced a situation of great insecurity. Newly emerging forms of patronage seemed one way for at least some economic and social safety—and a pathway for entrepreneurially minded individuals to use them for their own ambitious plans. The fact that these new structures became heavily interwoven with traditional kinship structures, on the one hand, and new forms of parliamentary democracy, on the other, is, in the author's reading, a concession to both the existing institutional and moral understanding, as well as to the challenges and international expectations ahead.

Ismailbekova analyzes and explains her material in a sophisticated way by making use of a somewhat unorthodox yet fruitful cocktail of theoretical ideas. Her starting point is in studies on identification and the rationale as to why actors ally themselves with specific others, and the price they have to pay for those alliances. This is complemented by borrowings from new institutional economics and the theory of social poetics. The occurrences in Kyrgyzstan are, of course, first of all a process of institutional change affecting all aspects of society. People thus have to adapt to new rules while simultaneously trying to influence the direction these changes take in order to better support their individual aims. In such processes there are inevitably winners and losers when compared with the previous distribution of benefits. And any change of rules is equally inevitably an obstacle for creating or maintaining societal trust and cooperation, as both rely to a certain degree on the stability of mutual expectations. To describe this phenomenon, institutional analysis in general and bargaining theory in particular seem perfectly adequate tools. And, in turn, patronage is a highly illustrative institutional device for the ongoing transformation process in post-socialist Kyrgyzstan. Yet how people manipulate and promote specific institutional pathways of change is influenced by traditional understandings of doing things the

appropriate way. To describe this, Ismailbekova utilizes the concept of social poetics, basically saying that manipulative rhetoric people use to persuade others to
support their aims must be embedded in existing perceptions of appropriateness.

But anthropology always subsists not only of good theorizing but also of
skillful and engaged ethnography. Here, Ismailbekova's book is also in the best
tradition of our discipline. Fieldwork was not always easy, as she explicates in her
introduction, owing to the fact that her status as a native of Kyrgyzstan and a
young mother did not make her, in the eyes of informants, the natural person to
do the kind of work she did. Much of the research was in fact teamwork with her
husband, Rufat, who accompanied and supported her. And while Kyrgyzstan is
certainly not a "typical" Muslim society, wherever one would find such one, and
gender relations are less strict than in other places in the region, to stay there as a
couple enriches the insights one gets enormously.

As a book, *Blood Ties and the Native Son* is borne by a special dramaturgy,
organized around a somewhat dubious character, the patron Rahim, and analyzes the specific economic and social configurations that develop out of the system he is able to establish. I will not give a detailed summary of the individual
chapters, as Ismailbekova does so in her own introduction, but will pick up a few
aspects that illustrate the strengths of the book. After laying out the theoretical
and methodological framework the ethnography itself starts with two chapters
on kinship and patronage in Kyrgyzstan. While the first provides more of a historical overview, the second introduces the reader for the first time into village
life and its everyday practices. Important to note here is that Ismailbekova takes
an intermediate stand regarding the segmentary lineage model so debated these
days in anthropology. While recognizing the limitations that earlier functional-
ist approaches had in this matter, she is—for good reasons—equally skeptical
of the deconstructivist undertaking of Sneath and Gullette, who claim that the
idea of a patrilineal kinship organization for Central Asian societies, such as the
Kyrgyz one, is more anthropological myth than reality. Obviously, ideas about
descent and lineages are socially or culturally constructed, yet like everything
else human societies take as their respective charter, but once created they are
all too real in their relevance for people's lives and as part of the political system.
This is certainly the case, as Ismailbekova describes, for the Kyrgyz in her study,
where social organization is based on the extensive knowledge of putative genealogical relationships. Manipulations do exist, but they take place within the rules
of the game in order to be acceptable and legitimate. One particularly striking
case is the process by which Rahim's lineage is turned into a noble one (a concept
largely absent from traditional Kyrgyz society), partly referring to his half-Kazak
background (where such a nobility does exist). The complementary takes place
when Rahim, lacking other close patrilineal kin, successfully uses his sisters and
female cousins by marrying them to important clients.

From here on the author moves to the implementation of a patronage system in the two villages where she carried out her fieldwork, Bulak and Orlovka. This is, on the one hand, the story of a former socialist enterprise, now dismantled and leaving people with little to make a living and, on the other hand, the rise of Rahim as a patron who brings new life into the settlement. He does so, however, in ways that do not necessarily make him the most likable person conceivable. Basically, after acquiring the enterprise, he decides that the inhabitants of the village seem unreliable to him and thus replaces them as a workforce with people from a neighboring settlement belonging to the same lineage as himself. These people now form the nucleus of the patron-client network, or "circle of trust," as it is called by Ismailbekova. The metaphor is so straightforward that it hardly needs explanation, but it points to the crucial role of patronage in times of crisis, namely, that of a coping mechanism based on solidarity within and mistrust toward the outside. This induces people to accept patronage in spite of its hierarchical character because it provides a means of access to resources. Needless to say, it also implies that there are people who are not part of the circle and thus less convinced of its usefulness and legitimacy.

The following three chapters each deal with specific events illustrating the workings of a patronage system and explain the broader dynamics of which it is part. It begins with a day in Bulak village where two parties oppose each other on the construction of a mosque. Rahim had other plans with the location and was able to find majorities to support him. This is the first time Ismailbekova utilizes the concept of social poetics in respect to Rahim's sophisticated manner to appeal to ideas of direct democracy (voting by a show of hands) and to the threat of Islamic radicalism about to spread. He is also able to manipulate the local state officials to either support him or stay away from the scene. This is followed by a description of the Election Day that results in Rahim gaining a seat in the national parliament (for the Social Democratic Party!). A lot of peculiar things take place from the perspective of Western democratic thinking, culminating in votes being bought and ballots being carried around by people who shouldn't until someone unduly completes them and throws them into the box. The line of events ends with a vivid description of the day after the elections, when Rahim throws a big feast to celebrate his victory as an affirmation of his position vis-à-vis his clients. To accommodate all his supporters and allure his future allies, he violates many of the etiquettes of a traditional Kyrgyz banquette, again using his social poetic skills to make people accept a bending of rules, for example, by seating guests according to their usefulness for his campaign rather than their social status.

As mentioned in the first lines of this foreword, all in all this is a book about kinship and patronage as interlinked institutions in contemporary Kyrgyzstan. It is thus also a history of changing social relations during Soviet and post-Soviet times when patronage came to achieve a new meaning in economic and political

life. Central to Ismailbekova's argument here is the role it has in the young democratization process in the country. In other words, is patronage part of the
problem or a reaction against a corrupt and already dysfunctional system? The
native son thus becomes a metaphor for an emic understanding of legitimate political representation. Who else if not one's patron and/or patrilineal kin would
care for one's needs and sorrows? And as everyone else acts in very much the
same ways, this is not only a smart strategy but also one morally justified. After
all, in democratic elections people are equally expected to give their vote to the
one they believe to act on their behalf.

But there is more to the story and analysis that provides insights for anthropological questions of an even more fundamental nature. The background to Rahim's rise and fall is, of course, the process of rapid social change in post-socialist
Kyrgyzstan. The ongoing disruptions and uncertainties have enabled people like
him to attain a position of power and status that would have been unthinkable
just a few years earlier. Thus, while such a patronage system may not necessarily
be representative for all rural Kyrgyzstan, the present conditions enable the rise
of people like Rahim in various places. Certainly, hierarchies and inequalities
existed before as well, but these were of a different nature and much more embedded in a (more or less) formalized structure. It is the specific post-socialist situation when the institutional framework and the corresponding punishments or
rewards for individual behavior were reconfigured overnight, thus allowing Rahim to become the kind of patron he was. In traditional Kyrgyz society he would
have been a usurper, during the socialist regime probably a criminal. Now, in a
situation of instability and social unrest, the circle of trust becomes an accepted
and welcomed way to deal with crises.

But the consequent fall of Rahim is an equal important lesson not only for
other Kyrgyz entrepreneurs who would like to follow a similar line but also for
anthropological thinking. What happens to patrons in a society where that particular way of acting is possible, enabled by specific historical configurations but
not embedded in the overall structure or ideology? To whom shall his clients turn
in search of a new safety network after the circle of trust collapses? There is little
historical precedence, at least in the living memories of people, on the thresholds
of acceptance or repudiation for usurping acts like the one Rahim committed.
And there is no socially proper way to remove people like him while maintaining
the system as such. If we compare his position and fate with classic anthropological accounts of Big Men or similarly organized societies, the new type of patron
in Kyrgyz society that Rahim represents lacks the necessary institutional character. Therefore, rise and fall, function and acceptance are not predictable, neither
for himself nor for anyone else.

Ismailbekova's book is a very important contribution to contemporary
Central Asian studies, dealing with a region that she describes as a "laboratory

of social change." Rahim is described here as a product as well as a motor of rapid institutional change so typical for post-socialist societies. As such it is illuminative both in its representative as well as in its exceptional aspects. As a much-needed adjustment to a dominant view expressed in much of the recent literature on statehood, tribalism, and clan politics, her description of the workings of patronage on the ground shows that things are much more complex when considered in detail. In contrast to these top-down approaches, she illuminates the individual motives, social constraints, and normative orders out of which people act and decide. This is ethnography in the best sense, and were it not for all the other merits described above, it would alone be reason enough to welcome this book.

—Peter Finke

Acknowledgments

My deepest acknowledgments go to my informants in Kyrgyzstan with whom I talked so many hours and followed across various settings. Thank you for spending those hours with me, for hot tea, and for delicious food. I am thankful especially for people's support and care. I was treated as an honored young guest, but the times people reminded me of my place in the community were helpful, as well.

Special thanks are due to several informants. Rahim's grandmother, Gulas *apa*, met me with wonderful memories, openness, kindness, and good treatment whenever I visited her. Eki, with astonishing generosity, openness, and trust, helped me collect deep and precise information, asking in return only that I include his name in this book. Dulan, one of the village chairmen, and Osmon, a milk collector, offered me their trust and much information. Thank you to Bakygul *eje*, for your hospitality. For the collection of genealogies, I would like to thank Jumagul *baike*. Even in a cold house, surrounded by several grandchildren, he offered his time, hospitality, and knowledge to me late into the nights. As my research developed to focus on the particular networks that surrounded Rahim, the trust of those who were close to him became critical; I remain astonished by the loyalty, gratitude, and trustworthiness Rahim's circle demonstrated toward him. My thanks are due also to Rahim himself for the interest he showed in my research and for having granted his permission to visit his private farm and events that he organized.

This work has benefited from the enormous support of academic disciplines and knowledgeable people in their respective fields, each of whom I would like to thank in turn. Because it originated in my doctoral research, I must express first my utmost appreciation to Dr. Günther Schlee at the Max Planck Institute for Social Anthropology in Halle (Saale), Germany. His ideas and thinking have greatly enlightened and penetrated my research and writing. Second, to Dr. Peter Finke at the University of Zurich, who led me to field research and helped me to build an academic career. Third, to Dr. Thomas Hauschild from the Martin Luther University Halle-Wittenberg for his interest in my project and critical comments, especially those directed at the concept of patronage. Dr. Michael Herzfeld has been a champion of this work from before it began: first by inspiring my courage to pursue social poetics in a course he taught as a visiting scholar at the summer school, "Building Anthropology in Eurasia," in Bishkek organized by Aida Alymbaeva and John Schoeberlein; second by reading my dissertation and—again—galvanizing my courage to go forward.

There are many other esteemed people who contributed to my field research and the original writing up with their knowledge, experience, and contacts. Dr. John Eidson, Dr. Joachim Görlich, Dr. Patrick Heady, and Dr. James Carrier became my best critics; these chapters could not have been written without their critical comments and discussions. Dr. Roland Hardenberg generously discussed problems that arose during my fieldwork, asked stimulating questions at the regional Central Eurasian Studies Society (CESS) conference, and read several of the original chapter drafts.

My field research was generously funded by the Max Planck Institute for Social Anthropology, and the Graduate School Society and Culture in Motion provided an initial writing-up fellowship. Funds for language editing also came from the Max Planck Institute for Social Anthropology. The Zentrum Moderner Orient (ZMO) in Berlin gave me the opportunity to transform the original manuscript into this book during my time as a postdoctoral researcher in the Crossroads Asia Competence Network Project. I would like to thank all my colleagues at ZMO for important interdisciplinary discussions, especially Privatdozent Dr. Dietrich Reetz, Prof. Ulrike Freitag, Dr. Mato Bouzas, Dr. Just Boedecker, Privatdozent Dr. Nora Lafi, and Dr. Hagen Findeis, among many others.

My utmost gratitude also goes to friends and colleagues who shared ideas and helped me in numerous ways during the years of research and writing. These are, namely, Aida Alymbaeva, Brian Donahoe, Eva-Marie Dubuisson, Eliza Isabaeva, Eeva Keskula, Jeanne Féaux de la Croix, Judith Beyer, John Schoeberlein, Milena Baghdasaryan, Malgorzata Biczyk, Mateusz Laszczkowski, Madeleine Reeves, Nathan Light, Nino Aivazishvili, Rebecca Reynolds, Rano Turaeva, Sophie Roche, Sergei Abashin, and Svetlana Jacquesson.

I also want to take the opportunity to thank Jennifer Cash for generously offering advice and criticism, helping turn the dissertation into a book, and outstanding language editing of the book. Anja Neuner and Anett Kirchhof helped repeatedly find necessary books and articles on time; Jutta Turner made the maps; Oliver Weihmann provided a variety of forms of technical assistance; and Cornelia Schnepel helped me with the manuscript preparation. Two anonymous reviewers provided invaluable guidance in the final shaping of the story told here about patronage and kinship in Kyrgyzstan, and how it relates to wider discussions in anthropology, political science, and area studies. I would like to thank, also, my editors Gary Dunham and Rebecca Tolen and their assistants Janice Frisch and Mollie Ables for their invaluable organizational assistance and help in preparing the final manuscript. I would like to acknowledge that I used portions of previous publications with Routledge, Indiana University Press, and the *Anthropology of East Europe Review* in this book.

Many personal thanks are due to my family and close family friends. These are especially to my father for his support and to my mother for her knowledge, understanding, and love. My mother-in-law took care of my son, who was born during the fieldwork. My father-in-law understood and supported us whenever possible. My brother, Askat, and sisters, Aida, Zina, Raya, Eliza, and Umut, have also provided endless support and encouragement. Professional life in Germany would not have been possible without Thomas and Claudia Sprung, who have been wonderful friends and introduced us to German village life.

I could not have written this book without my husband. Rufat Sultanaliev contributed his time, love, support, and constant encouragement. In the field, he helped me collect information that was invisible to female eyes. Thank you, Rufat, for your sharp eyes and communicative skills. I know you are a brilliant researcher. Finally, thanks go to my son, Akbar, and daughter, Aikümüsh, for making us happy. This book is dedicated to my family.

In the face of so much practical, moral, and intellectual support, I alone retain responsibility for any shortcomings in this book or the research on which it is based.

Note on Transliteration

Fɪᴇʟᴅᴡᴏʀᴋ ᴡᴀꜱ ᴄᴏɴᴅᴜᴄᴛᴇᴅ mostly in Kyrgyz language. Kyrgyz (Turkic language) Fieldwork was also conducted in Russian language. The Soviet linguists standardized the Kyrgyz language in the early Soviet years three times.[1] The first alphabet was Arabic, but this alphabet was not widely spread in pre-Soviet Kyrgyz Autonomous Republic because the representatives of higher social strata were literate that time. However, in 1927 Latin alphabet became the official alphabet of the Kyrgyz Autonomous Republic. Only in 1941 was the Cyrillic alphabet officially introduced by the Soviet Union with the aim to speed up the process of the acquisition of Russian language by Kyrgyz (Chotaeva 2005, 137–140). The translation of Kyrgyz (and Russian) words follow the standard American Library Association and Library of Congress Romanization Tables: Transliteration Schemes for Non-Roman Scripts (ALA-LC).[2]

As the Kyrgyz language knows phonemes that are absent in Russian, I use the following additions to the ALA-LC standard: Ө = Ö; Y = Ü; Ң = Ng. For example: Kyrgyz Y (pronounced as a long *u*, as in "rude") is transliterated as Ü. Kyrgyz Ө is rendered as Ö and is pronounced much like the German Ö (for example, Möhren). The words in italics are in Kyrgyz, both in the plural and singular forms. The words in (R) italics stand for the Russian language. Usually my informants used both languages, Russian and Kyrgyz, during the interview.

Notes

1. UCLA Language Material Projects (Kyrgyz language section), www.lmp.ucla.edu /profile.aspx?langid=62&menu=004 (accessed January 28, 2011).
2. Library of Congress and the American Library Association, ALA-LC Romanization Tables, www.loc.gov/catdir/cpso/romanization/russian.pdf (accessed January 28, 2011).

Acronyms

Acronym	Category
SDP	Social Democratic Party
NGO	Nongovernmental organization
NIE	New Institutional Economics
R	Russian
K	Kyrgyz
F	Father
B	Brother
M	Mother
Z	Sister
W	Wife
S	Son
D	Daughter
FBS	Father's brother's son
FBD	Father's brother's daughter
FBW	Father's elder brother's wife
FZC	Father's sister's children
MBS	Mother's brother's son
MB	Mother's brother
FS	Father's son
MS	Mother's son
ZC	Sister's children
FB	Father's brother

BLOOD TIES AND THE NATIVE SON

Introduction

The Native Son and Blood Ties

I̅t was cold on December 2, 2007, when I ran into Kanybek, a Kyrgyz man of thirty-five, on a crowded public minibus at the bus station in Tokmok, a small town in northern Kyrgyzstan. Both of us were on our way to Kyrgyzstan's capital, Bishkek. I already knew Kanybek—we first met when I visited his house in June 2007. When Kanybek got on the minibus, he saw me and sat next to me. Kanybek told me that he was on his way to Bulak, his native province. It was election time in Kyrgyzstan, and all the political parties were broadcasting their campaign messages over the radio. Sitting together on the minibus, we listened to the conversation of the local radio correspondents, which got us talking about the upcoming elections and the two leading parties. The Social Democratic Party (SDP) was commonly referred to as the party of northern Kyrgyzstan, while Ak-Jol Party was considered the southern party.

With great pride, Kanybek began telling me what he did for a living. He was a marketing and trade specialist for a large private company called Nurmanbet, which was located in Bishkek and specialized in various services related to marketing. Kanybek's boss, Rahim, was the president of Nurmanbet and one of Kyrgyzstan's leading businessmen. Kanybek told me that Nurmanbet was named after Rahim's ancestor, and had been in operation for only ten years. I had heard that Nurmanbet was one of the most prosperous companies in the country. According to Kanybek, Rahim's success both as a politician and as a businessman was due to his ability to adapt quickly to new situations. By buying a small piece of land, establishing a niche in the market, and slowly extending both his land-holdings and his market share, he had built the business up from the ground.

Keen to protect his business interests, Rahim had decided to become a member (*deputat*) of parliament. During the election campaign, Nurmanbet's workers were sent to their native northern villages as well as to southern Kyrgyzstan to campaign for the SDP. As a "responsible person" (*joopkerchiliktuu*) and a native of Bulak Province, Kanybek was assigned to go to the village of Bulak, the administrative center of the province, to promote his boss and SDP. As part of this task, he would fix the roof of the village school and build a bridge for the villagers with money given to him by Rahim. Kanybek was happy to take on these charges because it enabled him to visit his home village and to do something useful there, all the while representing his boss. At the same time, it provided him with the opportunity to increase his own status within Nurmanbet as his boss's representative in the village. Kanybek was hoping to recruit his kinsmen to help the campaign and to spread the word about Rahim's achievements in business and politics and his grand plans for the future.

On the road Kanybek showed me several copies of a recently published local history book that he was going to distribute in the village. The book told the story of the history of Bulak and was full of the genealogies and mythological stories about the famous ancestor Nurmanbet, for whom Rahim's company had been named. With the book Kanybek sought to show that he, the villagers, and Rahim all issued from the same lineage. Kanybek hoped that the book would generate support for Rahim in the elections, as people would be keen to support their "native son." While we were on the bus, Kanybek pointed to a genealogical chart with his finger and showed me how Rahim and he were related, just as he planned to show the villagers.

I found it odd that when Kanybek spoke about his tasks and responsibilities, he sometimes referred to Rahim as an elder brother (*baike*), and sometimes as a father (*ata*). Unlike in English usage, Kyrgyz kin terms are often extended to incorporate individuals who are not related through blood or marriage. The term *baike* is especially common and does not always refer to an actual brother. However, I was confused that Kanybek switched between the terms *baike* and *ata*; what kind of a relation did he have with Rahim? Kanybek explained that he used to call Rahim *baike*, but when Kanybek married, Rahim became his *ököl ata* (representative father).[1]

Kanybek supported SDP because it was his boss's party and because his interests coincided with those of his boss. Kanybek was loyal to his boss, who in return protected and guaranteed Kanybek's security and well-being. In fact, Rahim had supported Kanybek for many years. He had bought Kanybek some land in Bishkek on which to build a house; he had purchased the kind of shipping container used for local market stalls (sometimes stacked two high) so that Kanybek could build and open a stall in the bazaar as an extension of Nurmanbet's many activities. Rahim had also promised to cover the future educational expenses of Kanybek's three school-age children. Kanybek told me that Rahim was like a father to him, and quoted two well-known proverbs to illustrate their special relationship: *Atam ölsö ölsün, atamdy körgön ölbösün* ("May my father die, but not the person who saw him"; that is, "May my father's reputation outlast him"); and *Ökül ata öz ata, örkündöp össün kainata* ("My representative father is my father, and may my father-in-law be prosperous").[2] In return Kanybek was obliged to support Rahim during his election campaign and to carry out certain tasks for him, although this obligation was never explicitly stated. To attract support from his fellow kinsmen and keep hold of the power he had, Rahim, as a responsible (*joopkerchiliktuu*) businessman and future parliamentarian, sought to understand their needs.

The encounter with Kanybek led me to think about patron-client relationships, a term anthropologists might use to describe the relationship between Rahim and Kanybek. How, I wondered, do actors like Rahim secure the support of people like Kanybek? And, conversely, how do "clients" secure the support of their "patrons"? In the case of rural Kyrgyzstan, patron-client relationships are set within a framework of the kinship system (and its terminology) and future promise. Kanybek told me, "The Kyrgyz are quick at making kinsmen, but for that we need to know the proper ways." In practice, however, establishing a patron-client relationship is not so easy. Such relationships need to be legitimized and accepted by community members. This not only requires that patrons and clients demonstrate their shared lineage identity, for which genealogies play a crucial role, but in some cases may also require manipulative strategies and various symbolic actions, such as Kanybek's recitation of the proverbs mentioned above (cf. Schlee and Sahado 2003). Patronage relations manipulate and exploit other forms of social organization and values, but both patrons and clients actively participate in this manipulation, conspiring to somehow render the relationship a moral one. How do such manipulations inform the intertwined processes of political and economic transition or "development" in post-Soviet Kyrgyzstan?

Biography of Rahim

Based on a total of fourteen months of ethnographic fieldwork (March 2007–April 2008) in rural northern Kyrgyzstan, this book tells the story of the rise and fall of a man I call Rahim, an influential and powerful patron, and of how his relations with clients and kin shaped the economic and social life of the region. At the time of my research, Rahim had been building his role of native son for about five years. In this book, as in real life, Rahim is a man who wore many hats. He is the manager of an agricultural enterprise; a businessman with many other interests, some of which involved dubious financial arrangements; a local politician and successful candidate for parliament; and, most important, an active and influential member of a lineage that is extensively represented in one of the northern provinces of the country. Rahim's patronage network was effective—at least until his murder in 2008—because it was sustained by the many kinsmen and allies who were actively engaged in and benefitted from it. The spectacularity of Rahim's rise and fall was unusual even in the first decade of the 2000s, when such a trajectory seems to have marked a particular moment in the "transition" between the last generation of Kyrgyz leaders who were fully socialized during the Soviet period and younger generations who have been fully socialized in the post-Soviet period.

During the time of my field research, nearly a dozen prominent businessmen-politicians and public figures were killed in Kyrgyzstan. These men—who included Medet Sadyrgulov, Jyrgalbek Surabaldiev, Bayaman Erkinbaev, Sanjar Kadyraliev, Usen Kudaibergenov, Bahtiar Amirjanov, Tynychbek Akmatbaev, and Raatbek Sanatbaev—had profiles quite similar to Rahim's. Remarkably, all were of similar age and had been evidently supported in business and recruited into politics by highly placed individuals of the last Soviet generation. These older individuals saw the need for change and new forms of democracy in Kyrgyzstan; while the younger men were especially bright, talented, and energetic. The remarkableness of these younger men is especially noticeable, when considering that they were members of Kyrgyzstan's "lost generation" that was already in secondary school when Kyrgyzstan gained independence from the collapsing Soviet Union. These men initially followed the career paths imagined for them since childhood: they completed university studies in medicine, journalism, agriculture, and similar fields. Many of their cohort failed to navigate the new economic and political terrain with any success, and resorted in large numbers to petty trade, labor migration, and village farming. Rahim and other men like him were key in pioneering the "transition" from Soviet-style patronage networks to those of independent and democratic Kyrgyzstan. But they did not work alone: it is crucial to highlight the kin relationships and cooperation that developed between old Soviet patrons and new young patrons as evidence of both continuity and transformation in the post-socialist world (cf. Hann, Humphrey, and Verdery 2002; Köllner 2012)

I have drawn from the biographies of other murdered businessmen-politicians to partially anonymize Rahim himself. Maintaining the full anonymity of people and places, however, is neither possible nor wholly desirable. In some cases, informants wanted their real names included in this book; I have respected their wishes. In other cases, it has been important to convey the specific symbolic dimensions of geography and ancestral lineages in contemporary politics. And in yet other cases, the identity of public figures is too singular and well known to disguise. In such instances, I have revealed nothing about these individuals' selves or activities (however legally dubious) that has not been widely reported by local media. Whenever possible, however, I have disguised the names and identities of villagers. My intent is to tell the story of how local and national politics are connected through the intimacy of kinship without yet exposing the intimacy of personal lives.

During my year of fieldwork, I observed the activation of Rahim's patronage networks during the parliamentary electoral campaign that culminated in December 2007. By the time I met him, Rahim had become the leader of the whole SDP in Kyrgyzstan. Rahim was not only the favorite politician among Bulak villagers; he was also a fellow villager and a local "big man" to whom most constituents were linked through patronage relations. While villagers acknowledged that such relationships could call the validity of the election process into question, it was their active participation and moral investment in the event as such that constituted their sense of being part of this larger collective project called "democracy."

According to an election brochure from 2005, he graduated from the Medical Academy of Bishkek in 1998 with a distinction. He then enrolled at Kyrgyz State National University to study law, graduating from there in 2002. From 2000 to 2005 he worked as a surgeon at the institute of Ministry of Internal Affairs. His immediate family consisted of his grandmother, mother, sister, wife, and two sons.

Rahim's representative father, boss, and patron was Turgunbek, Kyrgyzstan's minister of public health. Before becoming his representative father, Turgunbek helped his "younger brother" Rahim by appointing him as a government official. In 2005 the prime minister of the Kyrgyz Republic appointed Rahim president of the Fund for Entrepreneurship Development and Crediting (R. *Fond razvitia predprinimatelstvo i kreditirovanie v Kyrgyzskoi Respubliki*). Rahim managed this fund for eighteen months and, together with his colleagues, contributed some 3.4 million som to the state budget.[3] In the election of 2007, which I detail in later chapters, Rahim became a parliamentarian, gaining direct access to state decision making, on issues of concern to villagers in the domains of agriculture, water, land, and electricity. With his election, Rahim's control expanded over village- and provincial-level access to jobs, education, hospital treatment, and relations with the police.

Rahim's business activities were similarly strong. Although elected deputies of the parliament are prohibited from engaging in entrepreneurial activities, there are many legal ways for them to continue business. For example, upon election, Rahim nominated his business to his wife. His holdings included a farm and canning factory in the village of Orlovka; the security agency "Ajax," the company "Niet-service," and one of the biggest construction companies in Kyrgyzstan, "Bishkek Kurulush." In addition, he operated a milk-export business in the Chüi Valley. According to my informants, Rahim's mother was ethnically Kazak, and his relatives across the border in neighboring Kazakhstan occupied "high positions." These relatives enabled Rahim to export milk to Kazakhstan with Kazakh companies, thus circumventing otherwise prohibitive tariffs.

The style of patron-client relations that Rahim employed is not necessarily representative of politicians or businessmen in Kyrgyzstan generally. Rahim was smart and ruthless; he manipulated and influenced his followers. In some villages there are stronger leaders who are more manipulative and authoritative than Rahim. In other villages one cannot find any obvious leaders at all. Patronage networks, therefore, vary from one case to another, depending on the patrons' interests, political motivations, and personal qualities. Patronage networks are widespread across Kyrgyzstan; they link local village life with national politics and economic developments, and they shape regional loyalties and constitutions. Generally speaking, the patronage networks of Kyrgyzstan in the early 2000s were like Rahim's in making heavy use of kinship relations and idioms. Such networks are the result of the rapid institutional changes that took place in Kyrgyzstan in 1991.

Politics, Patronage, and Kinship

This book is a study of kinship, patronage, and politics in Kyrgyzstan. For twenty-five years, political scientists have been concerned that corruption, nepotism, and patron-client relations would forestall democratization in Kyrgyzstan, but they have lacked convincing data about the role of kinship systems, genealogical relations, and local political practices. This book is an ethnographic study that investigates the intersection of kinship relations with political patronage. In it, I reveal how extensive kinship relations have enabled democratization, even as they also facilitate the forms of patronage that preclude the individuation of political opinion and action. At a theoretical level, *Blood Ties and the Native Son* reopens questions that political scientists and anthropologists once asked together, but that anthropologists abandoned with their critique of the modernization paradigm of development studies.

I use the term *patronage* to denote a social institution whereby two or more actors enter into a relationship characterized by trust, exchange, and mutual benefit that is nevertheless asymmetrical in the sense that the patron benefits more from the relationship than do the clients. Patronage provides safety for clients in times of uncertainty; a patron selectively distributes employment to and exchanges favors with his clients. Patronage has a contradictory nature: it combines inequality with the promise of reciprocity, and voluntarism with coercion. Bargaining power in the relationship depends on both symbolic and instrumental resources (Roniger 1994b).

Anthropologists have generally considered that patron-client relations function as a substitute for kinship, enabling people to access resources that would otherwise be inaccessible (Blok 1974; Eisenstadt and Roniger 1980, 1984; Foster 1961, 1963; Gellner and Waterbury 1977). Within the broader social sciences, dependence on both kin and patronage has been expected to decrease with the advent of "modernity"—that is, economic development and democratization. In post-socialist Central Asia, and Kyrgyzstan specifically, none of these assumptions hold true. In part this may because there are no emic concepts for patronage in the Kyrgyz language.[4] Rather, people tend to use kinship terminology when discussing practices, behaviors, and relationships that resemble patronage networks. When pressed, people distinguish kinship relations from those of patronage—so they are clearly not the same thing—but the categories are definitely complementary.

In Kyrgyzstan kinship and patronage are better seen as overlapping categories. Clients are recruited from among kin; kinship relations are manipulated to legitimate patronage; and patrons and clients often perform their relation as one of kinship due to the segmentary lineage system (discussed in Chapters 2 and 3). People manipulate genealogies, negotiate kinship and lineage identities, and strategically employ local practices such as hospitality to recruit clients from among kin, legitimate or reinforce relationships of patronage, and achieve other ends. The flexibility of the segmentary lineage system makes it possible for kinship to be the foundation of patronage networks.

The result is that both kinship and patronage develop apace with democracy, and "traditional" social relations are strengthened, not eroded, by modernization. Patronage and kinship relations may prevent individuals from developing and expressing individual political positions, but they also constitute the primary mechanism through which liberal "democracy" has become embedded in local cultural and social practices in place of "socialism." Of course, relations of kinship and patronage also enabled the functioning of socialism during the Soviet period. Thus the story of post-Soviet political transformation is also one of how patrons, clients, and kin simultaneously reconfigured their relations under new and old paradigms; the Kyrgyz became "democrats" (and "capitalists") at the same time they reasserted their "Kyrgyz" way of relating.

The emergence of this particular kind of patronage network is closely related to the historical changes and sociopolitical dynamics that Kyrgyzstan has experienced since the collapse of the Soviet Union. The patron-client relationship as an informal institution existed in pre-Soviet times. It not only survived the Soviet period but also took on new forms and meanings within the socialist system by integrating into Communist Party and kolkhoz structures. In the post-socialist period, the patron-client relationship also adapted to help people survive in situations of massive crisis. Rural Kyrgyz society has what one might term a strong patrilineal kinship system, values, and ideology, but these have been changing over time. Notably, patrons like Rahim who could provide economic support and stability to individuals and entire villages have emerged, forming patronage networks in a slightly new form.

Earlier generations of anthropologists expected that patronage would lose relevance when processes of democratization were implemented (Foster 1961; Powell 1977). More recent episodes of democracy building, however, suggest that actors involved in patronage networks have proven themselves highly capable of quickly adapting to "democracy." Political scientists condemn this adaptation in the strongest terms: patronage and kinship loyalties, it is said, are "a pre-existing frame which corrupts 'pure' democracy" (Juraev 2008, 253). Yet there appears to be no such thing as a pure democracy. On the contrary, in the post-Soviet context, Kyrgyzstan's patronage networks have been intensified as a result of electoral party politics.

In the chapters to follow, I develop a broader argument about the ongoing significance of patronage in Kyrgyzstan. From an emic perspective, patronage relations do not so much hinder as facilitate electoral party politics. However "imperfect" local forms and practices might seem to be from the perspective of the Western ideal of democracy, we must understand how "electoral party politics" become embedded in local cultural and social practices. No matter how problematic the observed expansion of patronage in Kyrgyzstan may seem to be from the perspective of the Western ideal of democracy, both patrons and their clients can and often do support democratic reforms. My focus, then, is on the political dimensions of patronage both in the local setting and with respect to their impact on democratization processes.

The questions I address include the following: Why has patronage not disappeared with democratization? And why and how has it persisted? How can patronage practices exist within the framework of a democratic state? Why do people vote along the lines of kinship and patronage networks? And, finally, how far can kinship be stretched to build patronage networks?

Questioning Clan Politics?

In the Central Asian context, the ambiguous and manipulative behavior of social actors like Rahim has been described by political scientists in terms of an oversimplified notion of "clan politics" (Collins 2002; Luong 2002; Schatz 2004, 2005). As such, it is presented as detrimental to the development of democracy (Collins 2002, 2004; Juraev 2008; Khamidov 2006a; Radnitz 2005, 2006, 2007a, 2007b, 2010; Schatz 2000; Sjoberg 2011). The term *clan* has become popular in not only academic discourse. Political scientists, NGO workers, and journalists have adapted the term, along with several derived from studies of kinship and social organization (for example, *clan networks* and *tribalism*), to describe the "failure" of whole subregions and societies in Central Asia.

Even local scholars have their own terminology, such as *tribalism*, which carries negative connotations (Dzhunushaliev and Ploskikh 2000). Dzhunushaliev and Ploskikh (2000, 116), for example, warn that a revival of tribalism may lead to regionalism and separatism, endangering the integrity of the state. In recent years some anthropologists have criticized the use of *clan* as an analytical concept in political science, averring that it is misleading and has no empirical basis (Finke 2002; Gullette 2010; Hardenberg 2009; Jacquesson 2010c).

Anthropologists have based their criticism of "clan politics" in part on empirical research on kinship. Kyrgyz social organization is built on both the *uruk* (a small group of kinsmen who share a common ancestor five to seven generations removed) and *uruu* (a larger genealogical grouping that can include a number of *uruks*) (Gullette 2010; Hardenberg 2009; Jacquesson 2010c). These units might be glossed respectively as *clan* and *tribe*. Yet as David Gullette (2010) demonstrates, neither unit is an empirically observable group in the sense of cohesive bodies of people; they are categories of relatedness governed by genealogical narratives. The apparent cohesiveness of the *uruk* and *uruu* is created discursively as people relate through kinship; common political interests and loyalty may accompany this discursive relationship but not necessarily.

United in their critique of political scientists, anthropologists remain divided among themselves over how to best study Kyrgyz kinship. Hardenberg (2009, 45–46), for example, criticizes Gullette (2006) on three points: he argues that Gullette does not sufficiently analyze the symbolic system or actual kinship practices; he faults the work for being devoid of ethnography; and, finally, he says it is impossible to understand genealogical relatedness without attention to its application to social practices. In his own ethnographic study, Hardenberg comes to the conclusion that the Kyrgyz social order appears to be a variation of a segmentary system based on genealogical, territorial, and ritual relations. The Kyrgyz, he concludes, do have a preference for genealogical relations and distribute territory according to descent, and people share an immense interest in these matters.

Although Hardenberg and Gullette both expand the concept of kinship in Kyrgyzstan to embrace the possibility of subjective forms of belonging to *uruk* and *uruu* as "segmentary lines," neither succeeds in addressing the political aspects of kinship. My aim is to extend and contribute to this discussion by taking into account how people use kinship discourse for their own purposes by manipulating kinship for economic and political gain. However, I build on works that have proposed alternative analytical concepts for understanding Kyrgyz kinship (Gullette 2010; Hardenberg 2009; Jacquesson, 2010a, 2010b, 2010c). And I develop alternative ways to think about kinship and patronage through social poetics, manipulative strategies, and strategies of identification. How do political elites and their followers manipulate kinship for their own purposes? How are certain people excluded or included into kinship groupings? It is these unanswered questions that I attempt to address.

The Study of Patronage

The anthropological literature on patronage, both recent as well as older, displays two trajectories for understanding and interpreting the concept. First, in many studies, patronage and kinship are discussed as exclusively autonomous domains (for example, Blok 1974; Gellner and Waterbury 1977). Patronage literature through the 1960s and 1970s primarily concerns the relationship between landlords and servants, and it describes the selective, manipulative, and strategic behavior that characterizes these relations (Blok 1974; Foster 1961, 1963; Gellner and Waterbury 1977). On the surface, it seems to have little to do with social relations in post-socialist Kyrgyzstan, where "support" is often rendered among kin and not across class lines. I also recorded many positive attitudes toward patronage, which is described in terms of helping and supporting our "native son," even though patrons and clients each knew themselves and the other to be selective and manipulative.

The combination of positive feelings toward the "patron" and an awareness of mutual strategizing led me to works by John Campbell and Eric Wolf, who described the overlap between friendship and patronage. In John Campbell's study of the Sarakatsani, a group of transhumant Greek shepherds, he described how "the unique values inherent in the Sarakatsani moral order" successfully transformed "a mundane struggle for subsistence and economic survival into a social system predicated upon incessant status competition" (1974, 262). A powerful patron outside the community helped the Sarakatsani in their repeated dealings with the inflexible government by drawing on his extensive informal connections. In return the patron gained social prestige and sometimes votes from those he protected. Self-interest gave rise to and shaped the nature of patron-client relationships among the Sarakatsani, but they were bound by the local moral system (Campbell 1974). For his part, Wolf (1966, 16) explained how friendship premised on mutual help could generate patronage: "instrumental friendship reaches a point of imbalance such that one partner is clearly superior to the other in his capacity to grant goods and services, and thus friendship gives way to the patron-client tie."

Second, many social scientists from the 1960s–1980s (Eisenstadt and Roniger 1980, 1984; Foster 1961, 1963; Gellner and Waterbury 1977; Schmidt et al. 1977; Weingrod 1968) argued that patronage systems would disappear with increasing modernization. In these older discussions, anthropological insights on kinship and social organization were considered valuable to understanding large-scale political processes at the national level. In the intervening decades, patronage has come to be viewed as an old-fashioned concept within anthropology. However, later patronage has proved to be omnipresent and very adaptable worldwide (Roniger and Güneş-Ayata 1994; Roniger 1994a, 1994b). My book shows that in Central Asia, patronage has not merely survived or resisted change; it has changed in response to the demands and expectations of every new social reality that has appeared in the past century, including the introduction of the *kolkhoz* (collective farm) system, communist single-party rule, post-Soviet electoral party politics, the collapse of the USSR, and the introduction of a market economy. In rural Kyrgyzstan, patronage is a process that quickly adapts to new situations and incorporates new principles to give new meaning to old forms in times of transition. I provide case studies of patronage, and highlight patronage in the context of the Kyrgyz elections, the party system, and business.

Earlier anthropological concern emphasized how mixing patronage with politics gives the latter the feel of corruption (for example, Gellner 1977; Scott 1977a). According to Gellner (1977, 3), "patronage may not always and necessarily be illegal or corrupt, and it does have its own pride and morality; but though it may despise the official morality as hypocritical, fraudulent, or effeminate, it nevertheless knows that it is not itself the official morality." In a similar vein, Scott (1977b, 495) states that clientelism can be illuminated through studying corruption because patron-client ties sometimes involve "payoffs" to clients, brokers, and patrons that violate the formal law. Gellner and Scott wrote with the assumption that patronage operated only in restricted domains, and on principles other than those of "official morality," so that most people could recognize it as "corrupt" behavior. In rural Kyrgyzstan patronage is fraught with paradox: while perceived as manifesting itself in negative and selective behaviors, the patron-client relationship is underpinned by important cultural values such as respect and trust.

Since the old anthropological interest waned, social analyses of patronage have been sparse. The edited volume by Simona Piattoni (2001) demonstrates both the potentials and limitations of recent work. First, the volume expands geographic scope to address the evolution of clientelist practices in several Western European countries. Second, the contributors base their analyses on a neo-institutionalist approach; while this tightens analysis, it also overfocuses on the economic aspects of patronage. Similarly by focusing only on patronage within party politics and the institutions of "civil society," the concepts of both patronage and clientelism are stripped of their capacity to describe actual cultural practices and values. They even lose their individual meanings, as *patronage* is used interchangeably with *clientelistic politics*, and both tend to be associated with ambiguous and manipulative behavior (rather than social organization per se). In contrast to such a narrowing of focus, patronage is best understood by widening the scope of attention. The older authors all agree on three things: that the patron-client relationship by itself is a "narrow concept" (Kaufman 1974); that there is a lack of a strong explanatory theory on the phenomenon of patronage (Clapham 1982); and that patronage is interwoven with other phenomena (for example, social exchange and social networks).

The Genealogical Construction of Identity

To understand the behavior of the various social actors involved in patronage, I illustrate how kinship can be "stretched" by the patron and his kinsmen by manipulating genealogies and kinship terminologies for their own purposes. I then show the importance of the segmentary lineage system, and how the genealogical construction and negotiation of lineage identity can assist with the construction of patronage networks.

E. E. Evans-Pritchard (1940) produced the classic work on segmentary lineage systems with his study of the Nuer. The Nuer's social order was maintained through community values and a system of segmentary lineage. Thus, segmentation was the main principle of the lineage system, which was revealed by a clear relationship between kinship structure and political organization. A clan (*sib*) was divided into maximal, major, minor, and minimal lineages, each with its own distinctive name linking it to a single (mythological) ancestor. All individuals then traced their relationship to this ancestor through a unilateral descent system.

The segmentary lineage system was a locus of debate for many years, both in terms of its existence among the Nuer and its possible appearances elsewhere. Kuper (1982, 92) considered the model to be the invention of anthropologists without any understanding of social reality. He argued that Evans-Pritchard had not described the reality of Nuer social life but instead had provided a highly abstract account of the purported patterns of Nuer social organization (Kuper 1982). F. G. Bailey (2001, 48) described Evans-Pritchard's account as an imaginative construct of Nuer society. Numerous anthropologists were nevertheless influenced by Evans-Pritchard's work, and societies across the Middle East and North Africa were also determined to be segmentary. In the late 1980s, some criticized this model (for example, Caton 1987), while others continued to apply it with modification. For example, in his study of the Yemenite, Dresch (1986) applied Evans-Pritchard's segmentary lineage model, but differentiated between people's values and their actual behaviors. Dresch argued that segmentation is an expression of the local ideas and values that may lead to the formation of groups, but these remain far from corporate in character.

With respect to Central Asia, the interest in segmentary lineage systems has been linked to the study of pastoral nomadism. Khazanov (1984, 146) argued that the segmentary lineage system fit the historic forms of social organization among nomads in the region, and enabled these groups to subsist in the harsh Eurasian steppe environment by segmenting into sublineages and uniting again in times of need and mutual support. Others have agreed that the segmentary lineage system is pragmatic for multiple Central Asian peoples (Finke 2004; Hudson 1964; Werner 1997). But Khazanov himself (1984, 147–148), also distinguishes two complementary sides to segmentation among nomads: the ideological and practical.

The Central Asian system is usually described as a stratified segmentary lineage system because it consists of a vertical structure, unlike the egalitarian system that Evans-Pritchard described for the Nuer and Middle Eastern societies (Lindholm 1986, 341). In Central Asia, the genealogies incorporate generational

distance and birth order to both express and determine rank, legitimacy of seniority, and internal differentiation. The degree of hierarchy involved in the
Central Asian systems is contested, especially concerning the ethnic Kazakhs
(Finke 2004; Hudson 1964). The Kyrgyz kinship system combines genealogical
segmentation going back many generations with seniority, the differential status
of co-wives (the senior wife and younger wives called *tokol*), seventh-generation
marriage prohibition (exogamy), patrilocal residence, prestige and status of elder
uruu members, and solidarity group action in times of life cycle events (Abramzon 1960, 1971; Krader [1963] 1997, 1955; Hardenberg 2009, 61–62).

In the nineteenth century, ethnic Kyrgyz recognized patrilineal descent
when they formed corporate groups. In practice, patrilineal descent has not been
the sole active principle since the arrival of the Soviets (see more in Chapter 1).
Nevertheless, ancestors, patrilineage, and genealogies constitute identity for the
Kyrgyz, and are thus the repositories of political identity. Political identity is
formed through common patrilineal descent, as expressed through appealing to
one's genealogy. Thus the Kyrgyz claim that they should be able to name everyone in the previous seven generations of their lineage. This form of social organization has been customary and stable for many years; therefore, it is one that
the Kyrgyz people consider natural or given. The Kyrgyz themselves say that their
customs and beliefs have never changed: they originated with Kyrgyz ancestors
at the time that God sent them to the earth.

On the one hand, genealogies persist over time by virtue of people's representation or belief in them. On the other hand, owing to internal or external constraints, it becomes necessary to change the rules of genealogy formation to fit
the roles that people perform in Kyrgyz society. Over a long period of time social
actors reproduce the same form of genealogy, and decisions for change depend
on practicalities in the present time. From the point of view of the Kyrgyz people, genealogies are primordial, but I follow the view that identity is constructed
through historical or social processes. It is therefore possible to consider genealogy as a continuum and as bridging the gap between the inherited and the social.
Those who claim to share the same descent also consider themselves biologically
related; that is, that which is socially constructed is also represented as given.

Ethnic Kyrgyz construe their social world through the model of segmentary lineage. The lineage system is used to mark the degree and quality of relations among people. The social location of each Kyrgyz individual is defined
in terms of lineage and descent membership, which people usually showed me
through the use of genealogical charts, arguing that their main ancestor was
reckoned through patrilineal lines. Genealogy is of crucial importance in the
segmentary lineage system; however, it should not be expected to be an accurate
representation of either biology or history. As elsewhere, genealogies in Kyrgyzstan are socially constructed, manipulated according to the perceived interests

of individuals and groups, and subject to a continual process of contestation, negotiation, and redefinition (Baştuğ 1998; Bohannan 1952, 308–311; Humphrey 1979; Khazanov 1984; Schlee 2007; Shryock 1997). Genealogy is not to be taken as factual; instead, genealogies are contradictory and ambiguous (Baştuğ 1998, 101; Shryock 1997). In short, genealogies are social constructs in which both factual and fictional elements are taken into account. Thus the desirable connections are distinguished from undesirable connections, leading to both people's acceptance and denial of genealogical relations depending on the context in which their "connectivity" is considered. Genealogical connection also reemerges in times of need, just as it does elsewhere (Humphrey 1979; Schlee 2007; Shryock 1997).

There are, however, limits to the "identity work" in which individuals can engage. People are not free to claim kinship alliances without reasonable justification, and many lack the capacity to muster (or even imagine) alternative sets of relations to the ones they have always used. Schlee (2008) describes the motivations and limits to reconfiguring identity as double-sided:

> One has to do with concept and categories. The way in which people classify themselves and others tends to be of a systematic nature, and employs a certain logic and plausibility of structure. Wishing to be or not to be something is not enough; one also needs a plausible claim to an identity or a plausible reason for rejecting it. If plausible alternatives are lacking, one might be forced by one's own logic and the expectations of others to join the fight on a given side. The other type of reason concerns the advantages and disadvantages that may arise from such identifications and such decisions to take sides: in other words with the cost and benefits of taking sides. It is to be expected that the two types of reason interpenetrate each other. Where there is room for identity work, i.e. for people reasoning about their identities and changing them, categories can be expected to be replaced or stretched to fit the needs of actors. These needs often have to do with the size of a group or alliance: one either seeks a wider alliance or tries to keep others out, to exclude them for sharing in certain benefits. (2008, 15)

Schlee's (2008, 2009) perspective on identity work was developed with respect to how people align themselves during conflict situations, but it is more generally applicable to the processes of identification in kinship. Importantly, identity is manipulated when it is advantageous to do so and when there are plausible alternatives. The plausibility of an identity claim, however, is not determined by the claimant alone. In Kyrgyzstan a patron's claims to identity vis-à-vis other individuals or groups must meet certain widely known conventions to be plausible. Only a plausible leader can mobilize people or create solidarity. The patron and his kinsmen identify themselves using criteria of descent and genealogy as a source of identification within a system of patrilineal kinship. Drawing on extensive and profound genealogy based on oral tradition (*sanjyra*), there is clear evidence that among the Kyrgyz genealogy has long been manipulated—depending on the context and situation. That is, people were capable of narrowing or broadening their heritage but based on a shared scheme or model. The ways in which people identify themselves and their kin depend on the available resources and their specific interests, including the desire to establish patron-client relations. In such situations social actors creatively change the names of certain individuals in their genealogical chart. This change can be proven by genealogical data, and is validated by the local *sanjyrachi* (expert in genealogy).

The way in which genealogy is relationally constructed in rural Kyrgyzstan offers the possibility of extending kinship ties. This is done, of course, through marriage and contractual kinship. In the case study described in this book, the patron extended his kinship relations throughout the province by fostering relationships in the region and through his political party. These extended kin relations fostered communication and mutual support, creating a yet larger social network. The Kyrgyz say once an individual becomes wealthy and powerful his kinsmen begin to increase in number; as his kinship network increases in size, it strengthens the whole group. For the patron, the advantage of having many kinsmen is that he can mobilize a large group of people for political purposes. So in the harsh post-Soviet reality of Kyrgyzstan, wealth and political engagement have become complementary to one another. When an individual loses his wealth and powerful position, his circle of supportive kinsmen immediately decreases. Thus, in accordance with practical necessity and specific situations, a person's kinsmen decrease or increase in number.

Manipulative Strategies

In the following chapters, I pay close attention to the problems that seem to have bedeviled democratization processes worldwide for half a century or more. How is it that patronage persists through time as a component of the political system, even as it is transformed through the institutional development of political parties, civil society organizations, and other regulatory devices? Why do people continue to accept the legitimacy of patronage relations, despite their complaints about "corruption"? To answer these questions, I turn back to the insights of anthropologists such as Bailey (1969) and Barth (1967), who were among the first to consider the interaction of individuals' strategic choices and the constraints and incentives places on those choices by institutions. Bailey's (1969, 2001) continued efforts to develop action theory are particularly relevant to this book to the extent that I am concerned with the manipulative strategies social actors employ to gain and maintain power. As Rahim's antics so eloquently demonstrate, such manipulations usually garner at least the implicit consent, support, and even approval of the wider community because they rely on the creative use of existing rules and norms. As a "manipulation" of kinship ideology, relations, and terminology, patronage in Kyrgyzstan's political, social, and economic spheres remains moral and legitimate, even if it is contested. Similarly, for those involved in them, patron-client relations are a "manipulated" but not "corrupted" form of kinship.

Bailey's (1969) *Stratagems and Spoils* showed that similar principles and strategies characterized political competition among both "exotic" and "developed" societies. In a second book, *Treason, Stratagems, and Spoils*, Bailey added "treason" to his concerns to draw attention to morality—and "to ideas of duty and conscience—as a foil to rational calculations of advantage" (2001, xii). He thus attempted to restore attention to people's own representation of their beliefs and values through such political actions as controlling their followers and defeating their opponents. Both books by Bailey provide a conceptual tool kit for analyzing patronage in a kin-based society, by questioning whether kinship can be a matter of winning or losing.

The clearest application of Bailey's ideas would be to view Kyrgyz politics in general as a competitive game with agreed-on rules and an agreed-on goal, with political actors being divided into "teams." I take this view somewhat (see Chapter 5), but find more inspiration in Bailey's conception of normative versus pragmatic rules. Normative rules are publicly professed and usually vague (for example, honesty and fair play). Pragmatic rules address the actual winning of the game, and differ from those that are on public display. This apparent contradiction between professed and actual behavior can also be framed using Bailey's distinction between public and private interests. In Kyrgyzstan, patrons and their kinsmen exercise various forms of normative codes, strategic actions, and pragmatic behavior to satisfy their own interests; they also hide their very pragmatic reasons for action behind moral rhetoric. In Chapter 5 I describe the way in which the patron exploits the rhetoric of public security and stability to satisfy ends that are based self-interest. Through patronage, actors manipulate the situation for their own ends, thereby obtaining access to alternatives spheres of action, which people usually accept since options are limited. In the Kyrgyz context, patronage is thus a means through which people can satisfy their basic needs within the framework of the "native son," who will represent them in parliament.

New Institutional Economics

New Institutional Economics (NIE) offers a framework for understanding processes of change and helps us examine the role of social, political, and economic institutions over time, and what roles individuals play in these processes as they bargain for power and act on their differing intentions (Ensminger 1992, 16). In other words, NIE is an economic perspective that tries to extend the concepts of economic performance and distribution by focusing more on the social and legal norms and rules (that is, institutions) that underlie economic activities (Ensminger 1992, 17). This goes beyond earlier institutional economics (North 1990).

The importance of institutions in a world of opportunistic rational actors is their predictability (Knight 1992). Institutions help establish expectations about the future behavior of rational actors and how people establish mutual trust for cooperation (Finke 2004; 2014, 25). NIE is a useful conceptual framework to analyze nonmarket exchange; informal institutions include topics such as kinship, religion, ethnicity, state, and identity (Finke 2014), while formal institutions include topics such as organizational arrangements, property rights, and modes of governance (Ensminger 1992, 16). Framed in this way, the institution of patronage involves actors who deal with transaction costs and are influenced by the rules, ideas, and values of the institution.

Patronage, however, is an informal institution that is formed partly in response to formal institutions. The dynamics of patronage visibly evolve in times of need, uncertainty, and rapid change, such as those associated with regime change. In these times talented individuals adapt to new political conditions quickly; they learn how the new system works and provide alternatives to the formal state structures. Such individuals provide "imaginative constructs" of the ideal type of life and state structure and thereby satisfy their own interests. Patronage, like most institutions, is somewhere between a strategy or structural mechanism and a cultural peculiarity (Ensminger 1992; Finke 2014; Knight 1992; North 1990). Patronage is also an institution that may look traditional but is not; what the patron does is quite modern, since he and the relations he establishes are responses to a particular situation. Patronage builds on cultural models and institutions that have been around for centuries. In such an institutional framework, trust is important, as patron-client relations need to be built on trust and interdependence in the absence of contracts or formal written agreements that might otherwise provide security.

NIE puts great emphasis not only on individual actor-oriented perspectives but also on institutional constraints, and it specifically deals with the relationships between market forces, local institutions, economic performance, culture, and ideology. Each individual within the institution can affect the economic outcome (distribution and growth); individuals realize this and try to change institutions to "serve their ends more effectively, whether these ends be ideological or materialistic" (Ensminger 1992, xiii). The success of different actors derives in part from their bargaining power in the pre-existing institutional structure. This process often has unintended consequences, and by no means results in institutional arrangements that better serve the interests of society as a whole (Ensminger 1992; Knight 1992). After all, actors within any institution are involved in a bargaining game in which each uses different combinations of power and resources to achieve a particular agenda (Finke 2014). Although NIE draws attention to the rules of bargaining, it gives little attention to the culturally appropriate ways breaking rules or of influencing others to serve another's agenda.

Social Poetics and Performance

In understanding the culturally appropriate way of breaking rules, it is important to recognize that patronage is also grounded in cultural practices and local concepts, and that people construct their own realities through performance. I have found the notion of social poetics, as developed by Herzfeld (2005), crucial in understanding these constructions. Herzfeld (1985, 1992, 2005) devised the concept of social poetics to describe the play between convention and invention in social life. He developed this concept as a means for understanding how social actors seem to act by the rules but also often break them. As part of this, he explores how far social actors can go in breaking the rules before they become violators of the rules rather than creative artists. There is a small difference between breaking certain rules in a way that looks clever, and makes one a master of those rules, and breaking them in a way that looks stupid, and suggests that one does not know how to behave. Usually social actors manage to be creative in a way that they violate what appears to be a letter of the law. But breaking the rules is also about recognizing the tensions at work between the conventions of society and invention.

Social poetics is a means of exploring the social rules identified by anthropologists and the people they study, how people play with those rules, and how actions are slightly twisted, bent, or manipulated in ways that lead to changes in the rules. Social poetics enables us to explain the relationship between the micropolitics of everyday interaction and long-term cultural change. In this book, I apply the idea of social poetics to election practices (see Chapters 6–7).

Outline of Chapters

In Chapters 1 and 2, I outline the basic patterns of social organization and kinship in rural northern Kyrgyzstan. Chapter 1 traces the interlinked relationships of kinship and patronage from the pre-tsarist period to the present. Here, I trace the meaning of patronage and its linkage with kinship through Kyrgyz history. I trace how one type of kinship and patronage in pre-Soviet times—described as patrilineal descent groupings—has evolved, then turn to its manifestation in the kolkhoz (collective farm) under Soviet rule. In times of transformation, patron-client relations constitute and shape both traditional and modern social frameworks. During the Soviet period, the framework was party-centered patronage in which favors were bestowed according to lineage or provincial affiliations. I then outline how the relations between kinship and patronage have changed in accord with the reorientation of Kyrgyz social organization toward nation-building projects, democracy, and a free market economy in the post-Soviet period.

Chapter 2 introduces my two field sites, the interlinked villages of Bulak and Orlovka, and their extant patrilineal and patrilocal forms of kinship. I describe how genealogical relationships in the villages are recognized, enacted, and re-membered. Thus I cover heterogeneous material including the organization of agnatic descent groups, cousin terminology, marriage and affinal relations, kin solidarity at funerals, spatial proximity of kin groups, and shared work and lei-sure activities. I also discuss the important role of genealogists (*sanjyrachi*) and oral genealogies (*sanjyra*) in people's everyday and political lives.

Against the normative, albeit historically changing, background depicted in Chapters 1, 2, and 3, I then document in the remaining chapters (4–7), the spectacular rise of the urban-dwelling Rahim as the "native son," not only of a few villages, but of a broad swath of northern Kyrgyz territory. In Chapters 2–3 I begin the story of how Rahim, a successful businessman and aspiring politi-cian, became the "native son" and patron of Bulak village. I show how villagers reconfigured Rahim's lineage into a noble one. The concept is largely absent from traditional Kyrgyz society but was known among ethnic Kazakhs in Kyrgyzstan; thus Rahim's half-Kazakh background was creatively manipulated. I also show how Rahim expanded his own kin networks against structural odds. Rahim had relatively few close male relatives (no brothers and only two patrilineal first cous-ins), so he built his kinship network in two ways: by acquiring clients from his more distant agnatic relatives and by brokering the marriages of his sisters and female cousins with important clients to substitute strong affinal relations for relatively weak patrilineal ones.

Chapter 4 describes how Rahim restructured the former collective farm (which had been populated mainly by ethnic Germans) during and after the privatization process. After Rahim took control of the farm, he disposed of the former members of the collective (both Kyrgyz and German) and replaced them with his lineage relatives from a neighboring village. Rahim also incorporated unrelated clients into his networks on conditions of future support, building a mutually protective "circle of trust" around himself. The chapter closes with a discussion of the significance of Rahim's mixed base of kin and "voluntary" clients. At the very least, this mixed composition helps obscure the recognition among clients of the extent of their exploitation within the relationship.

The focus on Rahim's successful manipulations continues in Chapter 5, where I describe the outcome of a public meeting in Orlovka village concern-ing the plans to construct a mosque on the central square. Rahim did not want the mosque, and he skillfully used his patronage networks and rhetorical de-vices to convince villagers to support his plan. I use this chapter, especially, to address the performative and rhetorical aspects of patronage. In this meeting

Rahim postured himself as a concerned citizen, and he appealed to a kind of basic democracy in which the matter should be decided by a show of hands. Of course, the individuals in his network supported him; few of his opponents could disagree with his appeal or the procedural dimensions of the meeting. But Rahim also made use of his privileged access to officials (who had already decided in favor of the mosque) to reopen the decision process in public. Thus, in this chapter I begin to show how democracy, kinship, and patronage are interlinked through social poetics and the performances of individual actors.

Chapter 6 takes as its topic the day of elections, which ends with Rahim becoming a member of parliament. It provides a close ethnographic account of the practices of "localized democracy" in which a "native son" is brought to power under dubious means that are then discursively legitimized. What would usually be labeled as "bribing" is recast by villagers as an "investment"; monetary payments secure votes for the right candidate that would otherwise be acquired in equally illegal ways (for example, the allocation of unused ballots) by another candidate. The democratic process is further rendered "fair" in local terms because the bribes are made fairly secretively and through patronage/kinship networks and because people do not necessarily vote for the person who bought their vote.

Chapter 7 describes Rahim's efforts to consolidate his political success with a victory feast after his election to parliament. This is portrayed as an affirmation of his position vis-à-vis his clients and others. At this political feast, the traditional rules and oratory that structure banquets are adopted to make the feast appear to honor kin (as in the banquets that accompany life cycle events), but are also violated in order to strengthen Rahim's political power (and to forestall dissent and counteralliances). Thus, the feast ignores rules of seniority, and places local elites and politicians in the foreground, placing the most useful people in the most prestigious seats.

Rahim's rapid climb to power ended abruptly in death. When he died his circle of trust quickly dissolved, and the system of patronage that he had built collapsed. His clients became unemployed and lacked protection. In the conclusion, I show how patronage offers a valuable safety net and coping mechanism for many people during the ongoing economic crisis of the post-Soviet period. Social scientists who view patronage as a sign of a weak or corrupt political system draw attention to the way that patron-client relations create hierarchies, favoring some individuals over others. But is patronage the problem? Or is it a reaction to an already corrupt and dysfunctional system?

For Kyrgyz villagers, democracy is not being built; it was instituted at the end of the Soviet period as a political system that was already pervaded by kin solidarity, patronage, and irregular voting procedures. For many, native sons like Rahim are the only people who publicly represent their interests, and they believe that their political support for such individuals is legitimate. The case of Rahim nicely illustrates how local politics functions within kinship society in which the role of genealogies, ancestors, agnatic descent groups, cousin terminology, marriage and affinal relations, and kin solidarity play a crucial role in building patronage networks and political loyalty.

Notes

1. Ökül ata-ene (lit. representative father and mother) is an established institution in Kyrgyz society that provides a framework through which a couple engaged to be married receives financial and emotional support before their wedding to help deal with anticipated difficulties and responsibilities continue after the marriage takes place.

2. Traditionally, representative fathers also took on the full responsibilities of support when the biological father died. Kanybek's father was dead, thus making Rahim even more of a father (*ata*) to him.

3. Local newspaper *Aalam* April 18, 2007.

4. There are terms and phrases in the Russian language that are known and used to designate relations of interdependence, the most popular of which is *blat*. The phrase "to be someone's man" more or less clearly indicates patronage.

1 Kinship and Patronage in Kyrgyz History

IT IS NOT easy to define "the Kyrgyz." As an ethnic group, and as an ethnically defined nation, the Kyrgyz are bound by bloodlines, claims of kinship, and mythical narratives about shared ancestors. People use all these forms of kinship to prove their own identities and those of others. The Kyrgyz kinship system has also been influenced by different economies and politics for centuries.

In the recent past, the intertwining of Kyrgyz kinship relations with politics was perceived by the Soviets as morally dubious, a "remnant of feudalism," and a sign of the "backward" nature of the Kyrgyz. Soviet policies were meant to transform Kyrgyz kinship relations, and they did: kinship relations were manifest in the organization and operation of the collective farms and the local Communist Party apparatus of the Kyrgyz Republic. Kinship relations were closely linked to employment relationships, economic networks, and access to state resources. As such, kinship simultaneously contributed to the emergence of informal networks and patron-client relations.

In the post-Soviet period, kinship has been transformed into an economically and politically necessary component of liberal democracy. At the same time, kinship has remained important in the private domain. On the domestic level, kinship provides members of the household with a constant source of mutual help and emotional support. Kinship in the public domain has been activated through political discourse and nation-building projects. Kinship has retained its complex character, rooted in both blood relations and the reckoning of them. But the reckoning of kinship, and particularly of lineage identities, has come under intense negotiation in the post-Soviet context as individuals and groups seek support from would-be patrons—such as Rahim—and would-be patrons seek potential clients. This chapter explores the temporary politics of kinship throughout the history of Kyrgyzstan and its changing manifestations.

The Pre-Soviet Period

The material below is drawn from the works of ethnographers as well as Orientalists, travelers, and military officers. As later studies have pointed out, such early writers often occupied more than one such role, which complicates subsequent attempts to distinguish the various levels of bias in their accounts (see Dragadze 1984, 2001; Gullette 2010; Israilova-Khar'ekhuzen 1999; Roy 2000).

Kyrgyz is an ethnic group mostly living in contemporary Kyrgyzstan (4,193,850),[1] as well as in neighboring countries such as Tajikistan (74,000), Uzbekistan (160,000), Afghanistan (1,100), China (232,000), Turkey (1,600), Kazakhstan (12,000), and Russian (800,000).[2] Kyrgyz are mainly Muslims belonging to the Hanafi Sunni school. The ethnonym *Kyrgyz* derives from the Turkic word *kyrk* (forty) and *Iz* plural suffix, implying a group of people consisting of forty tribes (Pulleyblank 1990). The Kyrgyz have a grand genealogy founded in both oral and written traditions, which links all ethnic Kyrgyz to a single ancestor—Dolon. However, on the origins of tribal groupings of ethnic Kyrgyz exist different legends. According to oral legends (*sanjyra*), Kyrgyz *uruu* and *uruk* accompanied the appearance of the first fathers. *Uruu* and *uruk* are units of kinship based on blood ties, but they are also basic political units based on several principles: common ownership of pastures, economic interdependence (particularly at times of life cycle events), and the practical requirement for kinship in daily life. Israilova-Khar'ekhuzen (1999, 130) defines the concept of *uruk*, which she says consists of a small group of kinsmen who share a common ancestor some five to seven generations back. *Uruk* are a group of people, related by blood or other kinship ties spanning seven generations, who are united by the principle of joint settlement in a community of general agrarian management. An *uruu* comprises at least one and usually several *uruk*, and can include native as well as nonnative members. That is, an *uruu* sometimes takes a subordinate (nonnative) *uruk* under its protection. Within the limits of its territorial borders, an *uruu* controls the cattle pastures.

Kyrgyz tribal divisions in the middle of the nineteenth century were arranged according to genealogical relationships and hierarchies that influenced collective labor and forms of ownership. In 1856 Chokan Valikhanov, an officer in the Russian army and ethnographer, visited a Kyrgyz area and stayed in the pastures belonging to the northern Kyrgyz nomads. He was interested in studying the social structure of the Kyrgyz descent groupings. He wrote down a Kyrgyz legend that explained the origins of the duality of Kyrgyz *uruu*:

> According to the folk legend, the origin and name of the tribal group (Russ. *rod*) came from the names of the ancestors. Because of this, the system of patrimonial division is closely connected to the genealogy of ancestors of the hordes. The first ancestor (*bai*) gave himself the name Kyrgyz. He had only one son, Ak-uul, meaning "white boy." Ak-uula, according to the legend, had two sons—Abla and Kabil. The posterity of Abla makes the right wing, and Kabil—the left. From the sons of Tagaja, a grandson of Abla: Bogorstan, Kojlaka, Kildzhira and Karachoro continued further tribes of the right wing. (1985, 40–41)

In her work, ethnographer Israilova-Khar'ekhuzen (1999, 136) gives further examples of genealogical organization from Kyrgyz *sanjyra*, a genre of orally transmitted information concerning the history, tribal structure, and genealogy of a lineage that is transferred from one generation to the next: "Kyrgyz divide themselves according to three basic groups such as *Ong kanat* 'right wing,' *Sol kanat* 'left wing' and *Ichkilik* 'internal.' The generations could be counted several tens to hundred in each tribal tree. The Kyrgyz genealogy was transferred orally from generation to generation."

The people located in the northern part of Kyrgyz lands (the central Tian Shan Mountains, basin of Lake Issyk-Kul, and the Chui River Valley) belong genealogically to the *Ong kanat* (right wing). This wing includes the tribes of Sarybagysh, Solto, Bugu, and Sayak. In pre-Soviet times, the inhabitants of the *Sol kanat* (left wing) were in the northern part of Fergana and in Talas Province (Abramzon 1960). The *Ichkilik* were located in the western Alay Mountains and in eastern Pamir (Geiss 2004). The ethnographic record suggests that the southern tribes and their genealogical relationships had been less coherently documented than those in the north (Vinnikov 1956, 137). It is not clear, however, whether this depiction is an artifact of ethnographic study. Influenced by Soviet ideology and being a member of the scientific group of the Soviet Academy of Science, Abramzon (1971, 180) described Kyrgyz kinship relations in the northern part of Kyrgyzstan in the following way: "A corporate group [R. *rodovaya*] of Kyrgyz was divided into descent groups [R. *rody*] and [R. *plemya*]. Such corporate groupings were headed by the *manap* and *bii.*" In 1959 Vinnikov made some efforts to fill the perceived gap in information through a second expedition to the southern part of Kyrgyzstan.

Kyrgyz lineages are organized according to myths of patrilineal descent through which members claim descent from a common ancestor. These claims are validated by detailed and extensive genealogies (Dzhunushaliev and Ploskihk 2000), but such genealogies can also be used for political purposes and to justify actors' involvement in political activities on the basis of myth and legendary stories. How this occurs in the post-Soviet period becomes evident in the course of this study, but it appears to have occurred in the pre-Soviet period, as well.

The local historian Djamgerchinov (1946, 35) documented the extensive genealogical material for the Kyrgyz that had been collected prior to the Soviet period. In the process of recording these materials, interesting manuscripts were collected that filled gaps evident in many published works on genealogy in Russian sources in the second half of the nineteenth century. Interestingly, the names of the tribes could be traced to their appearance in a variant of the *Manas* epic, the *manaschi*-Sagynbaj Orozbakov. There are names of various Kyrgyz descent groups (R. *rodoplemennoi*) and the unions that continuously formed and also broke up throughout history (Khazanov 1984). Djamgerchinov suggested that the names could be traced to show the changing interactions, ties, and political associations between patrilineal descent groups. Chuloshnikov

(1924, 196–198) asserted that in the majority of cases, the general ancestor for the hundreds of individuals in a *rod* was a fictitious person who had been invented to meet the demands of the already-well-developed custom of claiming origin from a common patrilineal ancestor for contemporary social needs. Further examination has revealed that the names of ancestors are not normally wholly invented and do refer to an actual person, although the exact dates they lived may not be known.

In some cases the basic structure was similar to that described above, but ancestral reckoning was slightly different. Pogorelskyi and Batrakov (1930, 108–109), for example, found cases when groups of households carried the name of the "third father" (i.e., grandfather) and called themselves an *uruq* (lineage). The three, five, or seven generations united under this ancestor were called an "extended family" (üibülöö). Pogorelskyi and Batrakov found that the extended family amalgamated its membership into political unity through voluntary (migrations and war alliances) and involuntary (employment, servitude, serfdom) means. On closer examination, üibülöö were rarely composed primarily of consanguineous or affinal kin, but members held common ownership of winter pastures and shared territory and formed a rather steady unit of several individual households. Kyrgyz lineages united through general assembly in response to external enemies—similar to the behavior that Evans-Pritchard (1940) described for the Nuer—but once the enemy disappeared, internal divisions would once again emerge among the tribes.

Ethnic Kyrgyz and Their Neighbors

What has been documented for the kinship systems of ethnic Kyrgyz in current-day Kyrgyzstan should be placed in comparison to what has been documented for their near neighbors. Most relevant are ethnic Kazaks (both in Kyrgyzstan and in Kazakhstan) and ethnic Kyrgyz outside Kyrgyzstan. With reference to the Kazaks, Hudson (1964, 21–22) claims, "The nature of social groups was that an *uru* of more or less close blood relatives in the male line usually had living and migrating with them members of other blood groups. But after a few generations people would become confused and the descendants of the original immigrant might come to be considered blood members of the group among which they were living." Hudson thus considered the term *uru* from two points of view: first, a group that is closely related, living together as an economic and political unit under one leader; second, any number of groups claiming descent from a common ancestor regardless of their genealogical relations.

In the period of the tsarist administration (1876–1917), ethnic Kazaks and Kyrgyz both were called Kyrgyz. When necessary the Kyrgyz were distinguished as Kara-Kyrgyz ("black Kyrgyz"). The distinction reflects common practice among Turkic-language-speaking peoples to use color terms to show division of the same group based on geography. In this case, the black Kyrgyz referred to southern groups.

In his study of a small group of Kyrgyz pastoralists and Wakhi agro-pastoralists in Afghanistan, Shahrani (1979) writes that the social structure of the Kyrgyz is organized according to agnatic descent principles. Kyrgyz in Afghan's Pamir Province trace their ancestry back seven generations along the male line, which is necessary for proof of identity and their claims to membership in a particular Kyrgyz *kichi uruk* (small lineage) or *chong uruk* (big lineage). Those who did not know their origins were considered *kul* or slaves, but this genealogical methodology was also used by individuals who were the descendants of mixed marriages between Kyrgyz and non-Kyrgyz and the offspring of Kyrgyz married to slaves (ibid., 150).

Shahrani's work is crucial to highlight here because the social structure of the Kyrgyz in Afghanistan was not subject to change under the direct influence of Soviet ideology. In contrast, social structure in Kyrgyzstan and Kazakhstan changed drastically with Soviet collectivization processes. Interestingly, Shahrani uses only *uruq* without referring to the larger unit *uruu*. Perhaps *uruu* divisions were uncommon because the number of Kyrgyz in Afghanistan was relatively small and they comprised only a limited number of *uruq*.

Without state intrusion, new groups emerged over time through generational fission. When a man's sons came of age, he usually provided each with a yurt (*boz üi*) and a share of cattle. The sons set their yurts side by side and continued to graze their cattle along with those of their father. During the course of generations, this unit would become too big or too small owing to economic reasons, such as inadequate grazing lands for an increasingly large group or lack of labor power. Part of the group would then split off and form a new group somewhere else. In the course of time, the new group would be considered a separate and independent *uruu*, usually known by the name of its common ancestor and still tracing its descent from the parent group (Abramzon 1960). Hudson (1964, 21) mentions similar processes in the case of ethnic Kazaks.

Social Stratification: Pre-Soviet Patron-Client Relations

Soviet scientists concluded that in nomadic societies, power lay in the hands of particular people. Among the Kyrgyz, such individuals were called *manap* (*uruk* leader), *bii* (judge), *bai* (rich man), and *bek* or *baatyr* (hero). These people resolved the political and economic problems of their communities. But their powers were not absolute; they were modified according to many factors—such as their age, experience, origins, and wealth (Israilova-Khar'ekhuzen 1999, 18).

In some areas of Central Asia, power accrued along what have been described as aristocratic and dynastic lines. In his ethnographic journal, for example, Lieutenant General Grodekov (1889) wrote about hereditary aristocracy among ethnic Kazaks. The Kazaks, he wrote, distinguished between aristocrats (khans and their offspring) known as "white bones" (*ak söök*) and common people, who were called "black bones" (*kara söök*). The white bones, he wrote, comprised a "ruling and owning class who enjoyed the highest prestige in Kazak society" (4–5). Such hereditary distinctions in status were not documented among ethnic Kyrgyz in the pre-Soviet period. Instead, *manap* and *bii* seem to have been positions taken up by certain talented individuals in order to further their political interests (Prior 2000, 2006). Prior also concluded: "The Kyrgyz were alien to the traditional structure of supreme political power in Central Asia, the lines of sultans, or putative descendants of Chingiz Khan from whom the Uzbek and Kazak raised their rules or khans. Tribal governance was, for the Kyrgyz, the top level of native rule: each tribe was led by its own *bii* or clan elders, who also acted as judges" (2006, 74). The extension of Russian imperial rule into Central Asia created an overall impression of nonaristocratic leadership, particularly through the introduction of local elections. These new electoral procedures were foreign across the Kyrgyz Province (Sneath 2007, 83). Russian rule weakened social distinctions within some groups. Grodekov (1889, 5–7) commented, "It is not unlikely that the rigidity of distinctions between Black and White Bones had been weakened first by the inclusion of persons distinguished for religious reasons and later by the collapse of the power of the khans and their families after the Russian conquest." Among the Kyrgyz, however, people were familiar with the concept of allying with one side and lobbying for another side.

The *manap* (*uruk* leader) was not an inherited position. Members of a community acknowledged the authority of a potential *manap*. If the son of a *manap* was malicious and impoverished, he could rarely become a *manap* himself. Nor was moral standing enough. A very good person, regardless of family background, could not declare himself a *manap*; his people also had to accept him as a leader (Grodekov 1889, 6). Yet even this "democratic" institution was naturalized in terms of kinship and lineage: the term *manap* is said to come from the name of the son of Dulas; Dulas's own father was Kilchi, and from Tagai (Kushner 1929, 85).

Influenced by Soviet ideology, Valikhanov (1961a, 1961b) found that Kyrgyz society was similar to that of the caste system, with the *manap* holding political, economic, and social power. The poor were the clients or followers of the *manap* and *bii*. The clients served the patron *manap* or *bii* in order to later inherit property (*inchi*), which would allow them to survive and to pay dowries. Following the dowry payment or on receiving an allotment of property, clients could continue serving the *manap* or *bii*, sometimes shifting to wage work for him. A patron's agricultural workers collectively received wages equal to the cash value of one-fourth to one-half of the total harvest; they ate at their patron's table, and he acted as a father to them, calling them "my sons." In return the worker was expected to pursue the interests of his patron (Valikhanov 1961a). Although patrons and clients were not related by blood, they nevertheless acted as if they were kin. Valikhanov's equation of the Kyrgyz social organization to the caste system is somewhat misleading because one's position within this social hierarchy was not inherited.

Similar relations of patronage existed across Central Asia (cf. Grodekov 1889). Although not hereditary, patron-client relations proved durable even with nomadism and migration. While one's security was generally higher among one's own kin, it was also evident that within strong tribes, poor people migrated with the rich. Richer kin groups protected poorer ones, and the poor paid with their labor (Grodekov 1889, 58). The entry of the poor into patron-client relations can thus be described as neither completely forced nor completely voluntary. The poor had needs, and the patron provided for his clients' basic needs and protected and helped them and their kinsmen.

Hudson (1964, 37) suggested that the nineteenth-century Kazak patron-client relationship was even less static than it appeared. He noted that the wealthy patron and poor relative frequently appeared in the guise of creditor and debtor. This suggests that the relation was primarily economic rather than social, and that the client was merely indebted to the patron for particular kinds of support. Hudson pointed out the wide terminology for different kinds of loans such as *saanchi* (loan of a dairy cow) and *malchy* (loan of a horse), and the common practice of borrowing animals from patrons to pay a bride price. Such loans were made in the presence of witnesses, and it was stipulated that the animal was to be repaid with another animal, while interest was to be repaid in the form of labor. If the debtor defaulted on his payment, he was obliged to work for his creditor without payment until the value of the loan was paid off at the rate of about seven sheep a year, which was the approximate wage of a shepherd (ibid., 37).

Bii among the Kyrgyz appears in the *Manchu Memorial from Kashgar*, a collection of manuscripts written by the assistant military governor in Kashgar, China, and translated from Mandarin into English by Nicola Di Cosmo (1993). These documents date from the early nineteenth century and cover the last six months of 1806 and the year of 1807. Ten memorials focused on the nomadic tribesmen called Burut (usually identified as Kyrgyz nomads), who came to pay tribute to the representative of the Ch'ing emperor. They had purportedly come with goods to trade, described as "horses, cattle, and various other things," especially brought by *bek* (warriors) of different ranks, described as Kyrgyz *manap* and *bii*. While the text testifies to the presence of trade and social differentiation among Kyrgyz, it provides no further details concerning relationships between the rich and poor.

According to the sources detailed above, Kyrgyz patron-client relationships were not necessarily blood based but often relations that had been crafted by integrating poorer households into the patrilines of richer ones. Those who were poor were also integrated into their adopted lineage as part of a process of new group formation by accepting and using major tribal names. These poor would use the official tribal name, but they also kept their own name for use among themselves. During this process of segregation and lineage alliance, the "true" blood lineages of both rich and poor could become forgotten, confused, or merged as alliances were successfully adjusted to new contexts and situations.

The Russian and Soviet Eras

At the end of the nineteenth century and the beginning of the twentieth century, nomadic Kyrgyz were forced to settle under the influence first of Russian colonial policies and then later by Soviet policies that stipulated they must withdraw from pastures, reduce the size of their herds of cattle, and settle permanently (Pogorelskyi and Batrakov 1930). Russian and Soviet sources tend to concentrate on describing the nomadic lifestyle of the Kyrgyz and disregard their political history. In reality the nomadic Kyrgyz controlled the Khanate of Kokand, a state that included parts of today's eastern Uzbekistan, southern Kazakhstan, Tajikistan, and Kyrgyzstan, from 1709 to 1876. Russian efforts to settle the Kyrgyz were thus not only part of the "civilizing mission" they proclaimed. They were almost certainly related also to the struggle for the independence from Kokand Khan, their alliance with Russia, and the expansion by the Russians into Kyrgyz nomads' territory—first into the north and then into the south.

As the Kyrgyz became subjects of the Russian Empire, they dealt with changes to forms of land tenure and mass settlement. The norms of customary law, which had regulated collective life for many centuries, were changed and partly eradicated under Russian rule. The Kyrgyz were initially incorporated into Russian Turkestan and experienced a direct form of colonial government that eradicated their traditional forms of political power and law. Yet this process was not simple because the social transformation took several years. While all authoritative, judicial, and executive powers were officially subordinated to Russian administration, people continued to observe former social hierarchies. For example, under Russian rule, *manap* still held preeminent positions in society (Prior 2006, 71).

Russian-speaking people also migrated into Kyrgyz territory, changing socioeconomic life (Arutjunov 1974; Israilova-Khar'ekhuzen 1999, 7; Roy 2000; Tishkov 1997). The Russian language became dominant, and cultural diversity increased. Assessments of the effect of Russian colonization and later Sovietization are mixed. For example, many of my informants positively view the linguistic and cultural effects, but negatively view the political and economic disempowerment of Kyrgyz and other Central Asians. Historians influenced by the Marxist prism of class, such as Abramzon (1971), tend to have a positive view of the effects of Russian rule. For Abramzon, this was a great opportunity for the Kyrgyz, giving them a prosperous future and a better life. Thousands of people had been liberated from the slavish conditions they experienced during pre-Soviet times, during which they were in constant battle. By joining Russia, the Kyrgyz rid themselves of the oppression of Kokand Khan's despotism and slavery (ibid., 169).

Thus from the second half of the nineteenth century, instead of being organized in terms of *aiyl* administrative units according to kinship and tribal affiliations, the czarist administration began to define the Kyrgyz population according to geographic units such as province (R. *oblast'*) and county (R. *uezd*). These administrative measures were designed to help liquidate the kinship and tribal ties of the Kyrgyz population, not only within the boundaries of the *oblast' and uezd* but also within those of the administrative unit (R. *volost*) (Aitbaev 1957; Argynbaev 1984).

Soviet rule brought three major changes: collectivization, nationalization, and indigenization (R. *korenizatsia*). The effects of nationalization have been particularly visible in Central Asia's late and post-Soviet political life. In the early 1920s, Soviet authorities aimed to create republics on the model of nation-states, in which each republic's territory would encompass a population that had a shared historical, cultural, and linguistic heritage. To this end, the Soviet Union established nationality categories that reflected a hierarchy of titular (majority) nationalities and minorities within the republics. The history of each titular national group became the basis for the history of its respective republic. Across the Soviet republics, these "national" histories all emphasized the bond between territory and people; such histories also created national cultural heritages as the achievements of writers, artists, scientists, and historical figures were ascribed to particular nationality groups. The Soviet authorities attacked alternative sources of affiliation, and thus the backwardness and traditionalism of the pre-Soviet past was contrasted with the enlightened modernity of the Soviet state. According to Soviet nationalities policy, all nationality groupings would follow a linear path of development from kin-based or clan groups, through tribes and tribal federations, to finally reach the stage of modern nation-states as represented by the Soviet republics (Abashin 1999; Akiner 1997a, 1997b, 1998; Bromley 1983; Roy 2000).

Throughout the Soviet Union, collectivization was meant to generate a new economy; in Central Asia, it was also meant to further destroy the power of extended family and kinship ties. Soviet ethics, legislation, and principles insisted on the importance of individual advancement by merit and professional qualities. Collectivization did change economic life; its effects on kinship were mixed and contradictory. In many cases, collective farms seem to have merely encompassed lineages and therefore enabled their continuation and strengthening. As such, the Soviet system accomplished far less of the total transformation of society than it proclaimed. Instead of creating a wholly modern society, Soviet practices reinforced many aspects of "traditional" social organization (Kandiyoti 1996).

One of the biggest changes was that many lineage groups were integrated into the kolkhoz structures. The majority of territories allotted to kolkhoz and sovkhoz farms in Kyrgyzstan were occupied by patrilineal kin groups that separated themselves according to *uruk* within the allotted territory. Thus kinship-based patterns of controlling pastureland were also integrated into collective farms. Similarly, although it was impossible to convert wealth in livestock into other forms of material wealth during the Soviet period, control over livestock continued to serve create patron-client relations (Isakov and Schoeberlein 2014; Jacquesson 2010a; Yoshida 2005, 220). Within the collective farms, "villagers" continued to identify themselves along kinship lines rather than those of class, nationality, or citizenship (Bacon 1966; Kushner 1952; Olcott 1987; Poliakov 1992; Snesarev 1974). The kinds of social relations that could be instrumentalized among the Kyrgyz increased and diversified beyond kinship during the Soviet period to include class and group mates, army friends, and work colleagues (Isakov and Schoeberlein 2014); such expanded social networks, however, could be reconfigured under idioms of kinship, as patrons like Rahim demonstrated so spectacularly in the early 2000s.

According to Abashin (2015), Soviet ethnographers were aware of the specificity of social transformation in Central Asia. They knew that Soviet reforms were not achieving their stated goals. Nevertheless, it was difficult for ethnographers to articulate the specific processes of change that were occurring because they were handicapped by their own conviction that traditional kinship relations were "fossils," unchanging remnants of the past (ibid., 20).

The Soviet policy of *korenizatsia* (indigenization) was a key component of extending Soviet rule in the early years, but it never fully succeeded in persuading people that the Soviet Union could really meet their aspirations. Through *korenizatsia*, titular nationalities were meant to become involved in the republican level of the government process by occupying managerial positions in the main party bodies and institutions of government, economy, social services, culture, and education. Initially new types of local solidarity emerged within rayons and oblasts, and poor young men gained power by joining the Communist Party, yet local rich leaders (*bey* and *khan*) retained their former influence. Over time, local leaders came to consider *korenizatsia* a "poor substitute for real political autonomy" (Olivier 1990, 78; see also Bilinski 1967, 23). In practice, Soviet authorities refused to fully extend administrative and party power to local populations lest they weaken the centralized power of the Communist Party and deprive ethnic Russians of power even in the non-Russian republics (Roy 2000, 93). As a result, *korenizatsia* also exacerbated animosity between Russians and non-Russians, increased Great Russian chauvinism, and generated local nationalism.

Soviet Kinship and Patronage

Gleason (1991, 613) claims that local elites in Central Asia had their own informal codes that interfered with their strict adherence to the rules of the Communist Party. Furthermore, local elites may not have had any influence in formulating all-Soviet policies, but they could influence how those policies were implemented in the republics. Local elites had "dual allegiance." As a result clever local elites could simultaneously pursue the interests of their native homeland, the Soviet Union, ethnic brotherhood, and their own personal interests. To the question: "The local official on the Soviet periphery is whose man?" a clever local elite could answer: "I am everybody's man'" (ibid., 614). In Gleason's analysis, the apparent duplicity of local elites appears to be restricted to Central Asia: "If one considers only their formal statements, many high Central Asian leaders have appeared truer than true, more committed communists than the most orthodox of their Slavic central comrades. Yet . . . the more they talked like communists, the more they acted like nationalists" (ibid.). The wider literature on patronage within the Soviet Union, however, suggests that local elites within Russia also had "dual allegiances."

Walker (2002), for example, demonstrates how the "circle culture" (R. *kruzhok*) of the Russian intelligentsia originated in the informal and haphazard institutional life of prerevolutionary educated elites. This literary intelligentsia had successfully established patronage networks and other kinds of relationship with the early Soviet state. The games of *kruzhok* culture took place in the domestic sphere, but nevertheless represented the interface between private and public life.

At the level of government, patronage was embedded into the system of professional appointment and advancement (Willerton 1992). Whether within the Communist Party or government bureaucracy, the official could not advance in the nomenclature without the assistance of his patron above. In return for assisting him by advancing his career, the client would carry out the patron's policies. Throughout Russian society, *blat* was an essential tool for obtaining goods and services through informal networks in the Soviet Union (Ledeneva 1998).[3] Some authors, such as Verdery (2003), argue for similarities across the socialist states based on how property was tied to professional positions, complex social relationships, social values, and political symbols.

The importance of patronage and other informal relationships is normally considered a function of the demand-and-supply networks. Since the state was the main distributor, some goods were not obtainable via the official local market. Additionally, since socialism operated an economic system based on shortage, hoarding and theft were necessary for the system to function (Humphrey 1998; Ledeneva 1998; Tarkowski 1983, 1981; Verdery 1996). Patron-client relations, reciprocity, and gift exchange were all conducive to the informal economy (Koroteyeva and Makarova 1998). As Kandiyoti (1996) argues, Soviet policies had the paradoxical effect of combining "modernizing" aims with traditional means.

To the extent that kinship had been important for obtaining access to resources prior to socialism, in remained so in the Soviet period. Across the Soviet Union, principles for reckoning kin and the ideologies associated with kinship proved remarkably resilient. In Buryatia, for example, Humphrey (1998) describes how a substantial part of economic life on the collective farms took place according to the rhythm of great socialist rituals, "socialist competition," and special campaigns initiated by the central government. Yet even as the rhythms of daily life became more agricultural, and beyond this more "Soviet," social reproduction at its most basic level remained little affected, "patriliny continues to operate as the cognitive principle of ordering kin relations, and this is despite the fact that in the Soviet period such agnatic kin groups no longer function as units of residence and production. The kin relations actually most important in practical life, such as the link between Namzhilov and his son-in-law Buyantuyev, are not necessarily patrilineal, but it is by means of an existing patrilineal structure that they are defined" (340). Kinship thus combined with patronage networks on the collective farms. It was not uncommon for the chairman of the farm to put his kinsmen in key posts as livestock specialists or foremen.

Similar tendencies toward continuity also occurred in the political domain. In Uzbekistan, "power relationships reconstituted themselves through a socialistic, Party rule idiom and ethos, but the players tended to reproduce long established forms of political associations based on that older social organization" (Zanca 2000, 7).

Kinship and Politics: Western and Soviet Scholarship

This ambiguous heritage of kinship has created a big discussion in terms of agreed and contested debates among scholars. There have been various ways of studying the kinship system underpinning Kyrgyz social organization during the pre-Soviet period. Yet there has been no agreement on the form that kinship took during this period. There has been contradiction not only between Western and Soviet scholarship but also among Soviet scholars themselves. These debates have often centered on the relation of kinship to overarching political and economic systems. The ethnographic studies of the kinship system during the late 1800s and early 1900s, for example, saw the kinship system as reflective of feudalism.

Earlier imperial Russian administrators, military officers, and travelers, however, had described the same system as opposed to feudalism.

Dzhunushaliev and Ploskikh (2000, 116) have recently criticized the Soviet preoccupation with identifying class relations through the study of kinship; they contend that many aspects of the more humane and civilized relations of the pre-Soviet period have been overlooked. Earlier kinship systems were also entwined with the rules of collectivism and collective responsibility, mutual support, intra-communal democracy, and the welfare of future generations.

This ongoing debate has left space for fresh views on the political dimensions of kinship such as that advanced by Sneath (2007). Sneath rethinks the conventional dichotomy between state and nonstate societies and envisages a "headless state" in which a pattern of statelike power was formed by horizontal relations among power holders, which was reproduced with or without a central head. His ambitious statement does not take into account the previous works on pastoral nomads of the Eurasian steppes and how these nomadic societies were based on idioms of kinship and descent (Finke 2004; Hudson 1964; Israilova-Khar'ekhuzen 1999; Khazanov 1984; Valikhanov 1985).

The Post-Soviet Era

In Kyrgyzstan, like many of its neighboring countries, people were reluctant to embrace independence when the Soviet Union collapsed. Starting from 1991 and onward, people in Kyrgyzstan suddenly found themselves without state support and lacking social protection. Economic strife accompanied the closure of factories and the dissolution of collective farms (Huskey 1997b; Kandiyoti 2003; Trevisani 2007). The collapse of such systems of social protection posed an enormous threat to people's existence and a challenge to rural and urban life. People found that they had to survive and meet the obligations of educating their children, organizing life cycle events, and contributing to social events without an income or access to many accustomed resources. They had to find new solutions for meeting an unpredictable and insecure life situation because previous means of accessing power and resources had expired.

Like other former Soviet republics, Kyrgyzstan has also pursued a program of economic reform designed to transform its centrally planned economy to one based on market principles (Anderson 1999; Pétric 2005). In the main, a successful transition to a market economy in Kyrgyzstan would depend on the implementation of reforms in the agricultural sector and in rural areas. Despite considerable progress with land reform and farm restructuring since 1991, the achievements fell short of the original expectations of international donors (Huskey 1997a, 2008). Despite the reorganization of collective farms into small cooperatives, most of the villagers still do not know how to use land in a sustainable and effective way, and

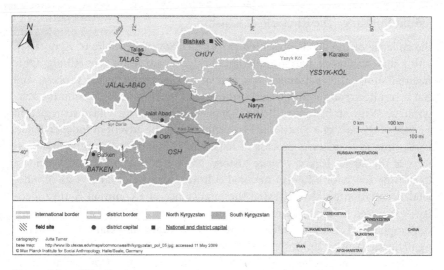

Map 1.1. Map of Kyrgyzstan.

they lack knowledge of how to exist in a market economy and produce goods for both national and international markets (Anderson 1999; Huskey 2008).

During the privatization period, people suffered moral crises and ethical dilemmas, and they searched for new ideologies (Anderson 1999; Huskey 2008). Corruption in the privatization process also led to widespread public mistrust, and many individuals became cynical of government and the conduct of officials. In the end mass unemployment, the reduction of state benefits and subsidies, the collapse of existing social and political infrastructure, agricultural privatization, and labor migration to Russia led to the deterioration of living standards. The resulting socioeconomic change led to social stratification and inequality between the poor and the rich, particularly in rural areas of Kyrgyzstan (Dudwick and Kuehnast 2002).

During privatization, communities and institutional structures were also transformed, and the Kyrgyz started to revive and reaffirm their local and traditional cultural values and apply them to structures of state power. People appeared open to the new ways imposed on them by international organizations (such as World Bank and IMF); in searching for alternatives, they began to manipulate the existing rules and norms. In short, people seemed ready to turn both to past experience and to acquire new skills to start a new life in the market economy. The anxiety resulting from these changes motivated individuals to seek personal connections and relationships that would provide them with greater security. In this way kinship replaced the state as the people's caretaker.

Nation Building: The Rhetoric of Kinship

The collapse of the USSR presented the former Soviet Republic of Kyrgyzstan with a dual challenge: nation building and democratization. My ethnographic material shows that patronage was crucial in this two-pronged process, and that it resulted from both internal and external pressures to refashion the Kyrgyz state. With no history of being independent, the Kyrgyz have struggled in the face of the loss of a centralized government. In the advent of independence, it was time to focus on a process of nation building and reexamine many aspects of the Soviet legacy, rewrite history, its political memory, and provide a flourishing space for a Kyrgyz national culture. During the early years of independence, nation builders stressed the importance of a common Kyrgyz identity—expressed through the metaphor "we are all brothers." At the same time, they emphasized civic and indigenous Kyrgyz cultural and social values, redefining national identity and fostering oral tradition (Akiner 1997a; Dzhunushaliev and Ploskikh 2000; Gullette 2008; Huskey 1997b; Light 2011; Prior 2000; Tolmacheva 2005).[4] Unintentionally, they also followed a Soviet way of defining the nation through primordial definitions of ethnicity and ethnogenesis (Gullette 2008; Marat 2008a, 2008b, 2006) (see Map 1.1).

On the surface of things, the major issues surrounding nation building in Kyrgyzstan have to do with its status as a multiethnic state. This means that the adoption of any particular national or civic ideology remains a problematic and contentious issue (Marat 2006). However, as Kyrgyzstan's citizens generally expect the state to generate new political concepts, the struggle for new political ideologies occurs in the realm of high politics. There is little input from "the public," but the political stakes are extremely high for contending parties and individuals.

Nation building across Central Asia, however, has generated more than the expected contest between ethnic groups vying for national representation. In nearby Kazakhstan, for example, post-Soviet nation building has placed sub-ethnic lineage-based identities at the center of political life (Schatz 2000, 489). This outcome was unexpected: "the privileging of ethnicity ironically helped to reconstitute the saliency of sub-ethnic identities. The post-Soviet state, through strategies of ethnic redress, encouraged a broad-based revival of Kazakh traditions, which included a rediscovery of genealogical knowledge and *ru* and *zhuz* (lineage-based) identities" (ibid., 491).

Similar processes have occurred in Kyrgyzstan through the actions of the state. Gullette, for example, claims that "the notions of 'clans' and 'tribes' were presented as important markers of Kyrgyz identity by local and government sponsored nation-building projects" (2006, iii). Successive governments have also used genealogies to construct the country's official history, which is played out in large-scale public festivities: "In the official narrative, ancestors are recognized as creating and maintaining an identity, for the Kyrgyz nation, and also for the state, which was elaborately marked in 2003 celebrations in honor of '2,200 years of Kyrgyz statehood'" (ibid.). And individual presidents and politicians, such as former president Askar Akayev, have legitimized their own power and authority through myths such as that of Manas (Prior 2000; Van der Heide 2008).

The nation-building projects of the post-Soviet period have been criticized for not establishing the best definition of statehood and for oversimplifying the political agenda (Tolmacheva 2005, 25). The lack of social rights and economic advantages for all citizens remains a significant obstacle in the creation of national unity (Ruget 2007, 81). Privileging ethnicity within the nation-building process has led to the utilization and politicization of kinship in social and political spheres, accentuated the country's ethnic and provincial cleavages, and exacerbated political instability.

Beyond the domain of official politics, the notion of a national culture has led people to freely investigate their belongingness. During the Soviet period, genealogical records were strictly controlled by Communist Party members, although people secretly used genealogies for their own purposes. Following independence, genealogy has become increasingly relevant in many domains, and is widely circulated in both oral and written forms. Local bookshops now carry numerous inexpensive publications about genealogy (Gullette 2006; Jacquesson 2010a, 2010b, 2010c; Kuchumkulova 2007). Ancestors became an important "dialogic trope" of serving and unifying communities as well we nations. Therefore, local leaders are actively involved in promoting and building "ancestral landscapes" that the state supports and even encourages (Dubuisson 2017, 14).

The North and the South Division

The division between the north and the south of Kyrgyzstan is especially important. The north and south are defined in relation to the mountains between them that make it difficult to cross from one area to the other. *The south* refers to the area around the cities of Osh, Jalal-Abad, Batken, and the Fergana Valley. *The north* refers to the area of the Chui Province, including the cities of Talas, Issik-Kul, and Naryn. The geographical separation is imperfect; Naryn, for example, would be better described as east of Osh, and thus logically "south." But the division is also based on communities of kinship, as described above, meaning that both kinship and the putative north-south divide combine in structuring all of the country's provincial divisions and the politico-administrative structure of Kyrgyzstan as a whole. The political opposition between south and north is long-standing, and the borders have become relevant to politics and identity in various ways throughout different periods. For example: the Toktogul Province during the Soviet Union was part of the Osh oblast, the Jalal-Abad, and even the Chui Province. Those residing in the north and south are mutually suspicious of each other, partly from the political dominance of each at various times in history (Huskey 1997b, 241; Juraev 2008, 259; Roy 2000, 97; Tolmacheva 2005, 25). The issue of the north-south divide first reemerged following the fall of the USSR over the issue of how to ensure a fair distribution of personnel according to provincial parameters.

Patronage Networks and Revolutions

Kyrgyzstan's postindependence experience serves as a productive point of entry for exploring the forms and local meanings of democracy and patronage networks in post-Soviet Central Asia. In the first years after independence was achieved in 1991, the Kyrgyz government took on strong patriarchal traits. In the first term of Askar Akaev's presidency (1991–2005), high posts in the state apparatus continued to be held mainly by representatives of the former Soviet administration. These high-level officials could use their official positions to obtain loans for establishing private businesses for themselves and others, especially in the privatization processes. With the support of old Soviet patrons, a new generation of patrons emerged who were active both in the public sector and in the business sector. Since the beginning of the transition period, state officials have tried to diversify their sources of income, and accordingly serve the state even as they operate as private entrepreneurs. Some were professional politicians, and others had another profession first and joined a business sector.

Widespread criticism of Kyrgyzstan's politics has focused on the uses of kinship by politicians. The newspaper *Delo*, for example, carried the following comment about the ongoing history of lineage-based politics on February 4, 2010:

> There were rivalry and struggle between the heads of the Soviet leaders. In post-war years, the Kyrgyz Soviet Republic was headed by Iskhak Razzakov, from the lineage *ichkilik*. Taking up the post of the first secretary of the Central Committee of the Communist Party of the Kyrgyz Soviet Socialist Republic (almost for a quarter of a century), he was replaced by Turdakun Usubaliev, who was from the *sarybagish* lineage. After Usubaliev, Absamat Masaliev was appointed from the *ichkilik* lineage. The first president of Kyrgyzstan became Askar Akaev from the *sarybagysh* lineage due to Moscow's personnel selection procedure. Once again, Kurmanbek Bakiev came to power from the *ichkilik* lineage, which looked like a historical revenge. Rivalry has continued since ancient times, for example, between the *sarybagysh* (dominating the north of the country) and the *bugu*—which is part of the right wing. And this rivalry is the main illness of the Kyrgyz, because as a result, by and large, the nation has not been developed.

The commentator's narrative of an ongoing duel between lineages with ancient roots that was preserved and promoted by the Soviets is not simply rhetorical flourish. The article was published five years after the Tulip Revolution and shortly before the Rose Revolution. Until 2005 the *sarybagysh* (dominating the north of the country) had been in power at the national level. For some fourteen years, southern leaders (*ichkilik* lineage) had felt themselves disadvantaged, but limited themselves to complaining about patronage and investment policies that they believed had created disproportionate political and economic power in the north, including the capital Bishkek (Huskey 1997b, 230).

On March 24, 2005, fourteen years after independence, the country's first president, Askar Akayev, was overthrown in a bloodless revolt known as the Tulip Revolution. For my informants in rural northern Kyrgyzstan, the Tulip Revolution signified the exercise of "people power" and offered some hope that there would be democratic change in Kyrgyzstan after a decade of increasing political and economic stagnation and an ever more visible concentration of resources in the president's hands (McGlinchey 2011). As the invocation of "tulips" in its naming suggests, the revolution was generally peaceful (Hiro 2009; Marat 2008a, 2008b), although there was some localized violence and a night of looting in Bishkek. Following the Tulip Revolution, a presidential election was held in July 2005, and the southerner Kurmanbek Bakiyev was elected to power. To avoid the division of the country along regional lines and to prevent civil war, a coalition was formed between Felix Kulov (from the country's north) and Kurmanbek Bakiyev after the election, with Kulov becoming the prime minister.

The Rose Revolution occurred on April 7, 2010. Like his predecessor, President Kurmanbek Bakiyev was also accused of corruption, appointing close family members to key positions in the government, and violating human rights. Not long after his election in 2005, people had organized various protests to express their dissatisfaction with the political situation, repression, their living conditions (which had deteriorated with a recent sharp increase in electricity and utility tariffs), and the sale of strategic state enterprises. People's concerns were ignored by the government, and the opposition gathered support until its leader, Roza Otunbayeva, succeeded (with the army's support) in demanding Bakiyev's departure.

As a result of this ongoing struggle between north and south, kinship groups are politically mobilized, and northern groups aligned against southern groups. Lineage affiliation in Kyrgyzstan tends to partially correlate with the country's provincial divisions according to southern Kyrgyzstan (*sol kanat* or left-wing), *ichkilik* (internal) and the northern Kyrgyzstan (*ong kanat* or right-wing) (see Chapter 2). Moreover, political parties are rooted in networks that coalesce around a leaders' province of origin and genealogical links. Parties are not reducible to lineages, but parties named for lineages (such as Dordoi and Ak-Jol) also suggest the idea that a party's obligation is to support (kin) members.

Kyrgyz politicians also use lineage membership within the party system to compete among themselves for particular positions. Those who are not related through kinship-patronage networks are often excluded. In this context, divisions between politicians along kinship lines can initiate and exacerbate struggles between groups, conflict over positions and power within the infrastructure of the state and over funds for development and education (Jacquesson 2010b, 2010c).

The discourse of kinship also links politicians to their "electorate." On the one hand, politicians scrutinize the family history of potential supporters in the hope of finding a common ancestor and then attempt to foster closer relations with newfound "kin." At the same time, kinship discourse is also utilized by people who seek to engage politicians (and businessmen) to help them to satisfy their own needs and hopes for a better future. People imagine and construct a union with these figures who might provide them with jobs, material, medical, and bureaucratic support. However, using kinship to claim access to new resources and power also contributes to the emergence of social cleavages along kinship (and provincial) lines.

Patronage in Kyrgyzstan: Continuity and Transformation

The patronage system was not weakened during the Soviet times; on the contrary it was strong and omnipresent. However, after the collapse of the Soviet Union, patronage emerged in a new form and was thus integrated into the new sociopolitical system.

The cultural logic of patronage in the post-Soviet period operates through an historical syncretism between pre-Soviet, Russian and Soviet, and contemporary practices. In the precolonial period, patrons held a traditional role as mediators in family and political negotiations. In the Soviet period, they helped bridge the gap between Soviet administration and local people. In the post-Soviet era, patrons are integrally tied to the democratic and nation-building processes. Forms of kinship-based patronage changed over time and were called by various names, but patrons were always drawn from those who displayed creativity and strategic cunning to establish political alliances and secure economic cooperation during hard times.

During Soviet times, the chains of patronage were hierarchical, descending through the Communist Party, state administration, and kolkhoz. In the post-Soviet period, the patronage system is tied to the state bureaucracy, political parties, and private business. It is less apparently hierarchical than during the Soviet period, but a patron's relative economic and political positions affect the number of clients he has among state officials, businessmen, and local people.

It is difficult to assess whether the new kinship-based patronage ought to be seen more as Soviet continuity, ethnic revival, or something else. Since independence, patronage through kinship has not been publicly suppressed or denied as in the Soviet period. Rather, kin-based patronage has gained momentum and credence in tandem with the state's pursuit of identity politics and nation building.

Yet the establishment of patronage networks is not as easy as it seems. The idiom of kinship greatly facilitates feelings of mutual obligation, but patronage has to be validated and made acceptable as an aspect of social life more generally. It is therefore common for aspiring and accomplished patrons to organize various political feasts and traditional sport competitions, to engage in gift exchange, and to display generous public hospitality. Such behaviors are linked to culturally accepted values for people seeking honor, position, and social recognition. Feasts and celebrations therefore dominate current politics. This situation resembles the prominence of public feasting and celebrations during Soviet times, but post-Soviet patrons distinguish themselves from their predecessors by posing as the sole initiator and personal financier of a voluntary and nonideological event.

Notes

1. National Statistical Committee of the Republic of Kyrgyzstan.

2. The emergence of minority groups in the neighboring countries is due to the historical and political situations (such as the suppression of the 1916 rebellion against Russian rule in Central Asia). In the contemporary period, Kyrgyz are in Russian, Turkey, and other countries as a result of labor migration, education, and business.

3. Although the term is now used throughout the former Soviet Union, my informants insist that they preferred to speak of "helping" one's relatives during the post-Soviet period. For them, *blat* connotes a specifically Soviet form of using connections.

4. For example, Chingiz Aitmatov, a writer and adviser to President Akayev, initiated a grand celebration of the one-thousand-year anniversary of the hero Manas. This had two aims: first, to revive the representative heritage of the Kyrgyz; second, to draw the attention of an international audience to bolster the Akayev government's authority (Abdykadirov, Sud'ba, items 64, 66, 68, cited by Prior 2000, 36).

2   Scales of Rahim's Kinship
Zooming In and Zooming Out

To grasp the interlinkage between patronage and kinship, it is important to situate Rahim's position in the wider Kyrgyz genealogical system that shaped his action and behavior. The use of kinship to build political power is not unusual for an ethnic Kyrgyz politician. The important question to ask is thus how Rahim's kinship profile made him poised to become a regional patron. How did Rahim's place in larger genealogical relations link him as a potential patron to multiple households, villages, geographic regions, and, indeed, a whole province?

Kinship relations are interwoven with questions of property, landholding and inheritance, local politics, employment relationships, economic networks, and access to state resources. This implies that kinship is integrated into the whole of social, economic, and political life among ethnic Kyrgyz, and in Kyrgyzstan more generally. In the following two chapters, I systematically link Rahim's position to the complex field of Kyrgyz kinship at different levels and scales. This chapter focuses on Rahim's deep engagements with the segmentary lineage system of the Kyrgyz. The system is flexible enough to allow for the manipulation of both individual and group genealogies.

As will be clear, almost all Kyrgyz individuals can claim shared descent with people from their native villages and regions. Almost anyone could become a native son. Only a few, however, make the attempt and engage so creatively in the reworking of genealogies necessary to find so many kin. Rahim did.

Locating the Field

Let me begin with a brief introduction to the village of Bulak and its kinship organization. It was here, in this village, that Rahim was most active and most fully integrated into the segmentary lineage system. And it was here that Rahim sought the status of a native son. "Bulak," by the way, is the Soviet name for the village. People use it interchangeably with "Nurmanbet," which is the name of the villagers' shared patrilineal ancestor (see Map 2.1).

Rahim was born and raised in Bulak among his father's relatives. Rahim's father traced his patrilineal descent from Nurmanbet (Suu Murun),[1] one of the two major Kyrgyz genealogical figures in Chüi Valley. When Rahim was

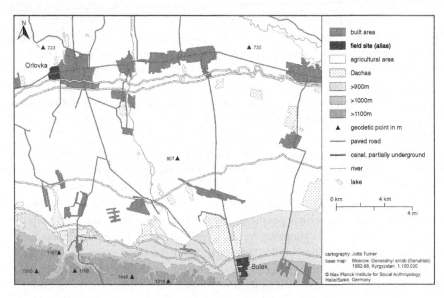

Map 2.1. Field site.

eighteen, his father died, and Rahim moved shortly afterward to Bishkek together with his mother and sister so that he could attend university. After Rahim
moved to the capital, he maintained ties with his natal village. So far there is
nothing very unusual in Rahim's story. His father's death weakened the social
status of Rahim's mother and Rahim himself. But it would be considered only
"natural" for any Kyrgyz to maintain ties with his father's village because such
a village would be the home to nearly all of his most important relatives, that is,
his patriline.

Bulak, too, is in many ways a typical Kyrgyz village. In 2007 Bulak officially
registered 5,042 residents distributed into 670 households,[2] but the real number
was significantly higher because people would not register some of the family
members to avoid paying taxes. Bulak, like my second research site of Orlovka,
just forty kilometers away, is located in Issyk-Ata rayon in the Chüi Valley. The
nearest large city to both Bulak and Orlovka is Bishkek. Orlovka, discussed further in subsequent chapters (especially Chapter 4), has a similar population size
of 5,800, but is more properly described as "semirural" than as a "village."[3] Most
important for this account is to note that Bulak has long been proud of having a
native son who takes care of them and provides basic needs in times of necessity.
Rahim was not the first native son of the village, but he was the first to appear
during the post-Soviet period.

Villagers in Bulak have needs defined by the village's economy. Located in a mountainous province, the village is cold and experiences heavy snows that often fall by December. Bulak has electricity, but in the spring it is cut off for twelve hours each day because of chronic mismanagement of the power grid at the Toktogul Dam. The economy is dominated by agriculture, although it is increasingly diversified. The number of people working outside the village for brief periods of time is steadily increasing, and the proximity of Bishkek makes trade a viable option for many.

Most villagers breed cattle and cultivate maize, wheat, and vegetables such as onions, potatoes, and carrots. Labor is divided along clear gender lines: men work in the fields and tend cattle, while women take care of the household and children, with the help of older children. Bulak produces more onions than neighboring villages, which people barter for potatoes. There are a few small shops (R. *kamok*), where shopkeepers sell largely on credit, recording names and indebted sums in thick notebooks. Debts are repaid as soon as a person sells milk, receives a pension, or has goods to barter. During my fieldwork, villagers sold their milk to a company owned by Rahim; the milk was collected every morning, and cash payments were immediately dispensed.

Villagers are stratified according to the categories of "rich" (*bai*) and "poor" (*kedei*). The category of "poor" includes people without livestock, machinery, and land. They make a living by working for the rich as servants or cattle breeders. The "rich" include many ex-kolkhoz managers and their kinsmen who profited from privatizing kolkhoz property before other villagers. The "rich" also include young businessmen active in the export of milk, wholesale of farm products, or who own private farms, cafés, or restaurants. Rahim's family belonged to the category of the rich, and, like all rich families, they had provided jobs to the village poor.

There is also a more or less economically stable category of the population who consider themselves to be middle class (*orto*). Schoolteachers, members of the village administration, and shopkeepers fall into this category. Such families have small incomes from state-paid or private work, but also cultivate land and breed cattle.

Kinship in Bulak Village

When one comes to Bulak village, the first question people ask is "Where are you from?" When this is clarified, whether they are from the south or the north, there are further specific questions: "Who are you?"—that is, "From whom are you descended?" And then more questions: "To which lineage do you belong?" "Who is your grandfather?" "And who is your father?" Through such exchanges, two Kyrgyz who meet for the first time are able to place each other, either as patrilineal kin or as affines in a segmentary lineage system in which both genealogically close and distant relatives are categorized together. Using these markers, people are able to decide who belongs to whom, and also one's own relation to the new acquaintance.

To summarize: Rahim belonged to Bulak. He was born and raised there, and as an adult he maintained his kin-based ties. His family was among the rich, and they had supported the poor before Rahim took up his turn. Yet his rise to the status of native son was not inevitable. As a young adult, Rahim had relatively weak kin ties. After his father's death, Rahim's closest patrilineal relatives consisted only of his father's brother—soon to die himself—and two mentally weak male cousins. How Rahim became the village's native son, however, involved a process of stretching kin relations, sometimes creating new ones, and taking up economic and social roles that matched the relations. Over the next several pages, I describe the basic framework of relations within which Rahim had to maneuver. Details of his profile and how he maneuvered then appear across the subsequent sections and chapters.

Kinship is the chief organizational principle for social relations in the village of Bulak, with both normative and practical aspects in the daily exchange of goods and services between relatives and neighbors. The normative model of Kyrgyz kinship includes details of descent, alliance, residence, cooperation, and inheritance. Ideally kinship is based on patrilineal descent. Thus descent is traced mainly through fathers, with each person's genealogy beginning with a founding male ancestor and stretching across at least seven generations. Such genealogies place an individual within lineage groupings of *uruu* and *uruk*.

The village of Bulak carries the name of the patrilineal ancestor, Nurmanbet (Suu Murun), claimed by all villagers. Why both names are accurate is beyond the realms of current memory, though one possibility is that Suu Murun was a nickname given to Nurmanbet by in-marrying women in the lineage who are forbidden to utter publicly the real names of their husbands' fathers, brothers, or grandfathers.

As shown in Figure 2.1, five lineages in Bulak (Karasakal, Shaibek [Ongko-goi], Sagyndyk, Kochokbai, and Ak Jol) trace common ancestry to Nurmanbet (Suu Murun). Several adjacent villages are also patrilineally related to Bulak, creating a dense network of kin relations in a compact region. Although Soviet policies sometimes succeeded in breaking the close linkage between patrilines and settlements, the general tendency in rural areas is for villages to be largely congruent with descent groups—like Bulak and its neighbors. The ideology of kinship obligations reinforces the cohesiveness of the community and facilitates mutual support; community solidarity is expressed in terms of active participation and support during life cycle events and the visible devotion of the majority to its community representative.

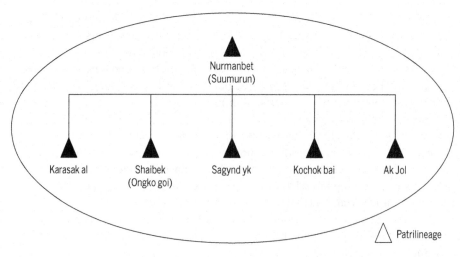

Figure 2.1. Simplified genealogical chart of the Nurmanbet (Suumurun).

Lineage distribution across Kyrgyzstan

Kinship belonging can be stretched to encompass wider regions. Kin and affinal relationships are mapped onto territory at the level of the household, the village, and the region—and they are also used to provide a conceptual framework for genealogical relatedness as distant kinsmen (*alys tuugan*). Rahim played creatively with the notion of distant kinsmen (*alys tuugan*) to stretch his kinship relations. While such play is theoretically possible for everyone, it is not easy to create extensive networks of distant kin because one's claims must be plausible and accepted by others.

It is important to draw more attention to the highest and lowest lineage levels and their close relationship. The kinship terminology of the Kyrgyz segmentary patrilineage system consists of two emic terms—*uruu* (lineage) and *uruk* (sublineage). In this system *uruu* is divided into several *uruk*, so that major lineages are segmented into small lineages. *Uruu* is a higher level of the lineage branch, whereas *uruk* is a lower level of branching. Each *uruk*—or lineage branch—consists of approximately forty or fifty households, each of which can be considered a stable social unit. The members of any one lineage, whether of a lower-level or higher-level segment, place great emphasis on being able to trace their patrilineal ancestors for seven or even ten generations in order to prove their membership in an *uruu* and *uruk*. Historically, those who could not prove their *uruu* membership were considered slaves (*kul*) (see Figure 2.2).

These minimal lineages often occupy specific territories, so that *uruu* and *uruk* are specific to a particular village or set of neighboring villages. Seen from

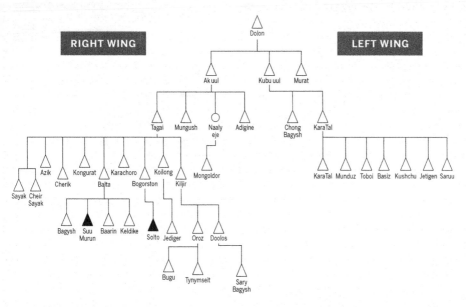

Figure 2.2. The genealogical structure of Kyrgyz (the right and the left wing).
See Abramzon (1960, 5).

the village perspective, this means that the lands occupied by these related villages up to the level of rayon or oblast "belong" to the head of the patrilineage. The majority of ethnic Kyrgyz in Chüi Province (*Chüilüktör*) would claim that they share the same ancestors—either Solto or Nurmanbet (Suu Murun) depending on whose descendants they claim to be. The descendants of the two ancestors reside in closely adjacent territories of the Chüi Valley.[4] However, the descendants of other major ancestors, such as Sayak, Bugu, and Sarybagysh, also reside in Chüi. Some of them have been integrated (*koshulduu*) into the sublineages of Solto or Nurmanbet (Suu Murun) and others not.

Analytically, I therefore classify Solto and Nurmanbet (Suu Murun) as the maximal lineages of the Chüi Province within the right wing of Kyrgyz lineages, which are segmented into minor lineages and thus distributed in the small villages across the Chüi Province. For example, Solto is divided into seven descendant lines (Söök murun, Besh Norum, Maak, Kungtuu, Kultu, Aituu, Chaa[5]) (see Figure 2.3). Descendants of Nurmanbet (Suu Murun) and Solto can consider themselves as the distant relatives since they share the ancestor Tagai. On the basis of the shared ancestor Tagai, Rahim nicely fits himself into an ancestral profile that makes him poised to become a patron for a whole region.

Nevertheless, despite being dispersed in various locations, descent ideologies are used at higher segmentary levels to conceptualize relationships between

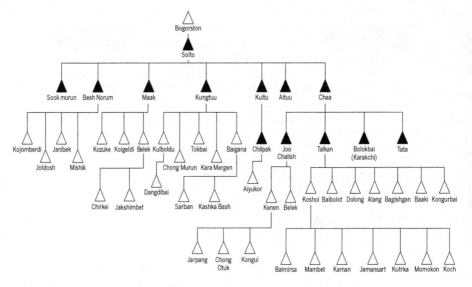

Figure 2.3. Genealogical chart of Solto.

larger segments. Thus several community members from diverse provinces can claim to be genealogically linked to the common ancestor Solto or Suu Murun, to share the same genealogical line and descent ideal.[6] These principles do not limit one's kinsmen to within the village framework alone, rather they go beyond the village and thereby stretch their genealogical relatedness to the entire region as well as the broader Chüi Valley as a whole. Its extensive history goes back some several dozen generations that include thousands of members. The main patrilineal descent groups were more strongly corporate, exercising political, economic, and social functions at once in the past, but we can now still see the subsequent formation of smaller groups from parent lineages.

As I said earlier, territory and kinship are congruent; therefore, there are also major patrilineal ancestors whose descendants are dispersed in different parts of Kyrgyzstan—Bugu, Solto, Sarybagysh, Tynymseit, Adigine, Kuschchu, and so on (see Map 2.2). The same genealogical system works in the same manner as in other places, in which patrons of other regions follow the same segmentation logic in building patronage networks along kinship lines.

Segmentation of Nurmanbet (Suu Murun)

The map of Kyrgyz descent groups does not show the complexities of the internal segmentation of lineage. Here I would like to zoom from a vast landscape of

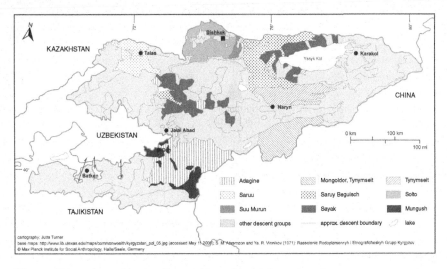

Map 2.2. Kyrgyz descent groups dispersed in various regions.

maximal patrilineages to a single patrilineal ancestor: Nurmanbet (Suu Murun) and his descendants, who have formed a unit in the Issyk-Ata region. The narrative genre of genealogical discussion around Nurmanbet (Suu Murun) is poetically driven by glorifying Nurmanbet as having an ability to do mystical things such as to forecast weather and earthquakes in advance.

At some point, this unit was too big because of economic reasons, such as a lack of pastures and animals. Part of the group would have split off and formed a new group somewhere else. As in Bulak, new areas were settled when relatives quarreled and moved away from one another. Whether led by a son or grandson of Nurmanbet (Suu Murun), the new group eventually would call itself by a separate name and form a new patrilineal descent group, although they continued to claim descent from Nurmanbet (Suu Murun). Depending on the demography, different parts of the group may have split off in different periods and formed units, giving themselves names after the son or the father of that group. Thus Nurmanbet (Suu Murun) is divided into six descendant lines: Oljobai, Asanbek, Duishom Tikuchok, Buchuk, and Karasakal (see Figure 2.4).[7]

Each of them in turn is segmented or branched in a pattern that is repeated down the lineage, and each is localized. However, the segmentation process in each period depends on the numbers of sons that are attached to the previous ancestors. Each of those sons' descendants in turn is segmented in a commonly recurring pattern of progression. In times of need, for example, the minimal lineage segments (see Figure 2.4)—Oljobai, Asanbek, Duishon, Tulkuchuk, Buchuk, Karasakal—unite and are then designated as a major segment Nurmanbet

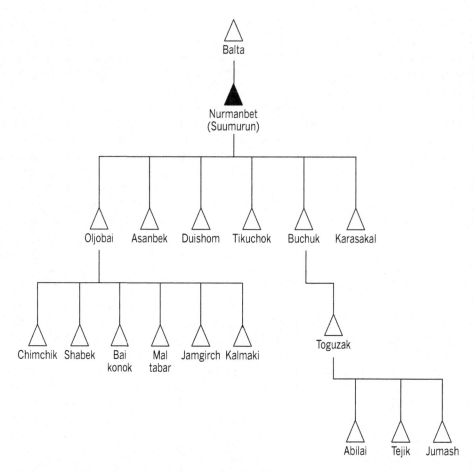

Figure 2.4. Genealogical chart 1 of Nurmanbet (Suu Murun).

(Suu Murun), opposed to the similarly constituted other descent group. In this line, what we see here how Evans-Pritchard's principles of fission and fusion of segmentary kinship fits the Kyrgyz kinship system. *Uruu* is divided into maximal, major, minor, and minimal lineages, each with its name linking it to a single ancestor.

Thus the segmentation process was a means of organizing effective social groups, effective in adapting to the challenges of the environment, maintaining order through patterns of interactions and customs and productivity across generations. During the Soviet times, several descent groups of Nurmanbet (Suu Murun) were brought up together and established a joint kolkhoz. Despite being under the Soviet kolkhoz, there has been constant internal split. However, the recent split in the lineage process was explained to me by a local village elder: "In comparison with the Soviet era, nowadays, the Ak Jol lineage consists of sixty households that can accommodate life cycle events independently amongst their own members. Whereas previously, representatives of lineages such as Sagindik and Karatai could help each other in times of need by sharing labor (slaughtering animals, cooking food, and distributing food). Now there is a split in the lineage system within the village as a result of the inclusion of very close sublineages and exclusion of those who are from genealogically remote sublineages." The number of lineage members has increased in Bulak Village, which has led to the division of the village along segmentary lines. Thus, lineages are constructed based on acknowledged descent lines and have various sizes depending on circumstances and also on generational depth.

The descendants of Nurmanbet (Suu Murun) reside beyond the village of Bulak. Only the descendants of five of his sons occupy Bulak, while descendants from his other sons reside in the neighboring villages and are scattered in several villages across the Issyk-Ata rayon, which itself comprises more than thirteen villages. The lineage of Nurmanbet (Suu Murun) can even be increased to cover almost all the eastern parts of the Chüi Province, depending on how one reckons genealogy. Normally the interaction between different descent groups in many villages and across the rayon is passive or uneventful. But because people in the thirteen villages were all related to Rahim through some genealogical lines, they could all claim a right to approach Rahim as a native son in times of need on the basis of kin relations.

Bulak's Five Lineages of Nurmanbet (Suu Murun)

While thoroughly investigating Nurmanbet (Suu Murun)'s genealogical tree, I noticed that some parts of the standard chart did not fit what I saw in the village. Lineage segments and branches, the names of lineages, and the descendants of the brothers and sons of particular "fathers" deviated from the ideal. Instead of clean lines of patrilineal descent, key male ancestors seemed to be scattered throughout the genealogical chart (see Figures 2.1 and 2.6).

Let us start with Nurmanbet (Suu Murun), who had four sons, Oljobai, Karasakal, Duishon, and Toguzak. Karasakal is one of the sons of Nurmanbet, which means that Karasakal stands one segment beyond the others in the genealogical chart. Toguzak, Nurmanbet's second son, had four sons—Jeirenbai, Shaibek, Buchuk, and Kemel. On this line, we can see that Shaibek is the grandson of Nurmanbet. However, on the same line there is also Buchuk, who has five sons—Jumash, Murat, Sagyndyk, Kochokbai, and Ak Jol. On this line, we can also see Sagyndyk, Kochokbai, and Ak Jol, who are great-grandsons of Nurmanbet (Suu Murun). Although new villages were sometimes founded as a result of lineage fission, it is not necessarily the only way in which villages became dominated by a single lineage. In Bulak villagers were members of lineages scattered throughout the genealogical chart. Some lineages originated with one of Nurmanbet's sons, while others originated with one of his grandsons or great-grandsons.[8] This may have occurred for a variety of reasons, including the possibility that some fathers died without sons or that intermediary lines have died out. Notwithstanding evidence to the contrary, villagers described the five sub-lineages as those formed by brothers.

Indeed, some of the ancestors, including Nurmanbet, may be fictional, but people believe they were real. I found that the character played an important part in people's decision making and that their idea of him influenced their actions and behavior. Thus the past is inseparable from present concerns, which are in turn linked to future generations.

There were also other gaps in genealogical knowledge. With many lineages, I found it easy to trace the relationship of my informant as "ego" back (or rather up) seven generations to a lineage founder. Yet with others, like the Karasakal lineage, there were irregularities. Karasakal was not lined up with his brothers and was in fact located one step below Nurmanbet. Also, because Karasakal occupies a place nine generations removed from my informants, those who claimed descent from him (within seven generations) necessarily overlooked some segments of their actual genealogy. No one seemed to know why Karasakal was irregularly placed, but offered several contradictory possibilities, including that the oral versions that people gave me were correct and the written chart I consulted had been incorrectly recorded. Mostly people told me that it would have been nice if I had come two years earlier. There had been a very wise man (*aksakal*) in the village who had known everything and could have explained it all to me. Unfortunately, he had died. The villagers gave me his written records but could not explain them further (see Figure 2.5).

Whether it is possible to explain the structural particularities of Bulak's five sublineages is less important than understanding the social importance of the structure. Why was the existence of these five sublineages, and their observable hierarchies and interrelations, important in everyday life? Why and how did they provide community members with a sense of belonging? At the very least, people understood their world through this structure and in relation to kinsmen. They knew by heart who belonged to each lineage and sublineage and orally transmitted this information from one generation to another.

The irregularities of the Karasakal lineage were not without their practical effect. The members of the Karasakal lineage were more respected than other villagers because their lineage was considered to be more senior. As a result, when villagers needed to appoint the head of the aksakal court of elders (*aksakal sotu*) in 2005, they looked to the Karasakal lineage.[9] As Beyer (2016) argued, the

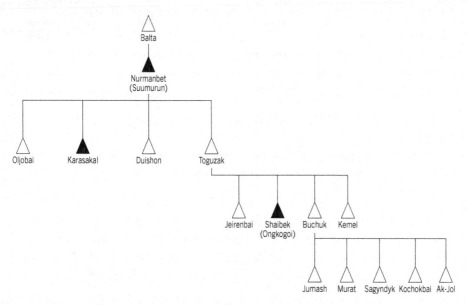

Figure 2.5. Genealogical chart 2 of Nurmanbet (Suu Murun).
See Abramzon (1960, 61), and see also more detailed genealogies of Nurmanbet (Suu Murun) from the villages Bulak and Saru, data taken from the history teacher and the genealogist of the village Ermek agai, February 2, 2008, drawn by the author.

authority of elders (*aksakal*), regardless of gender, was the result of individual accomplishments and respect earned over time and invested in social relations. In addition, in line with Beyer's argument, elders' authority was also the result of lineage status.

I gathered genealogical information from my informants and from written accounts, both published and unpublished. Accounts between sources were inconsistent, and people made sense of the inconsistencies in making or refuting their own claims. About inconsistencies in Bedouin genealogies, Shryock stated, "This contested area is also fertile ground for cultural analyses" (1997, 17). These gaps in genealogies were also critical for Rahim because he could be creative in making claims of possible kinship connections.

Remembering Genealogical Connections

While they are still children, Kyrgyz boys are expected to learn by heart and know the names of their seven forefathers. Ideally many boys should be able to name their seventh forefather, but this is not always the case. In any case, they can always approach a genealogical expert when this information becomes necessary. By middle age, however, men have become thoroughly familiar with their genealogy through their participation in various life cycle events. On such occasions, people depend on their genealogical knowledge to know whom to invite and whom not to invite according to lineage identity. Knowledge of one's lineage is also necessary to find jobs and in many other domains. Accordingly, Rahim should have been socially weak because of his lack of brothers and other close male relatives, but he used his genealogical knowledge to find "brothers" and other close kin.

The "official" genealogy of the village was in competition with oral accounts. Only male names are recorded, but female members of lineages are also sometimes important in the recall of patrilineal descent. Kyrgyz women have a significant role especially in transmitting oral genealogies and passing on stories to their children and grandchildren. Women are also actively involved developing "new names for the men" in the genealogical grid in order to use them exclusively by themselves. This is related to the fact that women are not allowed to utter publicly the names of their fathers-in-law or those of the brothers of their fathers-in-law (Ismailbekova 2014a, 378).

In my conversations with the sixty-some-year-old village historian Adyl, I soon became confident enough to ask specific questions about individual genealogies. He had compiled the full genealogical chart of the village. Knowledge of the full genealogy of the village was a sign of honor and status for Adyl because few villagers' knowledge was as complete. People respected him because of his symbolic capital. He was a university-trained historian and had been compiling the oral history of the village through his long-term genealogical research since the early 1980s. Because of his textual expertise and collection of oral history, villagers authorized him to produce their history.

Adyl also showed me the published book of the village that he found incomplete (*toluk emes*) and full of dry information (*kurgak*). The author of this book, he said, was not from Bulak. He had not taken the time to record everything in detail because he had been participating in a competition on genealogy. He had not interviewed anyone but had relied on the help of another genealogist in the village. Nor had he consulted with Adyl. He was not objective, removed many names, and distorted the genealogical grid of Nurmanbet (Suu Murun). Adyl would usually take the published book with him when he went to discuss genealogies with people so that he could show them the inconsistencies in the names.

I borrowed the published book for several days and compared it against Adyl's records. The main ancestor, major lineages, and sublineages matched in each account. There were, however, frequently different spellings of names; some segments of lineages were missing in the published account, and there were gaps where names had been removed or not included in the published one. Moreover, the published book did not take into account the importance of seniority within the genealogical structure that is that lineages were ranked according to the seniority of a line descent. Those whose lineage is senior would be senior to all members of junior lineages, but the author mixed up the senior with the junior lineages.

Eventually I came to ask questions about the relations between the patron (Rahim) and his clients and spoke with more than two hundred of the patron's clients who claimed to be his kin. The examples that follow draw from some of the most interesting stories concerning how people considered themselves to be related to the patron. They reveal some of the dynamics through which genealogies are remembered (and forgotten) in ways that make possible the strategic manipulation of genealogies, without rendering the resulting genealogies false.

I noticed another obvious inaccuracy while I was drawing the genealogical tree of Baikonok: when I compared a written version of the lineage and an oral version, I found that the written source documented the name Shaibek, not Baikonok as people had told me (see Table 2.1). The book recorded Baikonok as the brother of Shaibek, but people had told me that they use Baikonok as an alternate name for Shaibek.

It was eventually explained to me that the brides of the village were responsible for the use of Baikonok in the genealogies. They were not allowed to name Shaibek in public, so instead they gave him a nickname (that is, Baikonok), which means "too large and rich," as a clear depiction of his physical appearance (a person with a belly). This misfit between oral and textual sources was the arena for multiple negotiations of clients of Rahim in establishing closer ties to his own Ak-Jol ancestor in the genealogical chart.

Written and oral accounts each have their own authority, and each can be deemed "incomplete," while attempts at "correction" may be strongly contested. Even Adyl did not consistently include the names of newborn male children, which means that new members of lineages are introduced at various points of their lives. In these ways, even the "official" genealogical charts always leave room for people to negotiate their genealogy while remaining within the bounds of authority and truth. Thus, genealogy is a chart for action in the present, not a historical document.

Rediscovering Ak Jol—Bulak's Unique Aristocratic Lineage

Over a period of some five years, Rahim built up his kin relations and business activities in and around Bulak. Then, shortly before seeking a position in parliament in 2007, Rahim discovered that he was descended from a noble line (*ak söök*). He claimed that his father's father's father, Baiymbet, was a rich chief (*bai manap*) during the pre-Soviet period. The chieftain's lineage was disbanded by the Soviet regime and local people had forgotten about it. Rahim had discovered

Table 2.1 Common Ancestors: Descendants of Karachoro

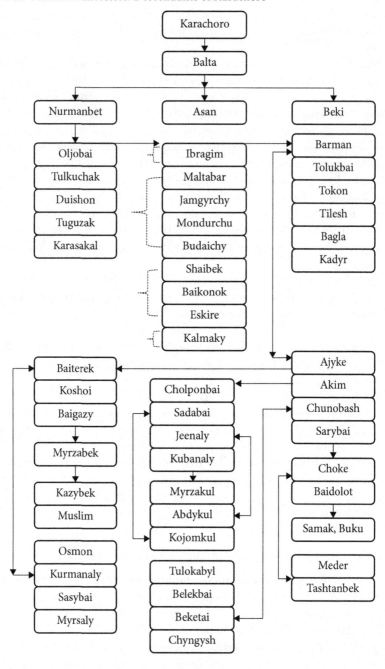

that this lineage of "white bones" (*ak söök*) still existed by consulting the village's extensive genealogy. Rahim also claimed Toguzak, renowned for powerful supernatural powers, as his great-grandfather in the seventh generation. As the descendent of nobles, elites, and sages, Rahim suddenly seemed destined to bring not only support but also glory to the community.

Ethnic Kyrgyz did not historically recognize noble lineages, so Rahim's claims to be *ak söök* might well have been challenged as preposterous from the outset. But people accepted even this claim because Rahim was politically and economically successful. In part people were willing to accept his claims to a noble past because of the material benefits of his patronage networks. But they also accepted the claims because they could be justified, if only indirectly. The Kyrgyz had, after all, recognized different statuses among lineages in the pre-Soviet period. The term Rahim used to describe his nobility, *ak söök*, was a Kazak term; his mother was from a powerful Kazak lineage. Indeed, people had forgotten much about Rahim's lineage during the Soviet period because those who had been rich were considered traitors of the people. Rahim's own story brought to the fore the more glorious elements of the pasts for several families, if not the whole village, that had also been silenced and forgotten during the Soviet era. And people were willing to believe that such noble ancestry, transmitted down the generations, might well have been the reason for Rahim's apparent luck and skill in the difficult world of post-Soviet business.

Such luck and skill had been necessary for Rahim. He could not rely on close patrilineal kin, as kinship ideology would have predicted. He simply had none: Rahim's father had only one brother, which is very unusual in rural Kyrgyzstan. Rahim's father and his father's brother were born following their father's return from World War II, but they had no other siblings because their father's war injuries led to his early death, and Rahim's grandmother did not remarry. As a result of poor health, Rahim's father also had only two children: Rahim and a daughter. Following the death of his father's brother in the early 2000s, Rahim's closest remaining male kinsmen were two mentally incompetent cousins, the twin sons of his father's brother. To build his career in business, Rahim had relied on more distant kinsmen (*alys*).

At the time I was doing research, Rahim asked the village elders several times to help him draw the genealogical chart of his fathers, and to discuss how rich his grandfathers had been during the pre-Soviet era. He wanted, he said, to make a new book of genealogies for the village because the existing one was not large enough to take into account the genealogies of the younger generation, including his own. He expressed his willingness to defend and preserve his version of the past for the future generation. The book was supposed to be published in time for the village's eightieth birthday in 2007, and its final results in a written text would have special authority (Shryock 1997, 243).

The discovered lineage justified a privileged status for Rahim within the village, his political power, and his position as a big man throughout the province. When I asked the villagers about Rahim's Ak-Jol lineage, they said that the uniqueness of this lineage was that it consisted of intellectuals and people who were ambitious, and that it was full of prominent leaders. Yet an odd contradiction emerged; while the ancestry that was discovered for Rahim gave him the right to govern the community, the elders whom he consulted conferred on him the modest name of öz bala (literally "own son") or the "son of the community." He was to be respected and honored because of his lineage, but his relative youth rendered him subordinate.

By self-identifying as a member of a strong, unique aristocratic lineage, the patron tried to claim a superior position and position in relation to members of his community. The patron used his identification with the community, ancestral land, and specific lineage aristocracy to legitimize and justify his actions and the support of his clients. The sources for legitimization did not come directly from him but had been synthesized on the basis of oral history, select published genealogical texts, and external experts. Rahim's status within the local social, political, and economic system became explained (and naturalized) as a result of his position in the unique lineage system. In Kyrgyzstan, as in other societies where genealogical reckoning is key, patrons considered the roots and foundations of ancestors as necessary components of their high social status and successful establishments of their political careers (cf. Shryock 1997).

As a patron, Rahim adopted symbolic forms associated with lineage identity to indicate his distinctiveness and to validate his high status. The kinship system allowed him a good deal of flexibility and room to manipulate symbols of descent but did not permit a wholesale reorganization of his kin relations. As Cohen states (1974, 59), "The traditional patterns of symbolic behaviour which maintain identity in the new situation, people try subjectively to invent new symbolic patterns of their own to deal with the new patterns of interaction."

Shifting Power: Native Sons and the Renewal of Lineages

Rahim was not the village's first or only "native son." The most important element of "native sons" from a national perspective in the post-Soviet period is their association with the dynamics of "corruption" and political patronage. At the local level, however, the appearance of native sons must also be understood in the context of shifting power dynamics between lineages, as well as the loss and renewal of particular lineages over time.

People would immediately give many examples of people of local origin who were entitled to respect on account of their privileged positions during or after the Soviet period: the person responsible for the State Treasury; the head of the

Academy of Science; the head of the university's geology department. People also added a few rich businessmen to this group, but they insisted on distinguishing between state officials as "big men" (*chongdor*) and those who were only rich men (*bailar*).

Rahim's appearance must therefore be understood also in the context of the village's recent loss of another native son, Sultan Toktonaliev. Toktonaliev had served as the minister of finance for twenty-five years, spanning both the Soviet and post-Soviet periods. During this time, he had been in ongoing conversations with the villagers. He helped Bulak by initiating the building of a secondary school, a technical school (R. *uchilishe*), and a department store (R. *univermag*). He also had helped educate a majority of the villagers by building the village schools, and had helped secure university places for many, especially those from poor families. People were proud that the village was full of specialized accountants who worked in the various business sectors that Toktonaliev had opened. After his death, the school took his name in place of its old name in 1993. Unfortunately, Toktonaliev had no sons. His house had been sold, and people regretted that the Shaibek lineage would not "keep his name alive" (*atyn öchürböi*).

By 2007 people had begun to talk more about Rahim's Ak-Jol lineage than the Shaibek lineage. Even newly married women proudly claimed to be the brides (*kelin*) of the Ak-Jol lineage, claiming Rahim as a brother-in-law and hoping to give birth to young leaders. Rahim was also invited to the various marriage ceremonies as a representative of the lineage to ensure that the bride was getting married to a good family with high status in the village and thus the parents of the bride were entering into a good union.

These claims to belong to Rahim's patriline were important to both Rahim and his clients. Rahim's clients, as shown in the following, were often creative and convincing in their efforts to reach their goals for securing his support.

The Case of Turdu

Turdu did not live in Bulak, but he was one of Rahim's clients. Turdu was from the Alamedyn rayon, and occasionally visited the Issyk-Ata Province. Turdu knew his genealogy because he had interviewed his now deceased father and read genealogical texts about Solto's descendants (from whom the whole Chüi are descended). In front of an audience in public, he would skillfully recount how he had met his younger brother (*atalash ini*) Rahim.[10] In his account, Turdu strangely called Rahim's ancestors by the name of the Suumurun ancestor. Technically this placed him in the Baikonok lineage. When I asked why he had not called the line by its official name as either Nurmanbet (Suumurun) or Shaibek (Baikonok), he told me that if he had used their official names, the villagers might have concluded that he had read too many genealogical books. Since he also had to prove he was an insider, Turdu's discrete approach in using the local lineage names was important. Later when I was looking at the picture of the genealogical chart, I worked out that under the name Nurmanbet, Suumurun was written in brackets. In other words, that person was right by claiming that his ancestor was Suumurun.

Turdu also mentioned that his grandfather had been born in Bulak, and he described how his grandfather had moved to the Alamedyn rayon as a result of the collectivization process in 1926. Turdu's grandfather does appear on Bulak's records, but he later associated himself with a lineage in Alamedyn Province, and Turdu himself remained part of the adopted lineage. When I asked why his grandfather had changed affiliations, Turdu explained that it had been necessary for integrating into his new home. Turdu remembered not only his grandfather's lineages but also his stories; in one of them, his grandfather had mentioned Rahim's grandmother, and Turdu himself retold this story when explaining his connection to Rahim.

Turdu's efforts to relate himself closely to Rahim were successful. With Rahim's help he became a parliament press secretary. Turdu and Rahim were indeed close and often seen together. Eventually close relatives to Rahim in Bulak objected to Turdu's claims and accused him of trying to access Rahim's resources through kinship. They consulted elders in the community, who provided evidence of the veracity of Turdu's claims. After this consultation, the villagers made no further objections.

The Case of Chopa

Chopa did not appreciate my extensive genealogical knowledge of the village. Chopa told me that he was a close kinsman of Rahim (*jakyn tuugan*), and I therefore expected that at least he would share the same grandfather as Rahim or that their grandfathers had been brothers. These were the normal relations that would have justified the degree of closeness that he claimed, and the Ak-Jol lineage was a large one in the village, comprising almost seventy households. To my surprise, Chopa's lineage coincided with Rahim's only six generations back. His paternal great-grandfather was a descendant of Karachal within the Ak-Jol lineage. I asked whether he and Rahim were related through this individual: Had his paternal great-grandfather been brothers with Rahim's great-grandfather?

Chopa exploded. He told me that I should not divide the Ak-Jol into several different brothers. Instead the Ak-Jol members are all kinsmen, and there was no need for specifying "which one was my brother or which one was your father." He was of Rahim's lineage, but he did not find any necessity to locate his exact relationship according to the genealogical charter. I was making, he said, "a big issue out of nothing." He did not have any precise information on the specific segmentation of the lineage, and it did not matter. "We are all Ak-Jol," he insisted.

In contrast to Turdu, Chopa benefited from a lack of specific genealogical information. He was more related to the patron than were other villagers, and he considered this to be enough. Early in our acquaintance, Chopa had denied that the patron helped his family, but Chopa's eldest daughter told me details that made it clear that Rahim did aid her father. He had helped her enroll at the medical academy (which she later quit because it was too hard for her to study in Russian); the tractor and other vehicles that Chopa used in his work actually belonged to Rahim. Chopa was Rahim's client, they shared a common ancestor, and they traced their ancestry for seven generations along the male line as a proof of their identity. Beyond this, part of the "contract" of their relationship required that they not interrogate the connections between them too closely (see Schlee 2010, 9).

Rahim and Chopa were also "related" through their grandmothers. I met Chopa after I had begun to visit Rahim's grandmother, who lived next to Rahim's grandmother. The women almost lived together on the same property; no fence had been built between their properties. Whenever I visited Rahim's grandmother, I often saw Chopa's children cleaning her house, and his wife also cooked food for her. Chopa was always there, too, cleaning his grandmother's garden and watering her cattle. Such closeness naturalized a relationship that might otherwise be contested by villagers because it provided two substitute relations (of grandmothers and neighbors) to that of patrilineal kin to explain the mutual obligations between Chopa and Rahim, and because the borderless property between the two women allowed everyone to "forget" who owned what (see Figure 2.6).

The Case of Maria

I met Maria on Rahim's private farm. Maria was the daughter of Chinibek, who was from the Sagyndyk lineage of the village. She was a divorced woman in her fifties with two children and had been working for Rahim for several years. Following her divorce, she lived with her parents. Then she approached the patron and asked him to help her find a job as an accountant somewhere in his office. She had always claimed to belong to the Sagyndyk lineage, but she usually referred to herself as "a daughter of the village." This category is not the equivalent of a native son, rather this would suggest that she was born in the village. While working for Rahim, her social status improved.[11]

In claiming kinship to Rahim, Maria benefitted from her membership in the Sagyndyk lineage. This lineage was only five generations deep. Normally, such

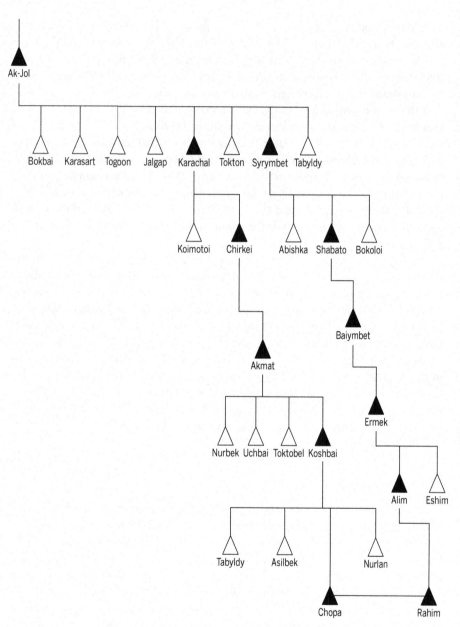

Figure 2.6. The relationship between Chopa and Rahim, who share a common ancestor.

shallowness of lineage might be expected to be a social drawback. But not always. Both the Sagyndyk lineage and the Ak-Jol lineage were descended from the same ancestor, Buchuk. According to Maria, her great-grandfather was a brother of Rahim's great-grandfather. She also managed to invert the relative age between herself and the patron; while Rahim was normally referred to by his clients as "elder brother," Maria identified herself as his "elder sister."

The Case of Kengesh

Kengesh was one of Rahim's workers. I had a chance to meet him while he was cleaning the private farmyard. As he told me, "Rahim immediately called me to work on the farm when I was working as a teacher at the technical school." When I asked how he was related to the patron, he told me that it was through Kanybek. Kanybek and Rahim were best friends and shared the same ancestor. But I learned more specifically from Kengesh how Kanybek and Rahim were related, and how he himself was related to Kanybek.

Kengesh told me, "My father is Kanai. My father had one elder brother, Nurbek, and four younger brothers, Mirzaid, Ormon, Esengul, Ynychbek. One of the younger brothers of my father is Ormon. Ormon has four sons, one of whom is Kanybek. However, Kanybek and I share the same grandfather; in other words, we are *bölö* [first cousins]. Our grandfather belongs to the Tolbashiev lineage." When I asked more about Kanybek, Kengesh stated that Kanybek was related to Rahim since both of them belong to the Sagyndyk lineage branch.

Kengesh could have claimed a direct relation to Rahim, but it would have been more distant than the one he could trace through Kanybek. The Sagyndyk and Ak-Jol lineages are equal segments in the genealogical chart, meaning that they are on the same structural level. But people consider themselves "close" brothers if they belong to the same lineage branch (*uruk*). In this context, Kengesh was related distantly to Rahim (*alys*) because the Sagyndyk and Ak-Jol lineages are considered as brothers only in the seventh generation (see Figure 2.7).

Analysis of Descent and Affinity as Frames for Patron-Client Relations

The main ancestor of the village, Nurmanbet, and his descendants are a crucial point of departure in this process of configuring genealogy and constructing patronage ties. In the village of Bulak, lineage identity was the normative code, and it was generally advantageous to belong to the patron's lineage. Bulak lineages, whether maximal or minimal, were not as rigid as they seemed, and there were multiple ways for individuals and family groups to shift from one lineage to another both over time and situationally.

Knowing the importance of genealogy for the Kyrgyz, both the patron and his kinsmen operated within the framework of genealogy and utilized their

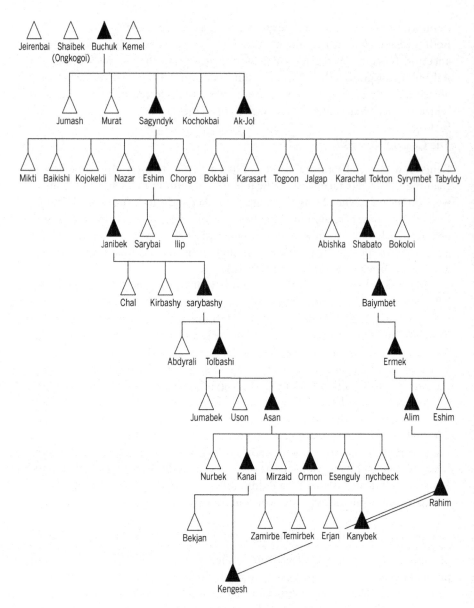

Figure 2.7. The relationships of Kengesh with Rahim through Kanybek.

kinships ties for various purposes. People looked for a common ancestor with the patron; this was the identity marker that implied their closeness to him. Potential clients became Rahim's close kinsmen both emotionally and practically by claiming they shared common descent.

People believed that their closeness was *biological*. Their feelings of closeness could result in or be a result of their repeated cooperation and a feeling of affinity and shared identity (Schlee 2009, 135). Kinship was usually governed according to mutual rights and obligations. Whatever intentions a potential client had in approaching Rahim, he or she needed to have a place within the lineage framework from which to claim belonging to the rights and duties that adhered to a particular descent group and position. In principle, a person should not refuse to help his kinsmen in times of need materially. Thus, throughout the course of their lives, individuals benefit from the help of their extended family. Kinship links, distant (*alys*) or close (*jakyn*), determine how and where one can get support. "Brothers" are among the most obligated to help each other, with older brothers being specifically obligated to be concerned with their younger brothers' basic material condition and social welfare.

Being relationally close to Rahim meant that his clients were able to access to his resources as a result of the simple code of the Kyrgyz kinship system—helping kinsman. In times of crisis and political instability, it is nevertheless hard to provide others with aid, even immediate kinsmen. This was obvious from the complaints many poor rural residents made about close kinsmen who did not help each other. During times when kinsmen seek material help, it is therefore advantageous for people to ignore the relations that make them distantly related. People constructed, changed, or modified kinship relations as a means of satisfying their interests.

Rahim and his clients manipulated genealogies to establish contractual relations of patronage. Claims to shared patrilineal descent doubled as claims to Rahim's resources for the clients and as a basis for loyalty for Rahim. Instead of being distinct from kinship, patron-client relations were an idiom of kinship. Kinship, and with it patronage, can be stretched to the wider household, the village, and the region level. Rahim's patronage networks thereby manifest the important role of genealogical thinking in the broader political culture of contemporary Kyrgyzstan.

Notes

1. *Suu Murun* is a nickname for *Nurmanbet*. Both names appear in village genealogies.
2. Village Census. Report on Bulak Village Statistics, Issyk-Ata rayon, Chüi Oblast, Kyrgyzstan, May 15, 2007.
3. Village Census. Report on Orlovka Village Statistics, Issyk-Ata rayon, Chüi Oblast, Kyrgyzstan, December 12, 2000.

4. For more detailed information on the exact locations of the residents of Solto and Suu Murun, see Valikhanov (1961b); Abramzon (1960, 21).

5. Among these are the Solto Jeti Kul, who were considered descendants of slaves. They are described as the "seven slaves inside Solto" (*soltonun ichindegi jeti kul*) (Abramzon 1960, 26).

6. For more detailed genealogies of Nurmanbet (Suu Murun) from the villages Bulak and Saru, see also Abramzon (1960, 61).

7. See Abramzon (1960, 61); for more on Suu Murun, see also the charts I developed during my fieldwork.

8. The pattern of division of kinship is described by Hudson (1964) in the case of Kazaks.

9. For more on the aksakal court of elders (*aksakal sotu*), see Beyer (2010).

10. *Atalash ini* is literary translated as "younger brother" from the patrilineal side. In other words, it means those who belong to the same lineage.

11. Her son was accepted by the National University to study, and his younger brother became a new director of the local school. She also bought a house in the capital, where she moved with her family.

3 "Renewing the Bone"

Kinship Categories, Practices, and Patronage Networks in Bulak Village

CHAPTER 2 OUTLINED THE basic frame of kinship relations with which Rahim established himself as a "native son" and patron in the village of Bulak and beyond. This chapter looks more closely at the ideals of family, kinship terminology, marriage, ritualized parenthood, and space and place that Rahim used to craft his role as the village's native son and to build patronage networks. In particular he built creatively on the relations of respect, consensual subordination, and forms of material support that are expected from kin.

To sketch out the ideals briefly: Households in Bulak are gerontocratic and patriarchal. Elders control things, and men tend to dominate. The ideal residence pattern has married sons living near their parents, while inheritance is based on ultimogeniture (house, land, animals). As marriage is lineage exogamous, daughters leave the village, and they move far away. Normally the youngest son should remain in the parental house and care for his parents as they age; in turn he inherits the family estate. Representative parents are chosen for each newly married couple to offer guidance and support (especially for the bride). The patrilineal ideology expressed by the logic of the Omaha-type kinship terminology is reinforced by the ideal of the extended agnatic family staying in spatial proximity and sharing much of their work and leisure activities. All of these kin and residence relations are activated through ceremonial occasions (especially life cycle events), and in various forms of mutual assistance, including labor exchange.

Kinship in Practice: Family (*Üi-bülö*) and Household Relations

To illustrate how the ideals of kinship are put into practice at their most thorough, let me describe one family.

During my fieldwork in Bulak Village, I lived with several patrilineal extended families, staying with each family for one month. I was particularly impressed by the reputation of one of these families. The family was the most respected in the village, its heads were among the most senior in the community, they were the most educated, and they were considered the most disciplined in keeping up traditions.

The family was headed by a grandfather and grandmother who were former schoolteachers. Tynych and Alma had educated their own children and grandchildren, but also all the community's children. The members of the family (that is, the children of one father [*bir atanyn baldary*]) resided in several houses (*üilör*).[1] Tynych *ata* had four sons; three lived in separate houses with their wives and children. My host, Murat, was the youngest son, and had remained in his parents' house in accord with custom; he would inherit his parents' property (land, house, and livestock) at the time of his father's death. The family also included unmarried daughters and the adult children of Tynych's brothers.

Murat worked as a sports teacher at the local school together with his wife, Aigul, a teacher of geography. When Murat and Aigul could not manage by themselves as a result of their work schedules; Murat's parents pitched in by taking care of the grandchildren (three sons and one daughter). However, the three sons were schoolchildren, so they would not be at home until 1:00 p.m. Murat's children usually helped with the work in the garden and with other home-based tasks that "required a young pair of hands."

As their sons came of age and married, Tynych *ata* had worked hard to provide each with a separate but nearby house. The four sons, their wives, and children gathered often, and extended family members would visit one another's houses almost every day, producing a constant flow of family members. The wives (*abysyndar*) would cook a common meal, and they would eat around one table. Sometimes even urban relatives, who often come in the summer to help with various tasks, would join the family.

In the fall Tynych *ata*'s sons would help each other with herding and collecting hay. They reciprocally celebrated and participated in the organization of their relatives' various life cycle events, such as weddings and circumcisions, by contributing both cash and labor. Tynych *ata*'s family had several hectares of land and livestock, and strongly emphasized economic cooperation between brothers under the command of their father. Before going to the field to herd or collect hay, Tynych *ata* would bring his sons together and ask them to slaughter a sheep, so that the extended family could come together, eat, and receive his blessing for the successful beginning of the harvest season.

In the village parental authority is broad. Tynych *ata* and Alma *apa* held authority over decisions concerning their children's and grandchildren's futures in terms of arranged marriages, the distribution of land, and higher education. They explained to me that they had taught their children to be obedient and respectful to their parents, and they had continued to do so as adults. Usually the children would not dispute or argue with Tynych *ata* and Alma *apa*, but would say, "You are right; this is my fault." In this way, the grown children remained obedient even when they did not necessarily do as their parents asked.

Tynych *ata* and Alma *apa* had decided that their eldest granddaughter would study at the medical university, and it was they who had sold the family's common livestock to pay the tuition. Most of the time, their sons did not give money from their salaries to Tynych *ata* and Alma *apa*, but when circumstances required it, Tynych *ata* could easily collect a large sum from his sons to use for common needs, like the education of grandchildren. The wives of Tynych *ata*'s sons were not particularly happy about this because they could not even save a small amount of money for their individual families. As the wife of the oldest son told me, there was mutual respect among brothers; if the father asked them to contribute money for some occasion, all of them would do so without open disagreement. While the father was alive, she said, he was in charge. But when Tynych *ata* died, his eldest son would inherit the status of father and become responsible for his younger brothers and unmarried sisters.

This ideal family demonstrates how kinship structures social relations in Bulak according to principles of hierarchy and respect. It is this kind of family, too, that provided a model for Rahim, as he defined himself as the village's native son.

In a Kyrgyz village, the ideals of family are expanded to the wider village level. The segmentary lineage system suggests this model. But people also imagine and value most social relations in the village in terms of kinship relations, even if they could be imagined otherwise (for example, as neighbors). Rahim shared this local view of the whole village through the prism of family organization (see Schneider 1984). Although he became a patron, he always acted in accord with the acceptable social roles of family. He was a "son of the community" or what I have rendered as "native son." He was considered to belong to the community and to be under the protection and guidance of not only his parents but also of all the village elders. As a native son, Rahim was expected by villagers to really care about the community; he was expected to offer sponsorship and also to demonstrate his belonging and his identity as a son.

Rahim creatively manipulated this identity as a native son, as shown in subsequent chapters, to become a powerful political patron. He mobilized the community to support him through kinship knowledge and skills. As he did so, an old symbol with historical relevance—the native son as a figure who serves and protects the community—was reinvigorated to serve the interests of Bulak people in the present.

An important manifestation of Rahim's identity as a son of the village was in his skilled use of kinship terminology in all his village relations. By addressing villagers as relatives, Rahim developed the relations of obligation and mutual support that pertain to a patron and his clients.

Kinship Terminology and Social Relations

Kin terms are extensive and reference subtle differentiations in the degree and nature of respect that should be shown between individuals. In general, kinship terminology among the Kyrgyz is of the Omaha type. It distinguishes between those who are related by descent, those who are affinal, and those who have quasi-kin or kinlike relationships. Patrilineal agnatic kin have one set of terms, and those related through women have another set of terms. Kinsmen are sorted according to their relative position of descent from common ancestors. It is a classificatory terminology, in the sense that they apply one kin term to more than one kin type, and there are parallels with Altai and Kazak terminologies (Broz 2005; Werner 1997). Gender, generation, and relative age are also marked. In the following section, I draw attention to the most salient features of kinship terminology, relations of respect, and the obligations of care and support that accompany them.

A father and his elder brother are classified under one kinship term (*ata*)—(FB=F).[2] Father's brother's children are classified as father's children, that is, brother or sister (FBS=B; FBD=Z). Accordingly, a man treats the children of his brothers in the same manner that he treats his own children and calls all of them "son" (*uul*) or "daughter" (*kyz*). Siblings, however, quite strictly mark distinctions of age: younger brother (*ini*), elder brother (*baike*), younger sister (*singdi*), and elder sister (*eje*). Also, how an elder male sibling calls his younger female sibling (*karyndash*) is different from how an elder female sibling calls her younger female sibling (*singdi*). Frequently, Kyrgyz add the suffix -*i*, for example, elder brother (*agai*), elder sister (*ejei*), mother (*apai*), to kinship terms for elder relatives and to nonrelatives to express a higher degree of respect.

The Kyrgyz have specific words for affines as a category; that is, ego's mother's patrilineage and maternal kin. This is reflected in the kin names of matrilateral relationships. For example, the natal family of the bride is called *törkün*. As in Omaha kinship, a number of relatives belonging to one's mother's patriline are grouped together, ignoring generational differences. Thus the same term is used for both one's mother's brother and one's mother's brother's son; mother's elder sister, mother's younger sister, and mother's brother's daughter are also called by a single term. This is related to the fact that relatives on the mother's side are of a higher status; therefore, the generational differences are ignored by putting them into the same category as senior relatives (for more, see Figure 3.1).

The Kyrgyz terminology further satisfies the defining criteria of Omaha-type terminology by classifying patrilateral relatives through female links with members of a younger generation and by equating same generation matrilateral relatives with members of a higher generation. In Kyrgyz FZC are called *jeen*.

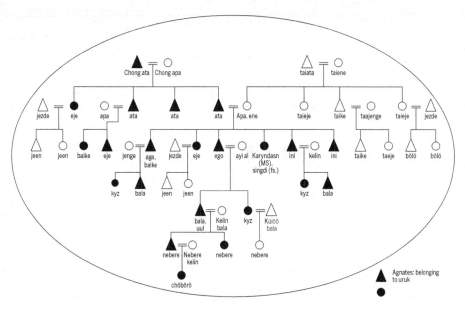

Figure 3.1. Kinship terminologies.
The Kyrgyz language is divided into northern and southern dialects, and there are also historical and cultural differences between the northern and southern Kyrgyz people. There are some regional differences in using kin terms, that is, in the Talas region the elder brother is termed *ake* and the elder sister is termed *apche*. At my field site, these were the terms my informants used (see the chart).

Similarly, ZC and MBS are referred to by the same term as ego's father and MB, namely, *taike*.

The terminology for cousins distinguishes between parallel- and cross-cousins. There are also different terms for parallel- and cross-cousins on the father's side and the mother's side. For example: parallel-cousins from father's side are merged with siblings (elder sister *eje*, younger sister *singdi*, elder brother *baike*, younger brother *ini*), whereas the mother's sisters children are called *bölö*. The cross-cousin terms from the mother's side cut across the generational division (*taike* or *taieje*), whereas the father's sister's children are called *jeen*.

In short, relatives on the mother's side of the family have more classificatory terms, while relatives on the father's side have more descriptive terms. This pattern stresses common membership of kinsmen in patrilineal lines. Ego's mother becomes a member of her husband's patrilineage, while ego's MB remains a member of ego's mother's natal patrilineage. There are also special groups identified that have authority and solidarity: the wives of the brothers are termed *abysyn*; ego would address his brothers' wives as *jenge*. These terms, *jenge* or *abysyn*, are used both as labels and terms of address.

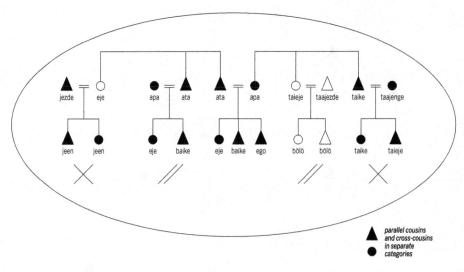

Figure 3.2. Parallel-cousins and cross-cousins in separate categories.

Kinship as an Idiom of Respect

Each terminology contains a degree of relatedness and distance, and it also labels social roles and status. For example, wife taking and wife giving are important categories because Kyrgyz show more respect for wife givers by putting the wife takers' position lower. To exemplify this, I use the ambiguous relationship between a mother's brother and sister's son (*taike* and *jeen*). Their relationship depends on the continuous process of performing duties by the sister's son (*jeen*) and of being respectful and helpful to the mother's brother (*taike*). The mother's brother (*taike*), then, is superior to the male ego's family, and it is expected that a male ego (that is, sister's son) will pay visits to his mother's brother.

Despite the respect due to the mother's brother and his relatives, the kinsmen of one's father are expected to be more important. Relatives through marriage form a third leg in this triangle of respect relations. They are to be more respected and are treated with more careful verbal and other formulae, precisely because links to them are considered more fragile. Given the obligation attached to these terminologies, each performs his social role as fittingly as possible. Avuncular relationships, for example, the relationship between the mother's brother and the sister's son (*taike andjeen*), are used to express relations of power. The status of *jeen* is lower than the status of *taike*, and the *jeen* must behave as a subordinate when he meets his *taike* (see Figure 3.2).

The *jeen* is usually metaphorically compared to a wolf cub. Even is a *jeen* grows up among his mother's patrilineage, he is expected nevertheless to return

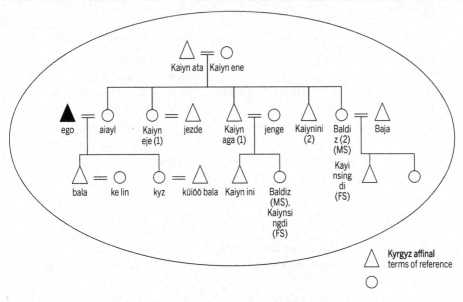

Figure 3.3. Kyrgyz affinal terms of reference from both sides.
FS stands for female egos; *MS* stands for male egos.

to the wild (that is, his patrilineage) once grown. Despite his mother's attempts to domesticate him and align him with her patrilineage, he belongs by nature to his father's side. Such a metaphor shows the ideology of the patrilineal side is strong. This is also shown by the negative term for the sister's son (sister's son will not take the side of matrilateral kin) (*jeen el bolboit*), which implies that the sister's son will never be as close to one as one's patrilineal relatives. This does not mean that the children of daughters are despised; rather this term stresses the daughters' children's place, that is, the patrilineal side of their fathers.

As a final example, a husband and wife each call the grandparents of the other *kuda*. The idea of *kuda* is closely connected to hierarchies, terms of address, and ways of showing respect to people. The *kuda*, however, are not only the biological grandparents of the couple. The term is also applied to a wide group of people treated with a similar kind of respect, including all the brothers of the bride's father (see Figure 3.3).

Complex relationships also exist between the wife's elder brother (*kainaga*) and her husband (*küiöö bala*). The relation is described as one of mutual respect, but the husband is subordinate to his wife's elder brother. This is structurally related to the lower position of wife takers to wife givers; the sister's husband took her away from her brother's patriline (see Table 3.1).

Table 3.1 Kyrgyz Kinship Terms (Bulak Village)

Tuugandar (Relatives on the Father's Side)	Taijak (Relatives on the Mother's Side)
Chong ata (paternal grandfather)	*Taiata* (mother's father)
Chong apa (paternal grandmother)	*Taene* (mother's mother)
Aba (the elder or younger brother of the grandfather)	*Taike* (mother's brother; both younger and elder ones)
Ata father (the elder or younger brother of the father)	*Taajenge* (mother's brother's wife; both younger and elder ones)
Apa (mother, wives of the elder, and younger brothers of the father)	
Kyz (daughter)	*Taieje* (mother's sister; both younger and elder ones)
Bala (son)	
Baike (elder brother, elder male relative in the same patrilineal lineage, father's brother's elder son)	*Taajezde* (mother's sister's husband; both younger and elder ones)
Ini (younger brother, younger male relative in the same patrilineal lineage)	
Eje (elder sister, elder female relative in the same patrilineal lineage)	*Bölö* (mother's sister's children)
Karyndash (younger sister [said by a man], younger female relative in the same patrilineal lineage)	
Singdi (younger sister [said by a woman], younger female relative in the same patrilineal lineage, father's brother's daughter)	
Neber (grandson; grandchild)	
Chöbörö (great-grandchild)	
Kybyra (great-great-grandchild)	
Jeen (father's sister's children)	

Kaiyn Jurt (In-Laws through One's Own Marriage)	Kudalar (In-Laws through a Child's or a Sibling's Marriage)
Küi (husband)	*Kuda* (male in-law)
Aiyal (wife)	*Kudagy I* (female in-law)
Kaiyn at (husband's father or wife's father)	*Kudacha* (younger female in-law)
Kaiyn ene (husband's mother or wife's mother)	
Küiö bala (son-in-law)	
Kelin (daughter-in-law; a young bride)	

(continued)

Table 3.1 *(continued)*

Kaiyn Jurt (In-Laws through One's Own Marriage)	Kudalar (In-Laws through a Child's or a Sibling's Marriage)
Abysyn (wives of brothers, younger co-sisters-in-law; co-brides)	
Jenge (elder brother's wife)	
Jezde (elder sister's husband)	
Baja (wife's sister's husbands)	
Baldiz (wife's sister)	
Kainaga (husband's or wife's elder brother)	
Kainini (husband's or wife's younger brother)	
Kaineje (husband's or wife's elder sister)	
Kainsingdi (husband's or wife's younger sister)	
	Contractual Kinship
	ökül apa (representative mother)
	ökül ata (representative father)
	ökül bala (representative son)
	ökül kyz (representative daughter)

The Use of Kin Terms

The Kyrgyz worldview is expressed in terms of kinship terminology, and, thus, patron-client relations are disguised behind a relationship of sister's son and mother's brother (*taeke* and *jeen*) or wife's older brother *and* younger sister's husband (*küiöö bala kayin aga*). Regardless of the degree of genealogical manipulation that is necessary to claim one of these roles, those who do claim them also adapt their behavior to match the corresponding rights and obligations of the role. All the kinds of relations encompassed in the attitude and conduct of a wife's older brother (*kainaga*), a sister's husband (*küiöö bala*), a sister's son (*jeen*), and a mother's brother (*taeke*) mean that a wealthy man can easily behave and be seen as behaving like a kinsman of appropriate rank and relation should behave. Thus, the Kyrgyz view the unequal relations of patronage through culturally accepted categories of kinship, expressing and understanding individual positions vis-à-vis others as if the only relations possible between people were those of kinship. An example follows of how this transpired between Rahim and three brothers-in-law he suddenly acquired.

A Wife's Elder Brother and a Sister's Husband

Rahim's father's brother had divorced twice, but the third time he sought to marry he was not given permission by the community elders. Without this permission, he could not bring his wife to the village and properly marry her. This nevertheless did not prevent him from forming an informal union, and his third wife had three daughters. These children were considered illegitimate, and when he split with their mother, they were still small children. They were raised in the Naryn District by their mother's natal family and considered to belong to her lineage. But when Rahim's father's brother died in the year 2000, the girls (now in their late teens and early twenties) visited his lineage's village during the funeral. There they met Rahim for the first time, and also became known to the men who would become their future husbands.

Sometime after this, the girls were kidnapped by their future husbands and taken to neighboring villages. At the time of my fieldwork, many villagers claimed that the sisters were kidnapped as a result of Rahim's high position in the province and his high status and renown in the Issyk-Ata rayon. They thought that the kidnapping was strategic on the part of men from nearby villages because it would enable their villages to access Rahim as a patron through his "sisters." They also thought that the weddings were beneficial to Rahim because they quickly increased his previously limited number of kinsmen. By having recognized his father's brother's daughter's as his "sisters" at the time of their father's funeral, Rahim stood to gain as his own affinal relatives the women's husbands, their parents-in-law *kuda*, and their extended distant kin.

As if indeed by plan, the sisters renewed their relations with Rahim's family to claim his support in their new predicament. As they were marrying into Rahim's province of birth, he decided to provide them with dowries. Once endowed, the previously illegitimate women gained legitimacy within Rahim's lineage. After their marriages, the three women continued to perform the social role of sister. They visited Rahim and helped him organize various kinds of feasts. Their husbands, too, maintained close links with the relatives of the *kainaga* category (that is, sister's elder brother). The relationship between Rahim and the husbands of his sisters was expressed strictly through kin terminology. That is, the wife's elder brother (*kainaga*) and the younger husbands of Rahim's sisters were called as (*küiöö bala*) and their elder husbands (*jezde*).

This particular kin relationship had embedded within it the seed of patronage. The wife's elder brother (*kainaga*) is always a figure of authority and superiority because the wife giver's lineage is always superior to that of the wife taker's lineage. It was seen as only natural that the sisters' husbands (*küiöö bala*) should be obedient and respectful toward Rahim. The sisters' husbands began to establish themselves as Rahim's clients. During my fieldwork, for example, the patron asked his brothers-in-law to be responsible for three important aspects of his business: the first one was responsible for exporting milk; the second one was responsible for breeding cattle; and the third one was responsible for repairing

Rahim's auto engines. In this context, the patron-client relationships fitted perfectly into a kin category, which was innately subordinate.

The Mother's Brother and the Sister's Son

The same relationship of authority and dependency can be found between a mother's brother (*taeke*) and a sister's son (*jeen*). Rahim and many of those who had become his clients expressed their relationship with these terms. In some cases, an actual kin relation had been (re)configured (as with the "sisters" above) so that the terms were accurate descriptors; in other cases, the use of the term was metaphorical but no less real in experience and expectations to those who used it. Bloch and Sperber (2006, 116) claim that the relationship between a mother's brother and a sister's son is special and interesting in patrilineal societies because these relations involve symmetrical and asymmetrical jokes and claims over various rights. In the Kyrgyz context, the relation is not a pleasant, "joking" one. Instead the relationship between a mother's brother and a sister's son attracts negative proverbs that are usually used by a mother's brother to offend his sister's son: such as, "Fur will never be a neck of the coat; sister's sons will never take the side of matrilateral relatives or of mother's patriline" (*toon jeke bolboit, jeen el boloboit*).[3]

In the Kyrgyz kinship system, a sister's son (*jeen*) has a lower status than a mother's brother (*taeke*). It is often the case that the sister's son is requested to occasionally visit a mother's brother and provide any kind of support that he needs. From the perspective of a sister's son, he does not usually feel comfortable visiting a place where he is not treated well, like his mother's brother's place. The ambiguity and asymmetry of these relationships serve the establishment of patron-client relations. Accordingly, when I asked workers at Rahim's farm how they usually referred to their relationship with him—that is, did they say "he is our mother's brother (*taeke*)," or "we are his sister's son (*jeen*)," or "we are mother's brother," or "he is our sister's son"—they would tell me that "our relationship to Rahim was like our *jeen*." They felt themselves to be on the subordinate side of a hierarchical kinship relation.

But occasionally clients claimed that they were Rahim's *taeke*. In such cases, the clients were dominant in kinship terms and told me that the subordinate Rahim could not refuse to help them. The dominance of wife givers over wife takers here introduces a paradoxical element into patron-client relationships, giving the actual clients a claim to a dominant position. Let me give some examples.

Rahim's mother was Kazakh, so he approached his *taeke* in Kazakhstan to enable him to extend his profitable business there. He wanted to export milk and also to extend his construction business into Kazakhstan. Evidently many of his *taeke* had been helpful and supported their younger Kyrgyz *jeen* in his new ventures.

Rahim's father's mother was also Kazakh and had numerous Kazakh kinsmen. These kinsmen also positioned themselves as *taeke* in relation to Rahim as a *jeen*. One of them was Amantur, who considered himself *taeke* and asked Rahim to assist him in organizing the wedding of his son. In this case, he used the proverb "*toidun korkun jeen achat, jakanyn korkun ton achat*" (the status of the event would depend on the sister's son, the importance of the neck of the coat depends on its fur), to argue that the status of the event would depend on the sister's son. Here we see the meaning of this proverb with negative connotations is reversed: the *taeke* and *jeen* relationship is used strategically within the framework of kinship categories. Rahim complied, and subsequently Amantur and his family began to visit and to help Rahim and his family. During life cycle events, they did not forget to visit Rahim, and they often visited Rahim's house to clean the garden, cook food, and cultivate potatoes.

People make use of mother's side (*kuda* relationships) for different reasons; however, in this specific case, the relationship between a mother's brother and a sister's son (*taeke-jeen*) was used for the establishment of patron-client relationships. Again, the kin relations are classificatory ones that may be only loosely connected to actual marriages and lines of biological descent. Claims made to relatives through affinal relations and the matrilateral line are somewhat less flexible than those made through patrilines. On the patrilineal side, it seems enough for someone to claim that they belonged to a particular lineage segment and to link this creatively to the lineage of patron. In the situation of affinity, however, one had to prove some proximity with Rahim's mother's side or at least his maternal grandmother's side to be accepted by a sister's son as mother's brother. But the most creative social actors prefer to keep patrilineal, matrilateral, and affinal options available, and depending on the context, stress one or the other.

Space and Place: Extending and Localizing Kinship

As indicated in Chapter 2, Bulak and its neighboring villages are often described as places through the use of kinship terminologies. With respect to one another, neighborhoods and neighboring villages are described according to the degree of their genealogical relatedness on either the mother's (*törkün jak*) or father's side (*ata jak*). When I asked Adyl, the local village historian, to draw me a map of the village and its neighboring villages, I got two interesting pictures. In the first map, he drew the village of Bulak divided into several streets. Those streets were divided into five blocks, and the lineage branches of each block were highlighted in red. Names of streets and other ways of defining "neighborhoods" were omitted. In the second picture, he drew in the neighboring villages. These he designated not by their official names, but as *kuda jak* (affines' side), *jeen jak* (sister's son's side), *taike jak* (mother's brothers' side), *kyz aluuchu jak* (wife takers' side), and *kyz beruuchu jak* (wife givers' side). This type of mapping lineages was not an isolated case; other people would usually also talk about the neighboring villages in kin terms.

On the one hand, this mapping of space through kinship reflects a normative and historical model of exogamous marriage and patrilocal residence. Prior to Soviet collectivization, Kyrgyz pastoral nomads used exogomous marriage to broker alliances with others to maintain grazing pastures and water rights for their animals (Abramzon 1960, 1971). By "exchanging daughters" (*kuda söök*), two neighboring kinship groups would form the foundation of economic relations. Their relations would often last for several generations, and it was said that wives had to be taken from the same bones (*söök*) as their mothers (Abramzon 1971; Kuehnast 2003, 592).[4]

On the other hand, this normative model facilitates extending and localizing kin relations that did not exist by factual descent. Thus space and place also becomes involved in the building of patronage networks. Any kin term can be extended beyond its strict application to kinsmen and benefit from the claim of being related. People strive to locate an appropriate kin term for a new acquaintance, offering the possibility for the instant integration of a person into the kinship-defined social network of a household, village, or region. Close kin terms are also metaphorically reapplied to both genealogically and spatially distant kin, so that distant relatives become (according to age and gender) fathers, mothers, younger or elder brothers, and younger or elder sisters. A man might treat all the youth in a community as his own "sons" and "daughters." Indeed, the terms themselves are often used to refer generally to younger generations within the village.

Such flexibility might suggest that accurate genealogical knowledge is scarcely necessary to construct and perform appropriate social relations. Yet this is not so; villagers are attentive to accuracy, as will become clearer in later chapters. Villagers habitually treat each other as relatives, and almost exclusively so.

This strong preference to construct all relations as kin relations became obvious when an elderly woman asked about my husband's lineage to explain my identity to her neighbors. She was not satisfied with my own introduction as an anthropologist, raised in Bishkek and trained in Germany. After I told her his lineage, she responded, "We are from his *törkün* (wife's side)." I was, she figured, the wife of one of her grandfather's brother's sons' children and thus *törkün jak* (natal side). Her assessment rested on the fact that she had been born in my husband's province, and on the fact that her grandfather's brother's sons still lived there. Because my own introduction had been so unsatisfactory in local terms, she had found a way to identify me through my husband's kin. The women sitting next to her then listened as she described the complete genealogy of her family in a chronological manner.

From people's own point of view, it remains possible to analytically distinguish close, distant, and ritualized kin regardless of the terms extended to them in social relations. As people would often say to me, close kin are formed through "biological" ties (children of one father and mother) and distant kin are formed through "social" ties (going back seven generations). Indeed, a term exists to distinguish the closest kin (*jakyn tuugan*) from all other types. The *bir atanyn baldary* (a man's sons) can include up to forty individuals who are closely related by blood and are absolutely obligated to help one another in times of need. As with all other terms, this one is flexible; it can include the sons of several brothers, or the sons of a common grandfather or great-grandfather. Rahim played with all of these possibilities to recruit potential clients as kin.

Obligations in Times of Hardship: Funerals

The ideology of kinship reinforces the cohesiveness of a community and facilitates mutual support within it. Community solidarity is expressed through active participation and support during life cycle events (such as funerals, weddings, and circumcisions), the contribution of money to assist in the organization of village events, and other signs of visible devotion of individuals to community elders (*aksakal*). In turn, the principle of descent is maintained by constant ritual practice. In addition to life cycle events, Rahim regularly made animal sacrifices for the spirits of shared patrilineal ancestors (*ata-babalardyn arbaktarina kuran okutaly*). During Eid al-Adha (*Kurban ait*) the members of a sublineage slaughter a sheep, pray for the ancestor, and share the meat among themselves.

In this section, I focus on funeral rituals I witnessed in which Rahim was actively involved. Funeral rituals differ according to region, and also between *uruu* and *uruk*. Funeral practices have also been in a process of constant change since the collapse of the Soviet Union, as a result of social, political, and economic transformations in Kyrgyzstan (Hardenberg 2010).

Closely related kinsmen, such as all the children of one father, are responsible for organizing life cycle events, including funerals. But distant kinsmen may help, and if a man is wealthy, many of his distant kinsmen will help him to organize an event out of respect, interests, and solidarity. My informants mean more than the literal when they say, "Everyone is related to everyone else in the village." As with child rearing and disciplining, villagers consider themselves as a part of a solidarity group; villagers influence one another by subjecting everyone to various kinds of obligations. This is done to act in the corporate interest and by ensuring that these obligations will be fulfilled, such as by attending a funeral, contributing cash, and helping with the organizational issues. A kin-based framework is the moral structure within which help is given and received since actors perceive themselves as always helping kin in need.

One of the elders of the community passed away in February 2008. The village was full of people from different areas of the village. Rahim attended the funeral to pay respect for the family of the deceased, and also because he was obliged to attend the funerals of elders because he had become by that time the village's native son. During that particular funeral, each man and woman of the village was expected to contribute at least ten som as a donation called *yntymak* to the family of the deceased.[5] Those who belonged to "wealthier" lineages, such as Ak-Jol, were expected to contribute fifty som. Higher amounts might be given by those who were close. For example, immediate kinsmen contributed between 500 and 1,000 som, and wealthy immediate family members might contribute up to 5,000 som. The village elders appointed assistants from each lineage to collect the donations. Usually these assistants had already collected some money within a few days and the sum was immediately given to the family of the deceased, or so that they could buy and slaughter cattle before visitors arrived for a funeral feast within their own lineage. Even though Rahim was not close to the deceased in most reckonings, he explained his generous contribution—a horse for the family to slaughter and helped to find the yurt for the family of the deceased—by saying that all the village was his family.

In daily life people usually do not distinguish between *uruu* and *uruk* and use the words interchangeably, which is quite confusing for outsiders. But when it comes to distributing cash and labor among sublineage members, the differences between them are emphasized, and people know who belongs to which sublineage. Those who do not want to contribute during the life cycle events or those who seek help begin to distinguish between themselves and others according to lineage. They start establishing how far back they are related and count the generations that separate their lineage branches and thus claim that they are genealogical distant from (or close to) the *uruk* of the deceased in order to pay less. But such economization has clear limits: when people do not have enough to contribute at their appointed level (for example, if there have been many funerals in the recent past), they will sell milk, fruit, and vegetables to raise the necessary funds. They know that they too will eventually be the recipients of *yntymak*. As Hardenberg (2010, 37) has argued, the cumulative effect of funeral rituals (mourning, preparation, gift exchange, commemoration) is the intensification of social relationships between both the living and the dead.

In general, funerals in rural Kyrgyzstan are among the events that bring together many people, creating an arena that can be used to manifest one's status and wealth. Support during the funerals is highly valued by many Kyrgyz families because of their difficult situations. Unlike other festive life cycle events, one's active participation during the funeral signifies respect for ancestors, living families, and the community.

Marriage: Affinal Distance, Respect, and Support

"Every good marriage begins in tears," said several of my recently married female informants, when I gathered them in a private place to talk about marriage. If a girl cries on her wedding day, it is taken as a good sign. A bride's tears demonstrate that she has been brought up well (*tartiptüü*). Tears symbolize a bride's resistance to marriage. Despite the proclivity for referring to nearby villages in terms of affinal relations, the general preference among ethnic Kyrgyz is to contract marriages across relatively wide distances. In Bulak at the time of my fieldwork, all the young brides were from distant villages.

Kyrgyz practice rules of exogamy, which specify the ranges and categories of relatives who are forbidden to marry members of their own lineage (*uruu*) within the village or anyone who shares a common patrilineal ancestor within seven generations. On one occasion a young couple who were related eight generations back along the male line provoked controversy, but they proceeded with the marriage. It is preferred that women marry into the village; the ideal marriage is one between people who are extremely distantly related, and this kind of marriage is encouraged. It is, of course, hard to marry someone with no relations at all, because this is presumed impossible if everyone is ultimately related to a common ancestor of Kyrgyz. However, a man who marries a woman of another ethnicity is especially valued. One can marry nonpatrilineal relatives, including first and the second cousins and distant uncles.

Kyrgyz provide an extensive bride-wealth payment, and upon the marriage a woman incorporates the lineage of her husband and moves to her husband's place (patrilocal). Women do not inherit any property from their fathers or their father's lineage; rather the fathers' sons and brothers' sons inherit the property. Usually the brothers should live side near the parents' house or within one village in order to share in agricultural and cattle-breeding tasks.

A new bride should not live close to her natal family because she would be constantly returning to them. The Kyrgyz say that when a bride marries nearby, her house is in chaos (*jakyndyn töshögü jyiylbait*). Yet I have also often heard parents express the wish that their daughters would not marry far away; if the daughter were to move to the southern part of Kyrgyzstan, they explain, visiting would be difficult. In practice, parents prefer to give their daughters as brides to men in a different province. In the Central Asian context, this is a considerable geographical distance: in the oasis of Bukhara, Uzbek and Tajik daughters rarely move more than a few hundred meters away at marriage (Finke and Sancak 2012). Even in Kyrgyzstan, the Osh Uzbeks frequently prefer to marry first cousins, producing local communities tightly bound by intermarriage (Ismailbekova 2013b).

In this village and throughout Kyrgyzstan bride kidnapping, *ala kachuu* (literally "grab and run"), is practiced. A bride who has been abducted should cry in protest and disagreement. In all weddings, the bride's tears reference this custom. Much has been written about this custom, and there is a lively debate about the extent of consent involved in most abductions (see, for example, Borbieva 2012; Handrahan 2004; Kleinbach, Ablezova, and Aitieva 2005; Werner 2004). In some cases, for example, informants told me that abduction is an acceptable guise for a man to lower the bride's price, or, that it can occur when a couple wants to marry but does not have parental consent. Regardless of the degree of consent to abduction, this custom is part and parcel of the relations of consensual subordination within marriage and kinship relations more broadly. It is this dimension that I want to focus on here, as it contextualizes the acceptability of patronage relations in other guises.

Whether abducted or simply married by arrangement, a bride must decide on her wedding day whether she will remain in or leave her husband's house. If she decides to stay, she accepts a white headscarf and sits down behind a specially prepared curtain (*köshögöö*). Once the bride accepts the white scarf, the parents of the groom receive congratulations for the attainment of their new family member (*bülöö*). The young bride usually does not remove the white scarf for many years and continues to bow to her husband's parents. In case of an unsuccessful abduction, if the girl decides to leave, a lot of older women will threaten her with curses that she will never marry in the future. Such threats often convince abducted brides to remain with their husbands, but when women do leave they are able to remarry.

The position of the young bride is expected to be respectful (*syiluu*) and subordinate to the husband's family. After marriage the young bride and her husband live under the same roof as the husband's parents, and she becomes affiliated with her husband's lineage. At death, her body is not returned to her natal family but buried by her husband's family.

The parents of the bride and groom also strive to maintain a relationship based on respect (*kuda*). Each side calls the other *kuda* or *kuda söök*, parents of the bride or groom. Of all kinship relations, this one is considered the most respected and due the most support. This relation is complex: it is described as "far" or "distant" (*alys*), referencing both the geographical and genealogical distance that should characterize it and nuancing the quality of respect that should be demonstrated. "Distance" should be demonstrated in the parents' relations toward one another and their respective kin groups. The groom's parents should never become involved in arguments with the bride's relatives, or vice versa. When marriages are contracted across provincial lines, even a whole province can be considered his *kuda* side because of the close connection between territory and descent groups.

Marriage creates new affinal relations for the marrying couple and their whole kinship groups. It also forms a relationship of ritualized kinship through the institution of "representative parents" (*ökül-ata-ene*) who are chosen for the couple at the time of their marriage. In terms of the range of material, emotional, and spiritual or emotional support that might be provided through the relation, ritualized parenthood in Kyrgyzstan can be compared to godparenthood in Latin America and Europe (for example, Gudeman 1975); however, while the *compadrazgo* relation stresses horizontal bonds between godparents and natural parents, the Kyrgyz ökül ata-ene stresses vertical relationships between the sponsor and young married couples. Representative parents are crucial for aiding the young couple with various problems. In advance of a wedding, a married couple is approached to serve as representative parents. They are chosen for their ideal qualities. The representative mother, for example, should be a good mother and wife, have a good relationship with the kinsmen of the prospective husband's parents, and not be involved in quarrels and fights. The prestige, authority, and respect of the representative parents within the community are requirements for their selection as *ökül ata-ene*, and their status only increases when they become representative parents. Refusals to undertake such a role are rare.

Representative parents offer guidance when there is a misunderstanding between the couple, or if there is a problem between parents and the couple, or between the young bride and her in-laws. Representative parents can also go between the respective families to find solutions in the event of conflict. Such figures are essential, especially for young brides, who are expected to withhold complaint, even in the face of great difficulties with a husband or mother-in-law. Brides who complain find little support from their own families, except in cases of overt domestic violence. The acceptable course of action is for a bride to turn to her ökül apa (representative mother). The representative mother, and village elders generally, are expected to help solve problems and regulate family life in ways that ensure that divorce is rare and that children are supported by both parents and their extended families. Representative parents and their assigned children also have a reciprocal moral obligation to provide one another with mutual assistance, generosity (by giving cash), and joint participation in rituals. As with the other categories of kinship, Rahim recruited his clients among his representative children.

"Renewing the Bone"

Rahim served as a representative parent for eight couples. His children were from poor families and considered themselves honored to have a wealthy businessman as their representative father. As such, the relationship between the rich and the poor was also wrapped up in kinship language. Yet the majority of couples sponsored by marriage belonged to his lineage or shared another common ancestor. It was hard for anyone to say that they were "clients" rather than distant kin, or that Rahim's choice to sponsor their marriages was other than an honorable and rightful way for him to support less fortunate kinsmen.

Here I would like to provide an example from one of Rahim's sponsored couples who married in 2007 after dating for several months. Muradil worked as a sport teacher at the local school. Zina did not work and after marriage remained at home to care for their children. They were a relatively poor family with neither extra livestock nor a big house, yet their elderly parents were dependent on them financially and physically. When asked about their choice of Rahim as a representative father, the couple told me that they asked Rahim and his wife to be their *ökül ata-ene* because of their economic stable positions in the village.

However, Muradil then told me that the main reason for appointing Rahim and his family to this position was to "renew the bones" (*söök jangyrtuu*) of Muradil's father, Chymyrov Aftandil, and the family of Rahim.[6] Following his military service in Russia during the Soviet times, Chymyrov had once asked for the help of a distant relative, Rahim's father. He asked Rahim's father, who worked in the National Police Bureau of Kyrgyzstan, to make him a sergeant of the Soviet Police Bureau in Kyrgyzstan. After Rahim's father's death, the connection between Chymyrov and Rahim's family was severely weakened when Chymyrov moved to a new city. With the aim of keeping this friendship, and of renewing the bond between the two distant kinsmen, Chymyrov's family had decided to ask Rahim and his wife to be responsible for navigating the newlyweds in their early years of married life.

The young couple did not want Rahim and his wife to be deeply involved in their private life. Therefore, they never asked him for any personal advice. Instead they asked him to provide the groom with a stable job at the credit company when Rahim headed the Kyrgyz National Credit Company. Such a stable job would enable Muradil to provide for his young family. During the wedding ceremony, the representative parents gave the couple gold rings, earrings, and some extra cash to pay the bride price. The *ökül ata-ene* promised to support the young couple financially whenever they required any monetary help or other related support.

The selection of the couple's *ökül ata-ene* thus followed all traditional expectations, although its practical negotiation focused on economic rather than moral support. According to tradition, only kinsmen are supposed to be *ökül ata-ene*, and only the parents of the groom have a right to choose the representative parents they feel are appropriate. All of this was followed: Muradil's parents initiated the appointment of *ökül ata-ene* and selected a distant kinsman with whom they wanted to renew the bones—that is, reactivate kin relations. The choice seemed particularly appropriate on moral grounds because Rahim's father and Muradil's father had been close friends. Nevertheless, the moral advice normally sought from the representative parents was replaced by a greater emphasis on economic security. This couple was the eighth couple that Rahim and his wife had sponsored, and Rahim almost refused, invoking the right of those with more than five sponsored couples to refuse further proposals. But it was the voiced desire to "renew the bones" between the two families that convinced him.

In comparison to other cases, Muradil could be considered a highly calculating client. For example, he told me how he approached Rahim as a brother (*baike*) before asking Rahim to be his ökül ata (representative father). Even before asking him to serve as a representative father, Muradil also sometimes called Rahim "father," switching the term of address and his tone to improve the chances that Rahim would grant his requested favor. The calculation continued into the new relation.

Zina and Muradil were aware of their subordinate relationship to their representative parents, so they limited their requests for "help" to financial support. Neither party was deceived by the moral and emotional trappings of the relationship. Yet the patron did not object to the financial outlay because the number of sponsored couples strengthens his status. Moreover, the sponsored couples were flexible and almost free labor when he needed them, such as campaign workers during the elections and as serving kin during life cycle events.

Another young couple (Timur and Nargiza), who were married in 2007, also had Rahim and his wife appointed as ökül ata-ene. Timur did not have a stable position, because he would change his occupation activities frequently. The couple did not have their own house; they temporarily lived with his parents until the younger brother of Timur got married. Timur said that he had always wanted Rahim to be his sponsor and suggested the choice to his father, who agreed. It was a big honor for Timur and Nargiza to have such an influential ritualized father. The main reason for appointing Rahim, they said, was to "strengthen kinship relations" between Timur's lineage and Rahim's lineage. Although Timur and Rahim were genealogically distant relatives, Timur nevertheless wanted to make sure that their kin relationships with Rahim were strengthened through ritualized parenthood. The newlyweds received financial support; one of the most expensive gifts was a baby carriage when their first child was born. However, the young couple did not want Rahim's family to be involved in their private lives; therefore, they never asked for any advice when they had problems. However, they respected and honored their ritualized parents. Rahim seemed not to mind the arrangement; he also did not have time to meet with Timur and Nargiza in a private atmosphere. Nargiza reported:

> I went to help Rahim's grandmother when she got sick. Rahim's grandfather told Rahim that I was a very good ritualized daughter. But we have not been to his house in Bishkek. I usually help only his grandmother in the village. But whenever we need something, first we tell the grandmother and she passes

the message on to Rahim. Being a part of this family is good for us; we feel included. Whenever we need their support, we can rely on them. We like our representative parents very much. (Interview with Nargiza, Bulak Village, January 18, 2008)

The young couple strongly demonstrated an affective bond for their patron as a result of the gratitude they feel toward him. And Rahim genuinely supported his ritualized children. Not all the behaviors are what might be expected: Rahim did not accompany the family of Timur to see Nargiza's family during the wedding ceremonies on account of business commitments. But two weeks after the wedding Timur was arrested by the police for drunk driving and fined a fortune, close to 10,000 som (approximately 150 euros). Rahim called the police and within three hours the matter was resolved.

By emphasizing emotion and by using kinship language to lend legitimacy to the ritualized relationship, the young couples created their own vision of closeness to the patron and sought to benefit from the relational tie. In this way the kinship system is not only a matter of terminological abstractions but also expresses forms of emotional attachment, security, and feelings of protection, which are revealed through such social processes.

Muradil, for example, told me how he once asked for a favor from his older "brother," *baike* (Rahim), but in the midst of asking changed his tone and addressed Rahim as "father," *ata*, to increase his chances of receiving support. By switching terms Muradil increased the respect he accorded to Rahim. Similarly, a young couple could be compelled to offer labor to their representative parents as a son or daughter. As with other forms of brokering kin relations, the selection of representative parents has been influenced by rising unemployment and economic hardship in the post-Soviet period. Thus, the desire for moral advice from ritualized parents has been replaced by a much greater emphasis on economic security. Ritualized parents can place their ritualized children at the university, find work for them, and provide money when needed. This gives the ritualized children a sense of security and stability. But this type of a relationship also creates anxieties. If the ritual parent is not supportive but demanding, representative children become much more like dependent clients on a powerful patron.

Kinship Categories and Kinship Practices

Patronage is concealed behind an ideal type of family, space, kin terms affinity, and contractual kin relations. The kinship-based social organization of ethnic Kyrgyz lends patron-client relations cultural legitimacy in three further ways. First, through hierarchical structures that demand obedience on the part of clients; second, through ideological kinship ties and extended kinship terminologies; third, through cultural values such as loyalty, deference, and solidarity.

I have argued that family affiliations, kinship terminologies, and affinity intersect with patron-client relations; they reinforce one another as a result of an ideological kinship system that permits considerable elasticity in the practice and recognition of extensive relatives. The kinship system can be stretched by social actors to establish patronage networks within the framework of kinship and ritualized parenthood. Thus there is the possibility to redefine the boundaries within a large reservoir of kinsmen.

Not all villagers had good relations with Rahim. Rather their relationships had to be established through a complex net of communication, gift exchange, and identifications. In the context of an increasing trend toward the privatization of resources, kinship ties in rural Kyrgyzstan have been strengthened. This became an alternative distribution of resources, which can compensate inequalities in access to wealth and influences. Alternative practices of support are being developed or kinship relations stretched in the context of rising inequalities between certain sectors of the rural population.

The subsequent chapters deal with the practices of patronage networks in business, politics, and religion.

Notes

1. The lowermost unit in a hierarchy is the category *bir atanin baldary* (BAB)—children of one father. It is presented in the form of a big family, because this is its economic basis. BAB can be situated at the same level as *uruk*, allocating it with its additional semantic characteristics. Realistically, these kinship ties reach three to five generations back (Israilova-Khar'ekhuzen 1999, 132).

2. A father's elder brother's wife is called "mother" (FBW=M).

3. This proverb references a traditional coat with a felt collar; the association of women with fur is both a sexual metaphor and an example of a common device in proverbs of juxtaposing humans and animals.

4. Ideas about bone and flesh are pervasive in discussions about the relative roles of women and men in kinship and descent relations. They are similar to those found among Mongolian and Tibetan groups, and posit that fathers transmit bones to their children through semen (*etsgiin töröl, yasan töröl*) and mothers pass on "blood" or "flesh" (*ehiin töröl, tsusan/mahan töröl*) (Diemberger 2006, 160).

5. Som is the Kyrgyz currency. At the time of research (2008), fifty som was equal to one euro. The average salary in Kyrgyzstan ranges from twenty to fifty euros per month.

6. "Renew the bones" (*söök jangirtuu*) implies strengthening the relationship between two distant relatives.

4 The Irony of the Circle of Trust

The Dynamics and Mechanisms of Patronage on the Private Farm

WHILE DISCUSSING KINSHIP and the importance of helping distant kinsmen with my informants in Bulak, the topic of the former kolkhoz in the village of Orlovka and its new owner—Rahim—often arose. In these conversations, people said that the new management was disorganized and fraught with internal competitions, and that the new farmworkers were suspicious, untrustworthy, and strange. At first I paid little attention because I was focused on Bulak, but as I learned that the kolkhoz provided many jobs for Bulak villagers, I also became interested and decided to visit Orlovka myself.

In this chapter, I specifically focus on the "Emgek" farm, still referred to as the "kolkhoz," even after the decollectivization process of 2004. Do the stock images of the farm in Bulak conversations merely express the conflicted feelings that still surround the dissolution of the kolkhoz and the founding of the new private farm? Or were local people correct in their perception that something was amiss at the new farm? The management of the new private farm appeared disorganized from the outside because it did not conform to conventional notions of business administration. This "space," which is referred to by insiders with unintentional irony as a "circle of trust" (*krug doverie*), is occupied by the patron and his clients, who on the basis of unequal power relations arrived at a way of coming to terms with one another that allowed them to meet challenges as they arose.

In Chapter 4, I unravel the basis of the patron's authority, the manipulative strategies that he employed, and the struggles of clients as they attempted to pursue their own ends, while maintaining or augmenting the patron's support. In doing this, I concentrate on what will probably prove to be continuous in the history of the province—a moment that is characterized by patron-client relations that inherently are neither forced nor voluntary, but intersubjectively constructed. In this moment the patron possessed access to political, economic, and cultural resources that were important for his client to fulfill basic needs. In exchange clients provided the patron with goods, political loyalty, labor, and other services. As elsewhere, patron-client contracts gave rise to a distinct power dynamic between two individuals with unequal resources, status, and power (Foster 1961; Gouldner 1977; Scott 1972a).

The new enterprise was a setting in which informal relations led to cooperation among actors, each of whom had various aims and intentions. Despite the diversity and complexity of these social relations, the common interests that bound clients in the "circle of trust" were the resources in which they were all interested, and over which they all competed.

The Setting of My Research Site

"Klara Tsetkin" kolkhoz was established in 1929 in the village of Orlovka. In the early post-Soviet years (1993–1994), legal changes made it possible to privatize land, but, like most farms, this one pursued a gradual path to full decollectivization. Because of the farm's long history and people's attachment to their kolkhoz, villagers initially decided to reorganize the kolkhoz into a cooperative farm (R. *kooperativnoe hozyaistvo*) until 2006. During this time, the name was changed to "Emgek" (labor).

Those who stayed with the farm were given credit for owning a certain number of shares (one share is about one hectare, and this is for one person), whereas those who left the farm received some kind of payment, in cash or in kind, corresponding to the shares that would have been theirs had they stayed with the farm. During my field research, I was told that none of the kolkhoz workers had given up their shares of the farm. Despite the decollectivization, local people consolidated the collective nature of the farm as long as possible by working without salaries for many years and keeping the previous head of kolkhoz as well as other workers in their positions. This kind of endurance of maintaining the Soviet style of farm organization can be found in other post-Soviet countries (Humphrey 1998; Lindner and Nikulin 2004; Nikulin 2003; Roy 1999; Zanca 2000).[2] The reasons for this continuation have been suggested most cogently by Humphrey: people prefer continuation of collective farms because the state failed catastrophically to meet the needs of the population. As a result of such conditions, "people are attached to collectives because they are the only thing that looks like a functioning intermediate institution and stand in for what is almost a nonfunctioning state at the village level" (Humphrey 1998, 461).

As a result of new policies that came into effect in 1993, the kolkhoz generated a debt totaling one million som and suffered from a massive loss in profit. According to the last head of the kolkhoz, Orlovka's village administrators had to slaughter and sell two hundred to three hundred cattle each year to meet the price of the lubricants, spare parts, seeds, material, and electricity needed to keep the kolkhoz alive. The high cost of maintaining a kindergarten, bakery, and a culture house was also prohibitive. While one possible way out of this financial crisis was to distribute the commonly owned farm property, people did not want this. There was no option but to sell the kolkhoz to those who could retain it. The difficulty lay in finding a purchaser who would buy the kolkhoz despite complicated bureaucratic procedures that surrounded its purchase.

Finding a purchaser for the kolkhoz was the responsibility of a former kolkhoz chairman, who took charge of the management of the kolkhoz. He was actively looking from 1993 to 2005. In 2005 the chairman finally found a potential buyer in Rahim, but he had to convince him of the farm's overwhelming prospects and opportunities. As the chairman of the kolkhoz said, he gave Rahim a tempting offer in terms of a low price for the failing farm. By buying the kolkhoz and paying off its debts, Rahim stood to increase his status and authority within the village and beyond because he would then be seen as helping people solve their problems. Moreover, Kyrgyz parliamentary elections were on the horizon and Rahim wanted to be elected as a parliamentarian for the Supreme Council (see Chapters 6 and 7). The chairman explained the farm's value further: even if the farm failed to turn a profit, the purchaser would not lose "one cent" because he could sell it in the future for the higher price than he had bought.

In the sale, Rahim bought only the nonland assets of the farm. He bought all the buildings (the house of culture, garages, gas storage, water supply, repair shops, barns); machinery (tractors, trucks, combine harvester); fuel; and livestock (cows and horses). As a further condition of the sale, Rahim had to give the workers and pensioners on the collective farm some money because they legally owned the nonland assets.

The Old Collective Farmworkers: Orlovka's Insiders

Thus, in 2006 Rahim became the owner of Orlovka's former kolkhoz and turned it into a private enterprise. Despite its bankruptcy and lack of productivity, many Orlovka villagers found it hard to believe that the kolkhoz no longer belonged to them. At the time of my research in September 2008, there was still confusion, fear, regret, and disappointment in the village. Villagers were still angry with the former kolkhoz chairman for his inability to manage the private farm properly, and they accused him of having attempted to take most of the property's money by not making the budget of the kolkhoz transparent. Some blamed themselves for voting in favor of the sale when asked whether the farm should be sold or not.

As Verdery (2003, 19) argues, property in post-socialist contexts goes beyond individualized property subjects. It incorporates "simultaneously a cultural system, a set of social relations, and an organization of power" that all "came together in social processes." So it was in Orlovka. The villagers attached social values and symbolic meanings to their kolkhoz and their life experiences in Soviet time, while the new owners and workers of the private farm viewed it in terms of economic productivity.

In 2008 there was confusion on the farm, as well. As a private farm, the former kolkhoz was meant to resume its specialization in dairy production and canned meat (R. *konserva*) with slaughtering, processing, and packing facilities onsite, both for domestic and export markets. At the time of my research, the farm was still failing to export its products beyond the village. The problems, it was said, were largely due to lack of motor transportation. The new head explained that the farm was also going to bring in new machines from Europe within a few months' time, specialize more intensively in the area of meat production, and increase its supply of milk to local dairy companies. But there were problems.

The privatization of the farm had been incomplete. The livestock had not been privatized, and other parts of the kolkhoz, such as the bakery, bathhouse, and the mill, had been sold to local people, but the property boundaries of the properties had not yet been fixed. The house of culture had been sold to Rahim, but people were dissatisfied with their lack of access to it.[3] The overall condition of the farm and related buildings, such as barns, the house of culture, and garages, were not good; roofs, windows, and doors all had to be replaced. Cars, broken-down tractors, old lorries, and big red combine harvesters were under repair. And management recognized that the conditions for new workers from Bulak were not good because they slept in cattle sheds and worked for many hours a day.

Some Orlovka villagers were concerned about their land. This was the only resource from the kolkhoz that they had actually received during the privatization process. Usually one family consisting of six to seven members had six to seven hectares of lands. By mutual agreement, the villagers were to rent their land to Rahim. But the monthly sum they received was very low, and they were unhappy. Most felt that they did not have another option because they could not cultivate their lands by themselves because of the high price of agricultural *machinery*. Only a few villagers tried to cultivate their land themselves.

The villagers of Orlovka complained constantly that Rahim had brought new and untrained workers to the farm. They said that he had replaced almost two hundred Orlovka workers with his distant relatives, none of them from Orlovka nor specialized in the rigors of cattle breeding. Of these, almost fifty were women, which was particularly egregious because dairymaid jobs were considered one of the main sources of household income. Men's incomes were not enough to provide for household needs, and women could not find other kinds of jobs. The new workers from Bulak verified that they had found their jobs by negotiating their lineage identities, but they did not intend to offend the previous workers by replacing them.

I could not help but notice the strange relationship full of misunderstanding and distrust between the villages of Orlovka and Bulak. People in Orlovka complained that they had been excluded, and did not receive support from the patron, while Bulak was included and received support from him. Moreover, they complained, Rahim had started to monopolize all economic activity in the village. Not only had he rented people's land; he had bought the main stores. And he had monopolized control of the key institutions in the village such as the *house of culture*, bakery, local garage, and kindergarten. Rahim did make significant contributions of occasional financial support for the school, hospital, and kindergarten, but conflicts still emerged between him and the villagers.

Individual Benefits of Cooperative Action

The majority of workers on the newly privatized farm were from Bulak and were part of the patron's lineage, Ak Jol.[4] There were also workers of other nationalities by ethnicity, mainly Meskhetian Turks, Dungans, Tatars, Russians, and Ukrainians on the farm. Out of twenty-eight farm workers, there were only four from Orlovka: three dairymaids and one male worker. Although he had fired two hundred workers, Rahim had hired only twenty-eight. Kalibek, whom I introduce below, told me that "the farm is in the early stage of development; therefore, at this point twenty-eight people are enough."

As can be observed in Table 4.1, the organization of the private farm was hierarchical. The chairman of the farm had the greatest authority, and the chief specialists under him were second in command. The unskilled workers were at the bottom of the ladder. The structure of the farm was divided into separate sectors following the Soviet model of "units" and "brigades." There were three sections within the farm: the governing committee, the production sector (of livestock and milk), and the unskilled workers service. The farm consisted of only one brigade that was responsible for milk production, crop production, and livestock, although it specifically concentrated on milk production.

The governing committee of the farm consisted of the chairman, the main engineer, the chief accountant, the economist, and the supplies manager, all of whom had responsibility for managing, supplying, budgeting, reporting, and making presentations during their meetings with the main director. On the second level were the chief specialists responsible for sectional production (milk production, haying, and cattle breeding); each was in charge of sections according to their specialization—such as mechanization expert, veterinarian, animal technician, agronomist, and machine operator. From time to time, some were engaged in other tasks, as well. On the third level were the unskilled workers; they were responsible for tasks such as guarding the territory of the private farm, milking, building, and repairs.

The farm also needed seasonal workers who do not appear on the chart. These were tractor drivers and harvester operators who were called on during times of sowing and harvesting. They were also responsible for irrigation, spreading

Table 4.1 The Private Farm's Organization and Administration, Orlovka, 2007

Labor Area	Specialization	Name	Age	Residence	Background (Lineage or Ethnic Group Added by the Author)
	Chairman	Rahim	34	Bulak	Ak-Jol lineage
Administration	1. Main engineer	Kalibek	34	Bulak	Ak-Jol lineage
	2. Chief accountant	Maria	47	Bulak	Sagyndyk lineage Sarybagysh lineage
	3. Economist	Dooronbek	52	Bishkek	Tatar
	4. Supplies manager	Alimjan	40	Tokmok	Turkish
	5. Personnel department	Farida	55	Orlovka	
Milk Production	Animal technician	Narinbek	52	Bulak	Ak-Jol lineage
Unit (*Molochnaya*	Livestock expert	Zakir	46	Bulak	Karatukum lineage
tovarnaya ferma,	Agronomy expert	Almaz	47	Orlovka	Tata lineage
MTF), Agriculture	Veterinarian (surgeon)	Efim	50	Tokmok	Russian
and Livestock	Mechanization expert	Burulbek	45	Bulak	Ak-Jol lineage
	Milk supplier	Oroz	46	Bulak	Ak-Jol lineage
	Machine operators:				
	1.Tractor driver 1	Muras	40	Bulak	Karatukum lineage
	2. Combine driver 1	Edil	43	Bulak	Ak-Jol lineage
	1. Tractor driver 2	Chopa	44	Bulak	Ak-Jol lineage
	2. Combine driver2	Salamat	39	Bulak	Kochokbai lineage

		Sabirovich	57	Bishkek	Ukrainian
Unskilled Workers	Builder				
Service	1. Cattle breeder	Nadir	34	Bulak	Kochokbai lineage
	2. Calf rearer	Altyn	27	Bulak	Karasakal lineage
	3. Cattle breeder	Chinar	33	Bulak	Ak-Jol lineage
	4. Cattle breeder	Marat	36	Orlovka	Tata lineage
	5. Livestock herder	Asil	26	Bulak	Tata lineage
	6. Driver	Alim	38	Bishkek	Dungan
	1. Dairymaid	Jyldyz	30	Orlovka	Tata lineage
	2. Dairymaid	Munara	40	Orlovka	Karatai lineage
	3. Dairymaid	Venera	24	Orlovka	Kenjebai lineage
	1. *Kolkhoz* guards	Omurbek	22	Bulak	Ak-Jol lineage
	2. *Kolkhoz* guards	Marat	44	Bulak	Karatukum lineage
	3. *Kolkhoz* guards	Chubak	25	Bulak	Karatukum lineage
	4. *Kolkhoz* guards	Ilich	29	Bulak	Sagyndyk lineage

manure, and cutting hay in the spring. Apart from performing various tasks in the farm, they lived in the village of Bulak; there, these same workers helped the patron's grandmother breed her cattle, cultivate a small piece of plot, make hay, and water her livestock. The workers' wives helped Rahim's grandmother clean her house and prepare food, and otherwise took care of her.

The majority of the private farm workers obtained their qualifications during the Soviet era. Owing to salary discrimination during the Soviet times, people in Kyrgyzstan were motivated to train as specialist workers. These workers had been actively engaged in the operation of the kolkhoz before the disintegration of the Soviet Union. However, since independence, their qualifications have not been as valued as they were during Soviet times.

Many of the Bulak workers had positions that were equivalent to those they had before in the kolkhoz. While they worked as they did before, they took up work this time with different intentions and expectations. However, the experiences of the Soviet-trained specialists, and the regular use of Russian terms such as order (*prikaz*), decision (*reshenie*), directions (*razporojenie*), and general plan (*orgplan*) in association with the management and regulation of the farm clearly indicated the continuity of certain features of the Soviet era.

Women are in the minority on the private farm: there are only four full-paid female workers, whereas there are twenty-four men, including seasonal workers. Private farm workers fell into two categories: those who were more experienced, acquired their qualifications during the Soviet period, and were aged between forty and fifty-five years old; and the majority, who were in low-service positions, mostly young men aged between twenty-five and thirty-five. Farm dairymaids were mostly from the village of Orlovka, since women from Bulak could not come to the kolkhoz because of tasks and responsibilities at home. The Orlovka dairymaids were considered experienced workers because they worked in the former kolkhoz. They worked only during particular times and then returned to their homes. Dairymaids worked year-round, while skilled workers had periodic work in split shifts.

Each worker was expected to concentrate on his or her specific job first, and then undertake additional work related to construction or repair. For example, during my farm visits, I noticed that one day a tractor driver might be cleaning the calf-house, and the next day he would be building a toilet or fixing windows. While I expected that workers would only stick to their specialist areas, the private farm did not have strict regulations and workers took on different tasks and responsibilities. Often workers spent their time cleaning, fixing, and setting up new doors, gates, and windows. This work arrangement was explained to me by one of the animal technicians, Narinbek, who said, "We need a smaller number of specialist laborers on the farm, which has a different economy now in comparison with the Soviet times when the kolkhoz had to create a lot of opportunities for its workers in a variety of areas."

Each sector of the farm was located in a different area. For example, the administration section was located in the main office in the center of the village, about fifteen minutes away from the farm by foot. However, the farm itself was situated at the end of the village, near the agricultural fields. Usually administrators visited the farm on Fridays to make general checks, but farmworkers rarely went to the main office. The garage, mill, and store barns were located between the main office and the farm, as were the farm machines, big trucks, milk equipment, and other tools. The farm owned some 120 horses, 150 cows, 16 pigs, 35 calves, and some sheep. Some of the animals had been transferred with the sale of the farm, but the farm also bred livestock seasonally. In winter the cattle were kept on the farm; in summer they grazed on open pasture.

Beyond the Salary

The salary of private farmworkers was defined according to experience, specialization, and references, but it was not precisely defined or guaranteed because workers had no contracts. The salary of administrators was 2,000–3,000 som per month (forty to sixty euros), chief specialists received between 1,000–2,000 som (twenty to forty euros), and low-service personnel received 1,000 som (20 euros). These sums did not begin to cover the cost of food, clothes, and housing for even a nuclear family. Moreover, although the salary levels appear to distinguish between levels of specialization, farmworkers claimed that their take-home amounts were almost equal. The highly qualified workers spent their own money copying farm documents or improving the farm's prosperity in other ways.

One might wonder why they spent some of their salaries for the patron, or, indeed, why they bothered to work at all. Workers had both short- and long-term work strategies. Such strategies were related more to life cycle events and family obligations than to daily wages. Also, by spending their own money, workers hoped to increase their status in the eyes of the patron.

The "salary" was a symbolic term that demonstrated the position of the worker and justified his position in the farm's hierarchical organization. Yet the real salary was absent or invisible. Salaries were not widely discussed inside or outside the private farm. For example, workers' salaries were once not paid for five months because of elections, but workers did not complain. Instead they continued to work as if they had an adequate salary, as well as financially contributing to life cycle events and traveling from one village to another. In these situations, people justified their lack of pay by stating they were helping a "brother" in times of need. Once the workers received free sugar and flour, which I thought was given to them instead of their salaries because the cost of sugar and flour was almost equal to their actual salary. But the workers assured me that these products were not considered their "real" payment, which they would receive at some point in the future.

While they received poor pay, the workers talked about the opportunities they perceived Rahim to offer them. They often claimed that the farm was the only place to which they could turn for survival, and that it offered a stable existence in an environment of instability. But such an answer hardly rings true. More surely, they worked for something that they rarely specified but often described as "beyond the salary" (*ailyktan syrtkary*). In the eyes of the other villagers, people had a reputation of working in the kolkhoz because they wanted to be financially maintained, and benefit from additional support from Rahim in times of need. Their responsibilities, villagers argued, had fashionable names such as "work" and "specializations," but these were only symbolic terms. Their status as "employees" legitimized their relationship with Rahim when compared with his relationship with other villagers.

Work on the farm indeed had some tangible forms of financial and material compensation "beyond the salary." For example, workers had access to farm equipment, such as combine harvesters, tractors, and trucks. Rahim permitted the machines to be used for the needs of other villagers, but farmworkers were the only ones able to drive and operate the agricultural machinery and they were the only ones with access to spare parts, extra fertilizer, or fuel. Because villagers needed the machines during the harvest in the fall and sowing in the spring, farmworkers could negotiate the price they charged to provide and operate the machines, skimming a bit to their own benefit.

The compensation that lies beyond the salary was also immaterial and required substantial personal investment, emotional engagement, and deferred compensation. Clients neither violated the rules of the community nor complained about their bad work conditions, low salary, or poor food. By working on the farm, they entered a "circle of trust" with the patron and his other clients. They supported the patron, and they relied on him in times of need. Their devotion went beyond immediate material gain as they sought support in a life that appeared uncertain, cattle for life cycle events, valuable material for housing, a network for medical treatment, and bureaucratic support when needed. In short, they sought to advance their lives. Their acceptance of a low salary was not an obstacle, but an invisible and rather justifiable tactic. The farm was therefore a demonstrative space in which people displayed loyalty to their patron by working hard, monitoring others, and contributing to the farm's development. And it was full of ambiguous relations and suspicious gazes from other workers.

Indeed, so great was the promise of the patron's support—and so uncertain were the prospects of some of the workers—that some workers did not receive a salary at all. Instead the patron provided them with shelter and food. There were two such families: the family of Marat (who was part of the Orlovka lineage

Karatukum) and the family of San Sabirovich (a non-Kyrgyz). Both families lived permanently on the farm, whereas the other workers lived and worked on the farm for five days, and spent two days at home. These two families also worked, not surprisingly, more than the other workers. The members of both families were neither part of the patron's lineage nor do had strong extended families of their own. They were truly dependent clients, yet even their relations were neither wholly forced.

Maratov's Family

This is the young family of Maratov. At the time of research, Maratov was in his thirties and had five children. He had fallen into debt and needed free housing for his family. According to Maratov, it cost 1,000 som, excluding electricity and water, to rent a room in the village. As a result he considered it better for his family to live on the farm premises in a shed with one adjacent living room, and to be provided with free electricity and water. The family looked after the farm compound in exchange for this free housing. Maratov had worked on the kolkhoz since he was a child, and had been rehired as a cattle breeder in the calf-house. Maratov's wife was usually a dairymaid, but during her latest maternity leave, she was assigned to be the farm's watchwoman.

The arrangement had been brokered by Maratov himself when he heard that Rahim needed a local person who knew the farm very well. When the kolkhoz was sold, Maratov asked Rahim if he could live on the private farm as his children were young and he did not have a house. In exchange, he offered his labor. The headman had agreed to take him on as a cattle breeder. His everyday responsibilities included clearing out the cattle sheds, preparing fodder, and carting away the cattle dung. In addition to carrying out the duties that came with this position, Maratov repaired empty sheds by putting down new floors and replacing doors, gates, and windows. Additionally, he was in charge of calf rearing and collecting milk from the private farm. He started work at three o'clock in the morning.

Rahim brought Maratov's children a cow for to milk and provided the family with a piece of land near the family's shed for private production. Maratov would also sometimes be allowed to earn extra money outside the farm. Initially Maratov had been very enthusiastic that Rahim had promised to help him build his own house, and that Maratov might even receive some building materials from Rahim. After some time at the farm, however, Maratov began to complain that he did not have sugar, flour, and tea at home. Furthermore, when I interviewed him, he had not received any money from Rahim for almost five months, even though he had been working like a "slave" (*malai*) doing everything that Rahim had asked; he had even repaired the houses of Rahim's close friends and relatives. However, while I was interviewing Maratov, his wife told him that Rahim was on his way to the farm. Maratov got excited and asked his wife to clean the yard. Talking to me a minute before, he had been angry about his patron's colleagues, but a visit from the patron himself seemed to change his mood entirely.

The house, electricity and water, and milk cow appeared to be strong incentives to work for Rahim. But Maratov also explained that he did not have much choice to make other arrangements. Nobody outside the farm could help him; he had nowhere else to go and no idea of where to work. He had been ostracized by his close friends, and his extended family had their own problems. He needed to support his family and deal with his own problems himself. His best option was to live on the private farm and to do what his patron had asked him to do. He was aware that a few words to the patron from the other workers would lead to his dismissal.

Early one morning, for example, Maratov had accidentally spilled five liters of milk, but he was accused by one of the farm chairmen, Narinbek, of losing fifty liters. He felt he could not protest, nor could he prove that it was only five liters. As Maratov said, the farmworkers could easily accuse him of stealing something from the farm, drinking vodka, or refusing to work. To justify his position on the farm, he would always listen to the farm administrators and do what they asked him to do: even when "his children were sick, and the administrators might order him to slaughter huge cattle during the night." To keep living and working at the farm, Maratov had to negotiate with and handle the farm administration with skill and also get along with the other kolkhoz workers as his position on the farm was always in question.

San Sabirovich's Family

San Sabirovich was fifty-six when I met him. He had been living on the private farm since 2006. He was originally from Ukraine. He came to Kyrgyzstan in 1999 to complete a big construction project, but his boss did not pay his salary and police took his unregistered passport. San was therefore forced to leave his job and find another one to earn cash to pay the fines for his passport and buy a ticket back to Ukraine. Rahim hired San to build a guesthouse for him in Bishkek, which he successfully completed within three months. Rahim also helped him recover the salary that his previous boss owed him. But Rahim did not pay San for his work.

According to San, Rahim's failure to pay was a good sign. It meant that he had shown interest in San; he also thought it was a good sign that Rahim had kept his passport despite promising to return it. Surely San had Rahim's support:

Rahim had organized a small wedding party for San and his new Russian bride, a young lady in her early thirties. This, said San, was an opportunity for the patron to offer his hospitality in place of the money that he owed San.

San's marriage was one of the main reasons he decided to take up the patron's offer and stay on the farm. At the time San was in crisis because he did not have a house, any money, or his passport. When Rahim offered him a place to stay on his farm, he had agreed. Officially his role on the farm was twofold: he took care of the sixteen pigs, and he was responsible for reconstructing the old farm buildings. But Rahim frequently called on San to do odd jobs, and San also had to carry out tasks outside the private farm—such as fixing the electricity in Rahim's guesthouse in Bishkek, renovating a shower and toilet in Rahim's grandmother's place in Bulak, or fixing the heating system in Rahim's brother's house in Tokmok.

San did not receive a salary, but he could make some money from buying and selling pigs. Furthermore, whenever Rahim visited the farm, he brought food, clothes, and extra money to San. San was proud of his ability to cope with several responsibilities at once: as a pig tender, a builder, an electrician, a fitter, a welder, and an assistant to others in mechanics or construction. In my interview with him, San told me that Rahim once politely asked him: "Father (R. *Batya*) please, help me to complete the farm project; after that I will help you with the housing and passport." Even though he was an ethnic Ukrainian, San had been moved by Rahim's appeal in kinship terms; although truly he did not have any other options.

Now we turn to the internal dynamics of the private farm to understand more why there were controversies and complaints among the workers regarding stealing and borrowing money.

The Internal Dynamics of the Private Farm

The cases above reveal that relationships on the farm were based on patron-client ties. The farmworkers provided services, which ranged from responsibilities as private farmworkers to participation at various events. The relationship between the patron and his clients can be schematically represented in the following way (see Table 4.2).

In the private farm context, clients can be categorized into two groups: local clients and dependent clients. These two groups remained separate, and workers did not move between them. The local clients were part of the patron's lineage and came from Bulak. Dependent clients, like Maratov and San, had no kinship claims on Rahim; some belonged to other ethnic groups, while others only came from different lineages.

Table 4.2 Patron-Client Network Pyramid

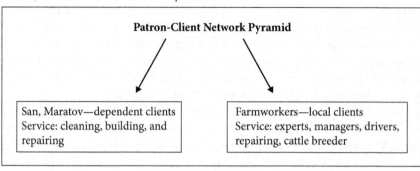

As Powell (1977, 157) points out, "Enforcement, compliance, and performance are bound up in, and limited to, the face-to-face relationship between the client and patron." Each worker was tied to Rahim in a different way, and his "contract" with Rahim was highly personalized, shaped by word of mouth, and informal agreement. The relationships between clients and their patron, most disguised under kinship terminologies, revealed mutual interpersonal relationships. Shared community membership and the use of kinship terminology such as father and son (R. *batya-sinok*) or younger brother and elder brother (K. *aga-ini*) reinforced their expectations of one another.

In such a framework, exchange becomes one of the main binding principles. A crucial aspect of this relationship is that the client perceives his or her interdependence as legitimate. In other words, for clients it is the *exchange* that makes the relationships legitimate. Any change in the balance of exchange can lead to a change in the legitimacy of the exchange network.

As noted above, the farm had two types of workers: the older, trained specialists and younger, nontrained workers. The experienced workers received support from Rahim during times of need in the past: such as in medical emergencies; when they required help enrolling their children at university; when they required money and cattle for life cycle events; when they were building houses; or when they wished to receive bureaucratic or official support in the form of informal connections for obtaining official documents, such as passports or drivers' licenses. In the future, when these individuals needed to educate their children, help them get married, find them jobs (*baldardy butuna turguzuu*), and help them settle in, they would also need the help of their patron. As such, a patron's support in the past results in a client's repayment in the present. In other words, clients feel obliged to work for their patron for little money and yet feel indebted to him.

In comparison with the older generation, the younger men were in the process of building their families and constructing their own private houses. Their future and plans were uncertain, but they felt that their options were limited as they lacked educational and professional qualifications. Therefore, they considered working on the farm the best option, since their future plans and the stability of their current position depended on it. Their devotion to their patron went beyond their immediate material needs or any salaries they received. Instead they looked to the future with expectation. For example, when they wanted to get married, young workers might approach their patron and ask him to sponsor their wedding and cover expenses such as bride price, the cost of slaughtering cattle, or the wedding party. In other cases, they obtained support from their patron in the form of transport, building materials, or medical treatment.

Variations of the Patron-Client Relation

Here, in the specific case of the private farm, there are social actors who decisively choose a combination of different resources to exchange. Patrons and clients are held together by the resource base of patronage, the resource base of clientage, the balance of affective and instrumental ties, and the balance of willingness and coercion (Scott 1972a, 1972b).

The Resource Base of Patronage and Clientage

Rahim brought together several different clients who assisted him on his farm as a result of his ability to not only to assist them but also to support them and their families in times of need. For his own purposes, he needed labor power to construct and transform the old kolkhoz into a profitable private farm.

The (nearly) free labor the patron received from his clients was of utmost value. For Rahim, the patron-client bond was beneficial because dependent clients, such as San, were talented and skilled in dealing with electrical wiring, cattle breeding, constructing buildings, and repairing the farm machines. Local clients also had their own specializations, and they were sometimes farmers able to supply their own unique services. Furthermore, everyone on the farm was responsible for providing the patron with additional services to meet his personal and professional needs both on and beyond the farm.

The Balance of Affective and Instrumental Ties

In the patron-client relation, affective and instrumental ties also play major roles. As Boissevain (1966, 18) points out, patron-client relations are based on "a self-perpetuating system of representation of belief and action grounded in the society's value system." In the case of the local clients, they stressed their shared lineage with the patron and manipulated it for diverse purposes. Their readiness to help is justified through kinship ideology, which allows them to expect from the patron houses, cars, cattle, medical treatment, or payment of dowry. The dependent clients had far fewer claims to Rahim's patronage; with few local family ties of their own, they had little hope of "discovering" a kinship link to him. Yet dependent clients also addressed (and were addressed by) Rahim with the kin terms "father/son" and "younger brother/elder brother." Dependent clients primarily expressed their loyalty by working very hard, demonstrating solidarity with the administration, and being honest.

Patron-client ties that were legitimized through kinship were characterized by greater freedom of movement on and off the farm. A kinship relation to the patron was also assumed to be one of affection. But, in fact, the affective bonds between the patron and dependent clients (such as San, Maratov) were stronger.

The Balance of Voluntarism and Coercion

There was also a difference in the degree of coercion and voluntarism in patron-client ties. In the case of dependent clients, they voluntarily entered into the patron-client relationships. The relationship was almost certainly exploitative because the patron required these clients to participate in various tasks without pay, and he limited their freedom of movement. Yet dependent clients still perceived the relationship as legitimate. Rahim took care to provide these clients with minimal forms of security (house, clothing, food, and access to limited cash); placed them in unique roles that made them "indispensable," and demonstrated his respect and appreciation when talking with them. This "balance exchange" (Scott 1977b) between the patron and his clients disguised the exploitative relations.

However, these relationships of exchange were also subject to change, as tensions emerged between a patron and his clients. In asymmetrical relations, actors' interests do not compete (Scott 1977b) because a patron's main interest is intangible assets (power, prestige, honor, cheap labor) whereas clients are more interested in tangible assets (money, cattle, work). At times of uncertainty, change, and economic crisis, clients work hard to gain their patron's trust and to have access to resources, so that they will be able to be independent from him. It is nonetheless possible to say that after a certain point, when the actor reaches the point where he deserves independence and acceptance, the patron attempts to retain and enhance his power by not giving his clients any further opportunities. For example, San worked very hard to return to Ukraine, but Rahim always found a way to keep him working at the farm, such as providing him with certain options, preventing him from contacting other patrons, and limiting his freedom of movement. When clients tried to advance their future prospects and pursue their own interests, Rahim attempted to keep them on the farm. Since the actions of clients were restricted, bound by a duty to reciprocate, and also bound by the rules of the farm, the patron could still control their actions outside the farm. Earlier promises and kinship terminologies emerged as tools that the patron used to act strategically and improve his own yield. As such, the patron enhanced his position and power vis-à-vis his clients by keeping them dependent on him, and their labor appeared finely balanced—neither forced nor voluntary.

The Irony of the "Circle of Trust": Balancing between Trust and Distrust

People who did not work on Rahim's farm talked of it being run by a "circle of trust." This circle was not talked about publicly at the farm, so I explored what was meant by this term through talking to people in private and observing their behavior. The workers, it turned out, knew the term from Rahim himself, who used it to regulate his clients and motivate them to work for him. By describing his farmworkers as constituting a circle of trust, Rahim assured them he had selected them because they were trustworthy; he trusted them to be intimately involved in his business affairs (which most certainly required circumspection in Kyrgyzstan's wild post-Soviet economy); and he trusted them enough also to require their services in his personal affairs and those of his close relatives. Because he trusted them, Rahim also assured his clients that they could trust him; though salaries might be small and delayed in the present, he would make up for these deficiencies in other ways. Significantly, Rahim's assurances were always made individually; he made one worker feel valued and trusted by suggesting, at the same time, that others might be less so. The circle of trust was constantly under threat from individuals who could not be trusted and might pursue their own interests at the expense of that of the "circle."

The rhetoric of the "circle of trust" fostered solidarity and loyalty, and provided Rahim's clients with a sense of hope that their needs and desires would be fulfilled. The patron played a skillful game with his clients—making their present unstable but promising a stable future. Because workers did not talk with each other about what Rahim discussed with or promised each, the "circle of trust" also functioned to divide and rule those who were included in it.

Will the "Circle of Trust" Be Broken? Competitive Interests

The circle of trust protected the patron, in large part by fostering distrust and exacerbating rivalry and mutual distrust among clients. While a patron provides his clients with resources in exchange for their trust, loyalty, and honesty,[5] clients are also aware that these resources must be shared among them. They therefore act strategically, and compete among themselves, to gain the patron's trust and defend their privileged access to particular resources. By way of comparison,

Putnam (1993) found that clients are in constant competition to get the best land on the *latifondo* or other available resources in southern Italy.

Distrust did not lead to the complete absence of social relations or cooperation between Rahim's farmworkers. Instead it generated a particular relationship alliance, which was likely to emerge between workers on the private farm based on their differentiated interests. In this form of integration based on differentiated interests, clients understood that they shared some interests in common. Thus while there was competition and misunderstanding between those whose shared the same interests and similar status, those whose interests were different tried to help each other to bring mutual benefit. For example: the interests of the chief specialists did not overlap with those of the lower-service personnel (guards, herders, and construction builders). In the following paragraphs, however, I consider the greater degree of mistrust that was generated among workers.

One of the strategies adopted by the "circle of trust" was a system of check and balance. Workers monitored one another in the patron's absence. This limited trust and cooperative action between clients. Clients regulated each other through gossip, informal talks, and biased judgments. However, one might also wonder how the patron knew what was true. If everyone was against everyone else, who really worked hard and who did not work at all? Clients were also classified according to those with whom he had good relations and those with whom he had bad relations. The classification of clients based on their integration and difference enabled the patron to understand the behavior of his workers and their respective intentions.

Here is an example: Oroz, a milk supplier, found out that Rahim's father's brother's son (Rahim's classificatory brother) Satilbek was adding water to milk to increase the volume of milk in the barrel. As soon as Oroz discovered Satilbek's dishonesty, he immediately informed Rahim that first-class milk had been decreased to third-class milk by Satilbek. This led to serious conflict between the two brothers. Rahim was at the stage of monopolizing the milk industry by purchasing milk from all the farmers in the Chüi Valley for a relatively high price because he had reliable buyers in Kazakhstan. It was crucial for Rahim to supply high-fat-content milk. His brother's dishonesty jeopardized this business plan.

The incident also strengthened Oroz's position because he had demonstrated himself to be a loyal worker. Oroz gained the patron's trust, and he was placed in Satilbek's former position as manager of the whole milk business. His responsibility was to manage his team, which consisted of twenty workers, milk collectors, milk experts, and drivers, and also to manage the collection of milk from several villages in the Chüi Valley, which was to be taken to the main barrel. Following this, he was responsible for monitoring the bacteriological testing of the milk, preserving the milk by cooling it on time, and exporting it to Kazakhstan.

Oroz's lifestyle visibly and quickly changed after his promotion, affecting his relations with other Bulak villagers. Within two years, the patron presented him with a nice car and supported him wherever and whenever it was possible. One Bulak villager told me how Oroz had changed since he started working for Rahim. First, he said, Oroz no longer greeted many of his former acquaintances. Second, he had started smoking Marlboro cigarettes. He previously had smoked only the cheapest local cigarette, *Polet*. He also used to ride a donkey. Now he drove a Soviet *jiguli*, was constructing a house, and educating his children. At the time of my research, Oroz was planning to ask the patron to help his daughter enroll in business administration at the local university. He was part of the patron's "circle of trust." He seemed quite happy with his position and pleased with his boss and future prospects, even though many workers did not like him.

In another case, Alim, a driver, and the dependent client San mutually accused each other of unfaithfulness, cheating, and stealing things from the farm. Once when maize was short on the farm, Alim accused San of stealing the maize for his pigs. On another occasion, the farm lost a milling machine, and Alim accused San again. In his turn, San has accused Alim several times of taking eggs from the farm to sell at the local market. In this case, San and Alim were of similar status and position, and neither was affected by the other's accusations. Or were they?

From my conversations with informants, it was clear that Rahim did not publicly disclose his opinion of individual clients. No client ever really knew whether he was more or less valued, more or less trusted. In a case like that between San and Alim, neither really knew whether Rahim believed him to be innocent or guilty of the others' accusations; both continued to seek Rahim's trust. It would seem that Rahim considered the gains to be made by keeping these two men in competition with each other to be greater than the value of the maize, eggs, or other farm equipment that each might steal. It is worth noting, for example, that each man told me that the patron had asked that he conceal the size of his salary from the other. In public the patron treated them equally, but never at the same time. On one day he worked with Alim, and the next day he gave attention to San. This uncertainty kept San and Alim guessing about their patron's true opinions.

Competition between equals also kept the administration relatively stable. Narinbek, an animal technician, sometimes performed a managerial role, but this role was also that of Maria, normally a chief accountant. They did not trust each other, and they did not like it when one interfered with the other's responsibilities. As a result, Maria (who has to remain in the office) always asked Jyldyz, a farm guard, to observe who worked, who drank, and who stole from the farm, and to specifically focus on Narinbek. Once Maria secretly told me that Narinbek was not a responsible person; he drank a lot and did not manage the farm appropriately. Moreover, she called him an easygoing person and said he did not

Table 4.3 Schematic Representations of the Relationships

possess leadership skills in management. Even though Maria and Narinbek distrusted each other, they shared many things. They were the same age, belonged to the same lineage, and had each gained the trust of the patron. They also both had adult children. The patron helped Narinbek's son get into an agrarian university, but Maria's son got a position as the main office manager of Rahim's crediting company.[6]

In fact, Narinbek's and Maria's interests overlapped because they protected the patron and both of them wanted to govern the private farm. If one could be excluded from the farm, then the other might have gained more responsibility and support from Rahim. In the situation as I encountered it, they had to share responsibilities, but sometimes the patron took into consideration one side (Maria), and at times the other (Narinbek). If one were removed from the farm, it would have created opportunities for the other. For example, on one occasion, the villagers came to a private farm during the harvest to sort fodder crops (maize and hay) in an arrangement called shared community labor (*ashar*). The main organizer of the community labor was Narinbek. He hired two minibuses and attracted mostly village elders and young village men to the event. Maria also recruited laborers, but she decided to attract schoolchildren because her sister was a school director. She wanted to demonstrate that she could influence the youth in the village as Narinbek influenced the elders.

The conflict between clients can be schematically represented, as seen in Table 4.3.

Conflict was likely to occur between clients at three interrelated points. Here, I would like to distinguish between more senior clients (who have higher positions on the private farm) and less senior clients (whose positions are low). In the category of lower-level clients, we can include the representatives of both dependent and local clients.

First, conflict arose in relation to the *system* of *checks and balances* described above. Oroz's case illustrated how, by competing with Rahim's brother, he complemented the social obligation to help his classificatory brother. Second, conflict arose when clients competed for a single task and also when their interests overlapped—a result of overlapping responsibilities and undistinguished tasks. Here, clients with equal status competed with one another, as in the case of Narinbek and Maria. As a result, the fluid responsibilities and overlapping tasks of clients coincided at a particular point where both had to control the available human resources. This could lead to the giving of contradictory orders and could also generate misunderstandings, further intensifying conflicts between clients. However, conflict could also create alliances, such as that between Maria and Jyldyz. Jyldyz was a simple farm guard, whereas Maria was the chief accountant. Maria and Jyldyz cooperated because it was profitable for both sides. If Jyldyz helped Maria by reporting on the internal life of the private farm, Maria helped Jyldyz to keep her position.

Third, conflict arose when clients consumed the same items. The case of the misunderstanding between Alim and San was a vivid example. Their enmity and jealousy arose out of their intense competition for the attention and the support of their patron. But an exchange between a client and the patron could be disturbed by other clients if their resources were in danger. Thus, at the level of the farm, exchange and mutual support were obtained through the actions of clients. For example, San and Alim cooperated to perform a limited number of joint tasks at certain times. Apart from this, they acted according to the *system of checks and balances*. Thus, the system of check and balance, the blurred or ambiguous division of labor, and interdependence of clients on the farm led to the situation where clients were made to defend their own interests as a result of the fact that the patron brought clients into his circle according to selective criteria.

The unskilled workers could approach the chief specialists in cases of urgency and need, to get some advice, or to inform specialists of other clients' behavior. In return the latter would always ask a *favor* of the former, either to bring something or to look after someone to reveal the mistakes of the other. Thus, clients who had more senior positions aligned with those who had more junior positions and cooperated to provide mutual support. Both benefited from intra-client relations because their interests did not intersect and they were of different ranks. To be accepted by and to obtain the trust of the patron, they acted strategically to monitor their competitors' work from outside and worked hard to further advance themselves. Within the "circle of trust," there were hidden patron-client relationships between senior workers and younger workers.

The relationships between employees and with the patron were not fixed, but fragile and vulnerable. In this game of conflict and harmony, Rahim's brother lost his job. Mirlan, the former head of the kolkhoz, was offered a less prestigious job once he had introduced the farm's operations to the new owners; he refused. Correspondingly, the farm's patronage was not fixed and structured. Rather, it was undergoing constant change, replacement, and reorganization. The dynamics of the patron-client relations were part of an open game, which increased the sense of challenge brought by any newcomers.

In summary, the "circle of trust" was established specifically under conditions of change, the recruitment of clients, and dynamic development of the patron's semilegal business.[7] Uncertain regulations and poor management gave rise to the emergence of diverse actors, who redefined their social interactions, reified their intentions, and struggled to gain the patron's trust. The rhetoric of the circle of trust promoted individual loyalty, but it also exacerbated rivalry. The rivalry brought some disorder to the farm, but it also resulted in the emergence of a self-regulated system in which Rahim's interests were supported by all workers precisely because each sought to improve his own position. Clients cooperated with those whose interests did not intersect with their own, but not with those whose interests did overlap. In this way, diverging interests also created joint interests.

Organizational Continuity of the Private Post-Soviet Farms

There is still some organizational continuity between private post-Soviet farms and Soviet collective farms (Hann, Humphrey, and Verdery 2002), but we also observe some discontinuity due to different political economies. The Soviet state, collective farms, and households were interwoven with other nonofficial networks, like kinship and patronage, but this "nonofficial" sphere was kept in the background as illegal. Nevertheless, people were not allowed to go out of kolkhoz or they did not have choices (Humphrey 1998).

The post-Soviet Orlovka farm, in the hands of a single economically stable owner, became an independent producer and distributer. The farm evoked qualities of security for close relatives of the patron in the absence of a strong state. Farm workers had the choice to leave the farm at will, but the patron-client dynamic functioned to make choices of working and not working neither free nor forced.

An overarching ideology of kinship governed the behavior of clients vis-à-vis the patron and lent social acceptability to the relationship. Clients emphasized the importance of work on the farm in terms of the security that such a job brought beyond the minimal and often delayed salaries. The structure and operations of the private farm left room for possible manipulative strategies, used by clients to justify and legitimize their positions, their dependency, and subordination in their relations with the patron. As a result, clients neither violated the existing norms of the private farm, nor changed them; instead they used them for their own benefit to satisfy their instrumental needs.

Actors pursued their own ends by developing strategies that were suitable in harsh conditions in which their options and expectations were limited. They also accepted the flexible and ambiguous rules of the farm, manipulated kinship ties and information about their backgrounds and qualifications, and engaged in exchange. Thus the ambiguous and diffuse characteristics of patron-client relations emerged, which combined moral and manipulative action, allowing actors to accommodate a wide range of situations. The "circle of trust" was a technique the patron used to convey to his clients his reasons behind patronage, with the aim of persuading them to consider their subordinate positions from a different perspective and accept it as providing future opportunities. The circle of trust rhetoric evoked an emotional response from clients, but there were also strategic reasons behind it. The goal of the circle of trust was used as an appropriate rhetorical device to construct the meaning of employment. Thus, I argue that within this network, clients constructed their relations, formed their own groups, and created competitive strategies to protect their own interests and positions and to creatively negotiate these in relation to the structure of the farm. However, patronage was not itself static or unchanging. Rather it was an ongoing process that demanded the creative engagement of actors who constantly reconstructed or reorganized their relations, once their aims were achieved.

Notes

1. For more on farmers' property rights in Kyrgyzstan, see Giovarelli (1998).

2. The new workers on the farm always used the Russian term *chastnoe hozyaistvo* (private farm), which denotes its current legal status, while previous workers called it "kolkhoz." I will use the terms *private farm* and *farm* interchangeably.

3. The house of culture was technically part of the kolkhoz and used for public celebrations and common needs (such as hairdressing and tailoring) in the village. Although land and livestock could be equally divided, the head of kolkhoz had difficulties dividing the house of culture among the three thousand farmworkers. In the end it was sold to Rahim, but people found it difficult to celebrate special days such as Victory Day without access to the building. Previously, the village hairdresser, club manager, and tailors used space in the house of culture to provide their services, and they were having problems finding other work space.

4. The farm was closed to outsiders, including me, so I was allowed only to talk to people and make observations and was not given any official documents concerning either the property of the workers or the quantity of the cattle. I could get only approximate numbers from kolkhoz workers.

5. More on cooperation, trust, and social exchange can be found from Cook and Cooper (2003).

6. When Rahim became a parliamentarian, Maria's son became his personal office manager.

7. By *semilegal* I mean that the private farm was registered as private property, but to some extent taxes were not paid. Permission and extension papers can be bought from the local tax collectors. If they are not purchased, tax collectors themselves start finding gaps in a business's activities. Similarly to Rasanayagam's (2002a, 2002b) argument for post-socialist Uzbekistan, entrepreneurship or other earnings in Kyrgyzstan cannot be categorized as strictly formal or informal because in practice a single operation can involve both legal and illegal transactions.

5   Patronage and Poetics of Democracy

In this chapter, I present a particular ethnographic moment concerning a dispute over land that reveals differing views on the role of religion in public space, the inability of the state to guarantee the enforcement of the law, and how the state is governed through creative uses of kin solidarity. The dispute resulted from a proposal to build a mosque in Orlovka. Community members with secularist views and business interests refused the proposal. The land on which the proposed mosque would have been built was zoned as public land, though in practice it was controlled by Rahim as if it were private property. I focus on the negotiations surrounding the formal arrangements of state and power, patronage networks, and the weak position of those who did not have access to informal networks of state officials. I explore the everyday life processes and strategies of these patronage networks, specifically how patronage was linked to state structures as private individuals negotiated with state officials to turn the law in their favor. Following this, I focus on how the entrepreneur motivated local people to become interested in the dispute by stressing different group identities based on religion and secularism and by promising key individuals support in times of need.

Formal and informal rules structure the social interactions of actors concerning access to and rights of property. In this case, there was a bargaining game between the patron and religious groups in which each attempted to mobilize the "state" as well as private citizens in the community. Each party had differential forms of power and resources at its disposal. In the game, the informal institutions of patronage networks sabotaged the formal institution of property rights. Each party found a way to "follow the rules" of the formal institutions which disguised the unlawfulness of their intent. Kyrgyz law has several layers, and it can be used to either legally support or reject the construction of mosques.

Such an institutional approach cannot fully help us understand the cultural appropriateness of the patron's efforts to break rules, creatively persuade followers, and influence voting. For this reason, I also apply Herzfeld's (2005) model of social poetics to the issues of power consolidation and legitimation by state officials. State officials adjust their behavior according to the norms of the community, such as reinforcing the local practice of voting. From the perspective of poetics, the patronage system has ambiguities and loopholes which allow space for creative movement. Indeed, diverse actors operate within or around certain logics, combine them, and sometimes dissociate or refute them.

Individuals acting in the name of the state have multiple and ambiguous statuses and roles because they are also members of private associations, economic complexes, kin groups, and other collectivities. The connection between the activities undertaken as private citizens and those conducted in an official capacity must be taken into consideration to understand how states function (Benda-Beckmann and Benda-Beckmann 2007, 208). When and how do individuals operate "on" and "off state" in their various social roles and activities? The mixture of state and nonstate activities should not be seen as a matter of individuals making sequential decisions about how to behave, but as the outcome of their application of more generally shared rules with which they conform. To this perspective, I add Goffman's (1959) concept of "front stage" and "backstage" behaviors, which suggests that social actors have two different modes of presenting themselves: the first one is when we are "on" for others (front stage) and the second one when we "let down our guard" (backstage).

Building a Mosque

On October 17, 2007, I sought to interview a lady in her sixties about her life during the Soviet Union. I saw a huge crowd of people, around three hundred, in front of the administrative offices of the private farm on Orlovka's main road. They were loudly discussing the construction of a mosque on a piece of land, some three hundred meters square. The mosque was to be constructed in the center of the village between the school, kindergarten, hospital, and the farm's administrative offices. Asking around, I learned that this sudden eruption of concern was due to the fact that a local religious association "Mutakalim," which consisted mainly of young people whom McBrien (2008, 14) refers to as the "new pious" (that is, scripturally oriented Muslims but not Islamists) had prepared the documents required to build a mosque in a public place. The final document had not yet been approved and signed by the institutions adjacent to the site, which included the private farm, school, kindergarten, and local hospital. Technically it seemed that the signatures were optional: when I interviewed the head of the State Agency for Religious Affairs, Toygonbek Kalmatov, he said that the neighboring institutions should negotiate their respective activities. According to the law, if the mosque did not impede the activities of adjacent institutions, then it could be built.

Despite the assumption of goodwill (*kudai bersin*), the religious group found its plans difficult to accomplish. The farm's new director, Rahim, had refused to agree to the mosque's construction and would not sign the paper; he said that the farm intended to build a private medical clinic on the same territory. The building plot was public property, and, according to the law, villagers might build any cultural or public institution subject to collective agreement. The "public" had already supported the religious group's plan, but Rahim was able to oppose the plan almost single-handedly. He withheld his permission to build as a neighboring institution, influenced state officials to convince state institutions to take his side, and eventually persuaded people to vote in his favor.

On that mid-October day, more and more people began to congregate in the center of the village. They gathered in a circle beside the Lenin statue—the usual meeting point for villagers, and the main location for people to gather to discuss pressing social concerns. Looking closer, I saw there were three groups involved in the emerging debate. On the right side of the Lenin statue, local state officials, elementary school teachers, the local hospital staff, and many community residents gathered and expressed their concern about Islam. The leader of this particular faction was a schoolteacher. On the left side, private farmworkers, elderly people, distant relatives, and private company bodyguards gathered. Both groups were against the mosque. To the front of the statue stood the religious group, consisting of young men with beards and white hats (*topy*) and veiled women, led by a man called Anar, who was allies with the village headman (*aiyl ökmöt*). Rahim and Anar had begun negotiating the mosque's construction one month earlier, but they had not been able to reach a consensus.

The First Position in the Dispute: Emphasizing the Importance of Islam

Anar was a local mullah in his thirties. To build the mosque, he had already mobilized a number of supporters consisting mainly of young people and had attracted a sponsor from Saudi Arabia who was willing to donate US$80,000.[1] The Saudi Arabian sponsor had told Anar that "if people were true Muslims, the mosque should be located exactly in the center [of the village] and in a public place." According to Anar, the sponsor had also promised that the mosque would be unique compared to others nearby because it would have a fence and be furnished with a toilet and shower. The sponsor was not involved in the dispute, though the representatives of the *Muftiate* sometimes appeared on his behalf. In general, Arab sponsors of mosque construction in Kyrgyzstan have little interest in the internal affairs of the community's in which they sponsor projects.

Once Rahim objected to the construction of the mosque, the religious group's aim was to convince (or remind) local people of the importance of having a mosque in the village. The group did this by drawing comparisons between Orlovka and other villages in which people regularly attended a mosque, prayed at life cycle celebrations, and performed the duties of a Muslim. The religious group and its supporters commented that this was a great opportunity for the village. Finally, they would have their own mosque where they could perform religious duties during family rituals and spread the message of Islam. The religious group reminded people that the land in front of the farm was the best site—it would attract not only young people and schoolchildren but also adults, who, faced with socioeconomic hardship, might rediscover their religious roots and identities. The leader of the religious group highlighted the responsibility and duty of each Kyrgyz Muslim to personally support the construction of the mosque.

Anar was the only mullah in the village. He officiated at almost every life cycle event, reading the Qur'an and performing religious ceremonies such as circumcision, birth rites, weddings, and funeral services. Anar had never refused to participate in an event, and was always supportive of villagers. Life cycle events (marriages and circumcisions) mostly took place during the harvest season, and sometimes he was not able to manage all the tasks allocated to him. When Anar was unable to perform his duties, he recommended other mullahs from the neighboring villages, but sometimes people chose to wait for him to become available. Anar was confident that the mosque would ease his schedule too: villagers could come to the mosque, and he could manage multiple life cycle events simultaneously.

On that October day, Anar told people that the mosque should be built so that young people could pray on Fridays and meet new people. This, he said, would prevent the alcoholism besetting so many village youth. He stated that fifty young men had died in the past year from alcohol poisoning and car accidents— almost one person every weekend, and alcoholism was a major problem in the village. Anar also expressed his personal opinion about how he found it hard to positively characterize the alcoholics when describing them to the community and family members during the death rituals (*janaza namaz*). These tragic deaths, he continued, should serve as a wake-up call to everyone in the village that the mosque would put young people on the right path by shaming the alcoholics and those who left them to die without any moral support.

Religious devotion, he argued, was required for people to clean their souls, but at the same time he felt obliged to fill the ideological gap for the younger generation. Another Representative of the religious association addressed people with a similar message of morality and shame: "Personally, I do not trust Rahim because Rahim was not sure whether his money was clean. How does he earn his money? Is it legal or illegal? We do not know about them at all. Second, see around [*showed by hand*], we have a casino, bars, and saunas. The businessmen buy such buildings and turn them into dirty places, thereby spoiling our daughters and involving them in doing bad things. How can we close our eyes while they are doing such things? How interesting that no one is interested in prohibiting their activities." The religious group was aware that the private farm itself did not have the right to prevent them from building the mosque. Yet they needed to persuade people to vote in favor of the proposal. They attempted to involve people in the moral order and convince them of the importance of the mosque by drawing their attention to the apparent disorder in the village. The group had high expectations because Anar believed in his villagers' support, and he believed in the importance of the mosque for the village. One of the leaders of the religious group, a seventy-five-year-old local woman, told people: "The land officially [R. *ofitsialno*] and morally [R. *moralno*] belongs to the villagers and not to outsiders who came three weeks ago and started to impose their own rules in a new setting. I worked on the farm for forty years; therefore, I have full rights to the land. You will leave someday, but remember that the land will never leave this place. People, wake up, we grew up together in this village and Anar is your son."

The Second Position in the Dispute: Performing Security

Rahim's supporters were standing in the shade close to the statue. Instead of carefully listening to the religious group's speech, Rahim's followers interrupted the group and started to harshly criticize its behavior, chanting antireligious slogans, and protesting against the construction of the mosque with some arguments. The meeting took almost three hours—a normal length for a public debate. Rahim's supporters highlighted the fact that the nearby shops were full of vodka and cigarettes. If the religious group was so worried about the casino, bar, and sauna, were they also prepared to rid the area of shops? Rahim's supporters praised his intentions for the village, such as replacing the Lenin statue with some modern lights, fountains, and marble stones.

Another of Rahim's supporters remembered that Anar had once served as a soldier in Batken, where an armed group of Hizb-ut-Tahrir began attacking a Tajik frontier post at Lakkon on the frontier between north and south Kyrgyzstan.[2] After his service in Batken, Anar became involved in religious activities and practices. Rahim's supporter thus attempted to rouse the people's suspicions about which side Anar had really served. The insinuation was that perhaps he had joined the Islamist forces he had been meant to fight. He had returned from military service with a changed physical appearance: he had grown a beard, started wearing a strange skirt and a hat. The worker told people that they should be fearful of Anar and look after their children's future. Anar might bring guns, hide them in the basement of the mosque, and teach the young boys combat skills. Furthermore, he emphasized that religious associations who wanted to establish *Hizb-ut-Tahrir* or Wahhabi started first by building mosques in the villages, and then gradually involved local people in covert activities.[3] Mosques were places where religious groups could hide their guns, narcotics, and bombs from Afghanistan, and eventually the religious group might even "turn off your mind" (*baaryngardyn meengerdi teskeri ailantyp kobosyn*). He gave several related cases from the southern part of Kyrgyzstan, where people had been arrested for such religious activities, not only for attempting to use the mosques but also for distributing books and various materials.

Yet another worker from the farm claimed that this religious group was being paid to assist with the construction of the mosque. Taking into account the value of one hundred American dollars by Kyrgyz standards, he stated that it was quite a lot of cash. In fact, it was likely that every member of the religious group was to be paid two hundred American dollars. Interestingly, he said, the Saudi Arabian sponsoring the construction of the mosque would also donate 80,000 American dollars for its construction—that is, the construction of a small mosque that was three hundred square meters. But it was unlikely that the mosque would cost that much. Calculating the cost of the materials, which were all usually cheap, only half of the money would be spent on the mosque. This meant half of the money would definitely be stored away in private coffers or would be distributed among members of the religious group. The worker concluded by saying that the main reason for the construction of the mosque was for people to earn extra money and that religion was perceived as a source of survival in a difficult situation. To illustrate what he meant, he explained how thousands of Kyrgyz had started to convert to Christianity as a result of lack of support from the state. The worker labeled these kinds of people "blasphemous" (R. *bogohylnik*)—that is, people were perceived as trying to resolve the dilemma of everyday survival through turning to God and by living for foreign dollars.

The worker's long-winded accusation of the religious group's intent to profit from the mosque building was an example of wider attempts to publicly discredit the newly religious in post-Soviet Kyrgyzstan. McBrien and Pelkmans (2008), for example, also documented such accusations in southern Kyrgyzstan that new religious groups are "paid." They argue that secularists' negative reaction to the new religious movements and their constant frustrations with them are the result of their efforts to protect Soviet era values; the locally popular notion that Muslimness is an ethno-national rather than religious identity; and their own legitimacy as new elites. Secularists, however, cannot rely on the state's strong institutional backup as during the Soviet period, so accusations of monetary gain are used to discredit religious groups.

The worker concluded his attack: "Building a mosque is the easiest way to earn money for Anar. In this case, Anar's family is an excellent example, because his whole family is involved in this conflict and interested in this project, therefore the mosque is a completely "free house" (R. *besplatnyi dom*) for his family. You are the supporters of religion; you really perform well in front of the public, but it is not good to pretend in front of God." Another farmworker (speaking entirely in Russian) put the local people in a dilemma:

> People, I would like to remind you that according to Muslim customs, one should plant a tree; instead you are cutting the trees in order to build the mosque. Do you know that in Saudi Arabia: people are not as religious as they

seem to us; instead Mullahs drink a lot like horses (R. *buhauyt kak loshadi*). They claim that while drinking wine, they relax. They drip milk onto the wine, after which the wine is not considered wine at all. Instead of building a mosque, Rahim thought it would be more useful if these sponsors built a hospital and a sports school. Do you need a hospital or a mosque—because doctors are also a kind of God?

Additionally, to threaten people and demonstrate the seriousness of the case, Rahim had invited special agents from the State Agency for Religious Affairs, the Interior Ministry, and the National Security Service (NSS) (that is, secret police). They arrived in a black Mercedes-Benz, creating a spectacle in the rural setting. Rahim had requested that people's proof of identity be checked. For thirty minutes, in front of almost three hundred people, the pushy and self-confident uniformed NSS men summoned leaders of the religious group for questioning; they asked for IDs, the name of the sponsor, and for other relevant documents for "security purposes." They also cross-checked the religious group members against the national black list, which includes known members of Hizb-ut-Tahrir.

The Third Position in the Dispute: Achieving Public Order

There was a fight between the religious group and Rahim's supporters, which led to the involvement of a third party, which was the so-called independent party. It seemed Rahim and Anar were interested in involving as many people as they could in this conflict and each strategically tried to encourage others to join their side. This third group consisted of the representatives of local state institutions, and was mainly made up of local doctors, state registry officials, and schoolteachers. This group of people supported neither Rahim nor Anar. Their concern was to maintain public order.

First of all, they expressed resentment and tried to convince the local residents that this land was not the best site for building a place of worship. They were afraid that the religious group might disturb the public order of the community by praying at five o'clock in the morning. Another reason why they argued that the land was not an appropriate site for a mosque was that there was not enough room to accommodate everyone who might come to the mosque for Friday prayer (*namaz*). There would be difficulties with funeral ceremonies; especially when people brought the deceased and more than five hundred cars might arrive. They argued that there would not be enough space to park so many cars on the small piece of land. Second, they did not like the idea of having a fancy toilet in the center of the village. Schoolchildren and kindergarten were very close to the area where the mosque was supposed to be built, and the smell of the toilet would not be pleasant, they said. Third, the teachers in the group argued that schoolchildren would attend the mosque instead of school because children were an easy target and often attracted by religion. They also emphasized what might happen if their children completely left their studies and focused only on religion. To achieve their objective of preventing its construction, the teacher immediately called for a written consensus. In the consensus, people articulated their concerns. Among them, they were concerned that the mosque would threaten the *secularity of the state* and the *attendance of children at school*. One of the teachers told people: "According to the Constitution of the Kyrgyz Republic, the Kyrgyz Republic is a secular country where state institutions should function without external religious influence. We do not support the location of the mosque because it would distract the lives of people in the morning due to the morning prayers; instead an alternative location is proposed a few kilometers away from the village. Please, religious group, show us the official and authorized documents showing us whether you have permission for building the mosque." One teacher asked both sides if the land was their private property, and she pointed to the adjacent borders. In fact, as noted in Chapter 4, the property lines had not yet been fully demarcated after the sale of the farm to Rahim, and the teacher was right to note that some of the proposed land might not be fully public land. If this was so, the religious group's documents would not be valid under law. And it would be necessary to measure the distances between buildings: according to the legal requirements, the mosque should be one thousand meters away from any school building, ten thousand meters away from another mosque, and twenty-two meters away from any other institutions. He said that first it was necessary to coordinate with the neighboring institutions to clarify to whom the borders belonged. The mosque would have been built near the major highway. If traffic accidents occurred because of it, they would become the responsibility of the villagers. Like the other speaker, he suggested an alternative location on the outskirts of the village.

Concerning the question of who granted permission to build the mosque, the religious group proudly exclaimed, *"Selsovet!"*[4] The group was confident of being supported by the village headman (*aiyl ökmötü*),[5] who not only chaired the *selsovet* but was also responsible for attracting, authorizing, and administering financial investment in the village, and for calling and presiding over any village voting. He was also the first who must give permission to build the mosque. During these important talks, the village headman was absent from the village on a business trip. His mother attended on his behalf. She was a local elder (*aksakal*), and gave a speech to people claiming, "This conflict was not my son's fault because he was asked to be silent. Please do not bother him with your questions and cause needless headaches [*bashin oorutpagila*]."

The Speeches

Rahim, Anar, and the representatives from the state registry entered the farm's administration office for an informal talk. After thirty minutes they came out and asked people to move closer to a site near the Lenin statue. Each side was going to give a final speech before they decided what to do and how to resolve the problem that they faced. The main task of the speeches was to express what had been discussed among them and to let people know the final outcome of their discussions about the problem. Three speeches were made, in this sequence: first to speak was Rahim; second was the chief executive of the state land registry; and third was Anar. Each had to state his opinion concerning the importance or lack of importance of building the mosque in this public place. The language Rahim and Anar spoke was Russian, since there were some Russian teachers from the school present in the audience. Anar had to speak in both Kyrgyz and Russian for the sake of the elderly and also his supporters. Schoolchildren or younger people were asked to translate the Russian speeches of the state official for elderly Kyrgyz women and men.

Rahim explained why he persistently refused to sign the paper and argued that a mosque should not be built on this particular piece of land. He continued to encourage people not to build a mosque in the center of the village, instead recommending a different place and a different setting. He argued that any praying at the mosque would hinder children's studies and the work of those at the state institutions. Since the mosque was a unique place, it had to be located or built far from these areas of dispute such as the business and state institutions. But, on other hand, he repeated that personally he was not against the mosque itself, and pointed out that he had even suggested building a mosque in a different site. He proposed to resolve the conflict by finding a site that was convenient for everyone, because in his opinion there were many sponsors who would agree to build the mosque. He said that he was concerned about the influence and proliferation of radical groups, such as the banned pan-Islamic party Hizb-ut-Tahrir, and he was obliged to prevent such a disaster. Rahim waved his hands several times while giving his speech in public, raising his voice to appear very confident, and making sure that his speech was simple and strong enough to convince people. His was dressed in a black suit with a golden watch, which gave the impression that he was a rich businessman with ambitious plans for future. Rahim spoke in Kyrgyz and Russian.

> The representative of the religious association told me that the local people had agreed by common consent to the construction of the mosque. I went to the Central Mosque of Kyrgyzstan in Bishkek and they told me that they had not given consent. Now local people claim that they did not give their consent. The village headman also claimed that he did not give his permission. In reality, it

turned out that this mosque was to be built through trickery. Local deputies, mainly older people, also claimed that they had not given their permission. Now, the state registrar [R. *gosregistr*] asserts that the paper that was brought before him for his signature; he had to sign it. It turned out that the permission for the building of the mosque was asked at the end; first, Anar should have coordinated with us, and then started collecting all his documents. We did not give you the territory. The local deputies were here[6]; how could Anar authorize the land without our consent? The religious group deceived us. Let us vote. We should not violate the rules; instead let us solve this problem together by voting through show of hands to indicate our choice and demonstrate whether we are "for" or "against" concerning the mosque. If a majority votes for the mosque, I will sign; if not, then of course there will not be a mosque. I warned you that you would be breaking the law if you decided not to seek my permission. I suggest that voting is the best way to solve the problem, only the people should decide whether the mosque is necessary for the village. I therefore ask you to decide for yourselves. I promise to build the mosque for you elsewhere out of my own money or I will find investors. I built a mosque in my own village. In general, I am not against the building of a mosque, but the mosque should be built on the outskirts of the village.

Right after this speech, the state official asked people to help Rahim to build the mosque through "common hands" (*bir kol menen*) and (R. *s odnoi rukoi*) and explained to them the reason why, right at the beginning, he had to sign the documents granting permission to build the mosque. What happened, he said, was that ten deputies of the village were meant to sign a document stating that they were not entirely against building the mosque, which they did, but one deputy was absent. Because of the absence of one deputy in the list, the entire validity of the process became unclear, and it was this moment, unfortunately, that had given rise to the current dispute. Despite that fact that the missing deputy had not signed the documents, the state official had to sign the document since the religious group showed him official agreement from nine other people. One of the state officials admitted that he had not given his approval to construct the mosque but only to design the mosque, which was an entirely different matter. Because of this, before laying out the foundations of the mosque, it would be possible to annul the document and modify it. He strongly advised people to resolve this problem together and also to accept his proposal "to vote by hand"; otherwise, the organizer would have to admit that they should have collected all the necessary documents from the beginning, and he would also initiate legal proceedings against building a mosque in this public place. For example, the state officials reminded people that the plot of land was a seismic zone; and it was legally forbidden to build on a seismic zone.[7] The three state officials also mentioned their ability to control licenses and land within the Issik-Ata District by categorizing and recategorizing district land. This threat means that the religious group did not have a chance to build a mosque on that piece of land. He concluded by casting doubt on the motivations of the mosque's proponents: "One more time we have to clarify whether this mosque was under examination. We have to register the name of each individual in the religious group. What was the name of the sponsor from Saudi Arabia? Why do people prefer to rely on foreigners?" Anar was the last to speak. He began by highlighting his frequent visits to the village headman and the way in which he had obtained approval for the mosque. He said that at the beginning of this venture, he had asked the village headman straightforwardly, "Is the land available or not?" The headman had assured him that the land was available, and officially registered as the site that villagers had the legal right to use for general purposes, as long as its use did not conflict with community affairs. Additionally, the village headman provided Anar with various papers and asked him to satisfy all the procedures by going through the main instances of the bureaucracy step by step. Anar said he had followed every instruction exactly. First, he got a signature from the director of the state registry and after that, he went to the Central Mosque in Bishkek in order to register the mosque. They gave their permission after which he went directly to the planning office; they also gave their permission. He has obtained all the documents. The final stage was only to get a signature from the state institutions adjacent to the mosque's location.

The three groups involved in the debate kept hold of their positions without taking into account one another's arguments and sometimes completely ignored the fact that other people were talking and kept interrupting their speeches. While Rahim proposed the public vote "for" or "against" the mosque, the majority of people agreed because it was a sign of conflict resolution that would take into account three equally strong and important arguments (the moral degradation of young people, security of the community, and the maintenance of public order). This method of conflict resolution was accepted by the local people, as well as the state institutions and the religious group.

People voted through a show of hands: the representative of the state registry asked those who were against the construction of the mosque on this site to raise their hands and counted the result. The same procedure was followed for those who were in favor of constructing the mosque on this site. The show of hands revealed the majority of people were in favor of *not* building the mosque on the site. This is because there were supporters of Rahim and people who thought building the mosque elsewhere was a good way to resolve the conflict. There were approximately two hundred outsiders plus forty local state officials, schoolteachers and kindergarten teachers, in relation to insiders, consisting only of fifty religious individuals. In the end the meeting swiftly dispersed, but people reassembled in small groups, consisting of locals and nonlocal residents. Some left to go home without any further exchange, commentary, or gossip, accepting their failure. Others preferred to stay a little longer and continue their discussions.

Debate around the Influence of Islam

The construction of the mosque aroused debate about the role and influence of Islam in the local community. State officials and Rahim creatively exploited the discourse of religious threat and imposed the rhetoric of competing public services (medicine versus religion) to mask their highly self-interested ends and to control the situation. Thus, the entrepreneur's actions were rhetorically justified on the grounds of appealing to a higher moral order: public order and the security of the community, which in effect invoked an alternative set of local practices that, he claimed, took precedence. Rahim also claimed to support the religious group; he was not completely against the construction of a mosque per se, he said, and pointed out that he had built a mosque in his own village. In this debate Rahim showed himself to be not unlike Russian businessmen in his attitude toward religion. Russian businessmen make substantial financial donations to the Russian Orthodox Church, often with the intent to exercise pressure over church activities or to support priests who do not criticize their business misconduct. Such businessmen treat the Russian Orthodox Church "like a client in the market' or 'spiritual service" (Köllner 2012, 29–30).

Islam in Kyrgyzstan is a valuable rhetorical instrument in political and social debate, but its utility depends on the situation. Every year, for example, parliament deputies raise the issue of legitimizing the actions of those who have more than one wife under the umbrella of Islam. But Islam is also suspect, as we have seen from the involvement of the National Security Service (NSS). While Islam is an important component of Kyrgyz ethnic identity, there are still many complaints about the presence and legal status of religious groups, and the law on religion is quite restrictive. Religious groups' activities are constantly monitored and there have been other warning calls by state officials, such as the police and the NSS.[8]

The invocation of the Muslim identity of ethnic Kyrgyz is sometimes convincing. Anar was initially supported, for example, in his call to strengthen religious involvement to prevent the degradation of morals and values among young people. But social opinion varies about whether the morals that should be upheld are traditional (ethnic) Kyrgyz ways, or "foreign" Islamic ways. Teachers and other state workers exploited this uncertainty in public opinion by saying that they were not comfortable with the possibility that schoolchildren might attend mosque activities at the expense of their schooling. The teachers argued that the presence of a mosque might lead to the Islamic radicalization of the village's children. Although they invoked the secular nature of the state in their support, their claims rested on the desire to distinguish Kyrgyz Muslims from dangerous, radical, foreign Muslims.

In the final debate, Rahim and the state officials built on the imagery of a "foreign Islam" that endangered local Kyrgyz Muslims. In this way, they supported the villagers' desire for public religious expression, even as they quashed Anar's initiative. The logic of their claim was the following: "Why should we attract foreigners when we have our own local entrepreneurs?" People stressed the point that the mosque was being built with Saudi Arabian money, and questions were asked about the donor's identity. A complete stranger, who was prepared to build a mosque and spend thousands of dollars on it—"Do we know him?" they asked. "How could we trust him?"

How Rahim Won the Dispute

The villagers agreed with all sides of the debate. They wanted a mosque, and in fact they liked and trusted Anar as a religious leader, even though some doubts always circulated in the community about what had happened during his military service. Like most Kyrgyz, they also feared the possibility that religious revival, especially when sponsored by foreigners, might lead to radicalization. They feared the challenge of strict Islamic rules to cherished aspects of both traditional and modern Kyrgyz lifestyles, and the "modernity" of Kyrgyz life that had been emphasized during the Soviet period. They valued education and public order (partly as a component of Soviet modernity), and feared the specter of terrorism raised by national and global media. When given the chance to vote on the construction of the mosque, they might well have voted more strongly in favor of the proposed plan. Or they might have been equally split. How was it then that the majority came to vote against the mosque?

Rahim controlled the dispute process in his favor, while placing responsibility with the villagers to decide democratically. This then, was a tremendous example of the social poetics of post-Soviet democracy in Kyrgyzstan: when self-interest was effectively hidden and advanced as collective decision.

Voting by a Show of Hands

A show of hands is a common voting method used in Kyrgyz committees and other informal or small gatherings for voting in times of injustice and uncertainty, and when the state is unable to resolve local community problems. As a code of practice, it is regulated by the elders of the village or sometimes a representative of the local consulate *Kengesh*. Usually voting is practiced in relation to money collection for village life cycle and other events. Such voting is a self-regulatory mechanism, and many resolutions are reached by a *show of hands*.

Voting by a show of hands is relatively informal compared to electoral voting. Each individual has one vote, regardless of his or her age, social role, or position, and people perceive a "show of hands" as providing the opportunity to express their own opinion without falsification or imitation. In practice, this way of voting is open to social pressure because everyone sees how others vote.

Using this practice, the sense of fairness and dignity of the local community is preserved. A show of hands is used to govern issues relating to internal affairs as it expresses general public discussion and it enables people to judge public opinion. In other words, voting is accepted as a procedure through which justice is served since the community can decide on its own affairs rather than its affairs being decided on by the state. Additionally, voting by hand in public is a transparent process and performance of "justice." This way of voting seems to be a sign that people's voices are being expressed and heard. But it poorly reflects the level of support or opposition for particular proposals. It is a practice that is most satisfying when it is used to pass resolutions where there is little or no opposition.

Using such practices, the villagers govern their own internal affairs. This practice can be switched, reorganized, and transformed in times of crisis or conflict according to the situation and circumstances, or depending on the influence of external actors, such as independent entrepreneurs or state officials.

Thus, the show of hands requested by Rahim and the state officials appeared to resolve the community problem in a *legal* and *transparent* way. This was an acceptable strategy for the community—and, furthermore, it resonated with the legitimate language of "democracy" propounded by the state. Yet Rahim initiated the process as an opportunity to "perform" the correctness of his position vis-à-vis the religious group. The state officials also used the voting to perform a local form of democracy, higher than the vagaries of law, that absolved them of the responsibilities either to adjudicate or to admit their earlier procedural mistakes.

Very quickly Rahim made the transition to voting. He gave people an ultimatum, stating that they had limited time to make their decision: (a) they must resolve the conflict today, or (b) "start the process from the beginning" (quoting the words of the state officials). He immediately called people to *vote* claiming that, since the documents no longer seemed to be legally valid, he would encourage people to express their opinion by voting with a show of hands. Rhetorically speaking, Rahim's position was temporarily neutral; that is, since he had asked people to decide themselves, he took up the position of an independent arbitrator, by being neither on the side of the religious group nor on the side of state officials. Rahim was a virtuoso performer: he was on the side of state officials (and the state officials were on his side), but he pretended to be on the side of the community.

In fact, Rahim held several roles and statuses, which combined to produce his self-interest. He was a state official (that is, president of the fund

Entrepreneurs and Crediting of the Kyrgyz Republic) and an entrepreneur. Initially he positioned himself as a businessman "protecting his own interests" in his refusal to agree to the mosque's construction. But, very quickly, he adopted a role that denied the importance of either of these roles, as he positioned himself as a mediator between the state officials and the local people. Rahim could have "won" the debate without a public vote. He was powerful and rich, and could easily have mobilized his extensive patronage networks at the local and provincial levels to stop the mosque building from "behind the scenes." The public vote, however, also enabled Rahim to perform his "honesty" against the corruption known to adhere to all bureaucratic procedures. As an "independent" actor, Rahim displayed his charismatic skills and his status as a state official and an independent businessman.

By proposing that people vote by a show of hands, Rahim navigated his dual roles of state official and independent entrepreneur. In reality each role informed the other, but during the debates, Rahim publicly performed an "off-state" position. People applauded the alternative form of governance that he suggested, even though it gave Rahim a chance to manipulate the situation to his advantage. Local people's concerns could be heard and taken into account by voting, but Rahim maintained the ability to manipulate the situation. He was, at the time, director of a presidential fund, and this official on-state position enabled him to operate freely off state. It was through his on-state position that he was able to leverage other state officials' approval or disapproval of the mosque building and its legal status. Voting helped Rahim win the case for his business, retain his authority in the village for his charisma, and gain respect from the state officials for his creativity.

Furthermore, during the vote, while some people were in favor of the mosque being built, the majority of people voted against it, and everyone had to accept this fact. In other words, the majority won without taking into account the voice of the minority, which is the case in situations where a compromise is hard to achieve. But people believed what Rahim told them: they made their own decision and could judge the outcomes of the voting process themselves. As a result no one could dispute the result, raise their voice, or express their disagreement or any dissatisfaction. Abandoned in the eyes of hundreds of people, the religious group was not strong enough to oppose the farm workers, especially without the support of the trusted headman. Rahim's success depended on his personal qualities, leadership skills and ability to convince state officials to change the rule of the game, manipulate existing local practices (to vote by show of hands), and urge people to act instead of merely judging and observing the situation.

The voting did not violate the rules and guidelines of existing law, and it was an accepted community practice for expressing public opinion and reaching consensus. By invoking it, Rahim strengthened the legality of his refusal. As attention shifted to voting, people were also encouraged to ignore the bureaucratic procedures undertaken by Anar. Anar, it seems, had followed the instructions he received in good faith (although Rahim initially cast doubt on this), but those in charge of regulating the procedures (the headman and state officials) had, at some point, misguided him or failed to follow the correct procedure.

Rahim accomplished far more than the mere obstruction of mosque construction. He simultaneously obtained the disputed land for building his dispensary. Legally it should not have been possible to build a private operation on this land, but, through the vote, Rahim made sure that his overall solution to the apparent problem was acceptable. Rahim stripped people of their full collective rights to the land, but in a way that was accepted and supported by the community as well as by state officials. Herzfeld's (2005) social poetics is helpful because Rahim managed to frame the situation by manipulating the rules in a creative way. By changing the actions of people in a way that was acceptable, this particular situation was governed with poetic effects. Rahim seemed capable of constructing the situation according to his own needs while not completely conflicting with or compromising the practices of the local community.

When a leader has power, he can force other people to do what he or she wants. The authority of the patron was perceived to be legitimate; therefore, people felt compelled to voluntarily comply with his wishes. The model of social poetics allows one to see the *technical* (that is, cultural and formal as well as social) aspects of performance that persuade others of the actor's virtuosity. He could legitimize his "illegal" actions, as people told me, representing them as legal, and justify them by framing them within acceptable principles. What was interesting about Rahim's strategy was that people accepted it as a means of resolving the problem without further complication or the involvement of outsiders. Rahim controlled and manipulated aspects of the *form* of social interaction by showing that he controlled the rules of the game by breaking them.

Rahim used his charisma to provide an alternative solution to the conflict in a situation of potential confusion, in a way that was perceived as diplomatic, and in so doing resolved an issue through voting. He also carefully crafted his speech, choosing carefully what to say and what not to say. He was aware of maintaining the support of this particular village and its value in the recent political elections. It was crucial for him to demonstrate his devotion and support of this community. He dealt especially well with local people, by continually asserting that he would personally help them build the mosque. At the same time, he empowered the representatives of the state by asserting that people should not violate the law. He did this through various strategies—by not disappointing people through the utilization of state corruption, but also by taking a piece of land in a way that did not violate the law. State officials and the entrepreneur managed to provide security for the community and display their protection. This was the task of the high officials, to rhetorically perform patronage in a socially and culturally acceptable way.

The Entrepreneur (Rahim) and State Officials (State Registrars)

Rahim's strategic position was between the community and bureaucracy, and Rahim's patronage networks extended in both directions. There were many factors that involved people in the dispute, but I limit myself only to the function of patronage. First, it is crucial to briefly discuss the situational alliance between the entrepreneur (Rahim) and the state officials to understand the reason why the state officials refused to register the mosque. The state officials could accommodate a wide range of interests as a result of privileges granted by the entrepreneur. One also has to keep in mind that protecting or supporting the entrepreneur is in the interest of the state officials because he masks their inabilities and makes up for their inefficiencies—that is, by sponsoring public institutions. But at the same time, we should not forget that the entrepreneur is neatly involved with the state officials because of the privileges he will receive on securing his private business. On the other hand, he enjoys the freedom and creativity of being an entrepreneur because of the security and support he receives from the state officials in times of need, such as in the case concerning the construction of the mosque. As Humphrey (2002, xxii) put it for Russia, "It *continues to be impossible to disentangle the 'economic' from the 'political.'*" State officials cannot cope without the entrepreneur and vice versa. Thus, a circle of state officials and businessmen are vital to the successful functioning of business life in Kyrgyzstan and securing one's position in the government structure where things are accomplished through weak institutions built on personal relations that keep functioning despite their intrinsic weaknesses.

When the state officials arrived, Rahim invited them to an informal but secretive talk. When the state officials emerged from the office, the state registrars tried to retract their signatures, seeking ways to falsify the legal documents and to justify their actions—as if the signature authorized, not the construction of the mosque but instead the architecture and design of the mosque. Thus, state officials came out of the battle unscathed by virtue of their positions. In Goffman's terms, the political/strategic manipulation of the situation played out in how state officials presented themselves on stage as concerned state authorities, while offstage they discussed their real intentions of falsifying the legal documents.

One of the state officials claimed that since the foundations of the building had not been poured, it was still possible to change the document at the "request of the people" or annul the document in a way that was legal. His ambiguity revealed two interesting interrelated points: on the one hand, the state official was legally right to sign it given the general consent by nine deputies to build a mosque; on the other hand, he had stressed that he could not sign it but had to sign it. In what sense was he required to sign it? The state official did not have the right not to sign the documents, because the documents were legally correct for the signature. Since the documents were in order, he could not annul the agreement. Yet the state official also made the situation more complicated, by persuading people to start the documentation process from the beginning. This was done to undermine the plans of the religious group and create additional obstacles. This ethnographic vignette clearly illustrates that there was ambiguity in the state officials' speech and that by virtue of their positions and connections, during times of need they used the existing space in the state regulations and law to manipulate certain cases and act with freedom within the state boundaries. Moreover, they were able to justify their actions and their activities as "honest." The state officials appeared to operate with freedom, able to change or write off the documents to retain their authoritative, representative, and legitimate position.

Let us take another statement. For example, when one of the officials said they would "change and modify the documents in an acceptable way" (*dokymenterdi jakshylap ongdop bytyryp koebuz*), he played with the construct of legality. Normally the manipulation of a document would be illegal, but, in this instance, doubt has already been cast on the legality of the existing documents. The official openly admits that he is prepared to engage in a normally illegal act to produce legality. In a single moment, he admits that state officials are "corrupt" but perform a higher form of honesty. In repeated and similar performances, the state becomes corrupt, while individual (and personally known) officials become the champions of justice and the people's voice.

State officials extend, narrow, and sometimes squeeze legal frameworks depending on the context. As Herzfeld (2005, 31; 1992, 67–68) argues, there is always some space in the state structure for officials to manipulate and deform it for their own purposes. A good bureaucrat is one who is accepted publicly, knows how to play the rules on the surface so that his behavior appears conventional, and who is inventive in the way in which those rules are applied to satisfy various interests at various times. To publicly uphold the power of officials, the state officials narrow or manipulate the legal system. In this context, the state officials asked the religious group to return to begin the process again but also indicated that they would fail. There was another and contradictory regulation that had been previously overlooked: the site was located in a seismic zone where new buildings were prohibited.

Further, I would argue that Rahim, as the owner of the private farm, and the state officials formed a temporary alliance in which they operated in tandem and supported each other so that both sides could take advantage of their cooperation. Thus, under the guise of the symbolic forms of the state, as the protector of the community, the state officials appeared to enjoy the freedom of manipulating already existing legal norms.

Nevertheless, some individuals became puppets of the big players (mullah and some of the local villagers), while the strongest players enjoyed the privileged position of appearing to govern the proceedings (Rahim and his followers). In this situation of conflict, the role of the entrepreneur and the state officials was fundamental since they were the ones who ruled people, calmed the situation, and played games according to their own interests. But these games excluded those who disagreed with the patron, and the religious group was left behind disappointed that their promise was unrealized.

The Excluded Party

There was one very important side effect in this conflict over the mosque: exclusion. Anar commented after the conflict:

> It is finished. When Rahim was aware of the fact that the documents were all right, he had to use his power and pressured officials to influence the decisions of the state registry. Yesterday, when we went to the state registry, the doors were closed for us. It is a pity that we lost our sponsors. Recently, there was a call from a rayon governor to the village headman to change the decision. It is useless to do anything with the documents. We wanted to work for people, but it did not work out. The sponsor also told us that he will not interfere in our internal affairs. What Arabs do is to provide money. Even though this land belongs to the village we cannot do anything with this land. We are powerless. These state officials do whatever they think to do. Who are we? We are just simple people. The construction of the mosque depends only on Rahim, if he says yes, then the mosque will be constructed, if he says no, then the mosque will not be constructed. Power and money played a great role here.

As the head of State Agency for Religious Affairs, Toygonbek, pointed out, Anar had behaved appropriately and gone through all the right channels to construct a mosque. His documents were complete and correct. But local people did not support him, even those from the same village. In a time of conflict, Anar had faced steep challenges; he was between two extreme parties, secular and religious, who attacked him from both sides. This not only reveals there were recurring conflicts between the secular and religious groups but also displays a history of contradiction. On the one hand, state officials depicted religion as a danger to secure their own position and retain power. On the other hand, religious sponsors emphasized Kyrgyz *Muslimness*. In this situation, Anar, a young religious leader, became a vulnerable pawn, used by both of these extreme sides. As a result, he lost his strong position, since his position as a mullah was dependent on both the financial support of religion and the bureaucratic support of the state.

On the way home, I had a chance to talk to several local Kyrgyz men, who commented on the event. Musa *ata*, a seventy-five-year-old pensioner, summarized: "At present, the past is coming back where the rich can rely on their resources and the poor cannot protect their rights. These capitalists came and destroyed the plans of the religious group. To find a site on which to build a mosque will take local people another five years. The mosque was not intended to be built for old people; instead, it would have been for the younger generation. Before, it was better because people believed in something, nowadays the thoughts of the young are empty; they do not know how to have motivations." The pensioners were unhappy and disappointed about the failure of the local villagers in attempting to build the mosque in their own village. They did not believe Rahim's promise that he would build the mosque in the future. Rather they were confident that Rahim would destroy their square with Lenin and the old building of the kolkhoz and instead build something "strange" in its place. They were also afraid that the community itself would not be able to preserve its own history, which is tidily connected with the Lenin statue, the contested plot, and the old kolkhoz buildings. Moreover, when I asked their opinion on the behavior of their own local state officials, the elders simply shook their heads. They did not want to talk about them.

The Entrepreneur and His Kinsmen

Many people participated in the vote itself. Yet those who actively participated in the conflict were mainly Rahim's followers; they played a decisive role in the outcome of the vote by convincing local people to take Rahim's side and by involving themselves in the voting process. The majority of these people were from Rahim's private farm, but it was also arranged that a bus would bring volunteers from Bulak. These followers were brought with the aim of increasing the number of people voting by making sure that most people objected to the construction of the mosque. By involving his own people in a "mass" protest, Rahim was able to creatively minimize the support for a community mosque. These people came only to support their native son by playing the role of the "masses" and demonstrating their loyalty and solidarity in times of need. No one could object to the participation of the farm workers. The active participation of his own people was also important for Rahim because, by his actions, he could convince his followers that he was not afraid of being punished or of "illegality." It seems people respected those who show they can handle uncertainty, so-called illegality, and corruption. Since the whole state system is corrupt anyway, people explained, it is critical to be able to rely on a person who knows how to follow this system and can also help his "own people." Consequently, the patron did not simply reveal his strength and power of leadership within legal or illegal frameworks; it was important for him to demonstrate that he could cross and blur the boundaries to achieve his own ends.

Explicit and Implicit Siding with the Community

This ethnographic vignette captured the workings of patronage expressed through social poetics. When Rahim, as the new owner of Orlovka's former collective farm, found himself in conflict with a religious group over plans for how to develop public land in the center of the village, he arranged to have the dispute decided in public. As a powerful patron, active in both the worlds of business and politics, Rahim could have won the case in numerous ways, including through illegal manipulations of bureaucratic channels. Instead he chose a public route in which his chance of losing was nominally equal to that of his opponent. The social poetics that unfurled as Rahim debated Anar, culminated in Rahim's proposal to *vote* by *show of hands*. The resolution appeared to be transparent, fair, and the will of the people.

Yet relations of patronage were present. Rahim succeeded in sending the headman out of the village for the day, and bringing not only local state officials responsible for zoning laws and construction projects but also the NSS. Patronage brought the "law" and the "state" into the village, and both came to serve the will of the patron.

The subordination of the state to the patron was possible because the state officials could adjust their behavior according to the norms of the community, such as the local practices of the villagers, and propose people vote to ensure that it appeared *as if* the event were transparent. In doing so, they violated the rules in such a way that this violation was accepted by the local people. This was done creatively using the local practices of the community in a timely and creative way—that is, *voting* by a *show of hands*.

Moreover, Rahim took both sides at the same time: explicitly siding with the community and implicitly taking the side of the state officials. In the end, despite the fact that the site on which the mosque was to be built was public property, state officials and entrepreneur secured the land with the help of the people themselves.

Thus, the tangle of state and nonstate activities reveals that neither morality nor legality could resolve the conflict. The conflict was resolved using the patron-client relation, which as it turned out accommodated a wide range of cases swiftly and transparently owing to its flexible character. Thus, personalized patron-client relations proved instrumental to the development and resolution of the situation and thus contributed enormously to the success of the case. Rahim's active role of constructing the local democratic election using the hands is visible, but the topic of Chapter 6 is the villagers' active role of constructing local democratic elections in the processes of building parliamentary party systems.

Notes

1. The new mosques, *madrasah*, and Islamic centers are mostly financed by Muslim organizations from Saudi Arabia, Iran, Turkey, and Pakistan. Since religious institutions mostly rely on foreign investment, constructing a mosque means an additional source of funding from the Middle Eastern countries. However, there are also local businessmen who support constructing mosques in other parts of Kyrgyzstan.

2. Hizb-ut-Tahrir is a banned Islamic group operating in several Central Asian states. In the media, Hizb-ut-Tahrir is described as a self-styled international Islamic political party aiming to re-create an Islamic caliphate. It has violently antidemocratic and anti-Semitic views and is strongly opposed to core human rights such as religious freedom. It was considered, along with the Islamic Movement of Uzbekistan, one of the possible groups responsible for the border attack in 1999. In the attack, three Tajik border guards and six Kyrgyz officers were killed (see www.iwpr.net/?p=rca&s=f&o=324242&apc_state=henprca).

3. The Central Asian governments view Wahhabi as a single fundamentalist religious group and accuse it of causing conflicts in the Fergana Valley.

4. This is a Soviet term, taken from the Russian for "village council" (*selskyi sovet*).

5. One has to take into consideration the significant local power and privileged authority of the village headman. It is he who governs the community and also attracts international development organizations that work on the infrastructure of the village. Furthermore, he is in charge of organizing public meetings, and without his jurisdiction neither voting nor meetings should be organized.

6. Local deputies (*aiyl kengesh*) consist of elderly people of the village, but their authority is weaker than village headman. One of the members of the local deputies was the mother of head of the village.

7. Suddenly state officials turned this spot of the mosque place into a seismic zone.

8. See "Kyrgyzstan: Crackdown Follows New Religion Law," *Forum 18 News Service*, Oslo, Norway.

6 The Return of the Native Son

The Symbolic Construction of the Election Day

Parliamentary elections were called by President Kurmanbek Bakiyev in Kyrgyzstan on December 16, 2007, after the constitutional referendum on October 21, 2007, approved a new electoral system and constitutional reform proposals. The constitutional referendum enlarged the parliament from sixty to ninety members and introduced a party-list voting procedure. It aimed to grant candidates from different financial backgrounds, and of different gender and age, equal chance of election. In this sense, the party system stipulated candidate lists should include at least 30 percent women, 15 percent minorities, and also some young politicians. Furthermore, the party-list system was designed to restrain divisions along kinship lines within the country.

It is in this polarized political context that the parliamentary elections of December 2007 were held. These were the first parliamentary elections after the revolutionary upheaval of 2005. The widespread hope at that time, both inside Kyrgyzstan and beyond, was that this new election would steer Kyrgyzstan back toward a "normal" political future after months of demonstrations, road closures, and political assassinations. Various parties were contesting the election, but the campaign was dominated by the newly formed Ak-Jol Party, which had been established by Kurmanbek Bakiyev just two months before the election, as an explicitly pro-presidential party. To my informants in the village of Bulak, Ak-Jol was seen as a southern party because Bakiyev was a southerner. By contrast, northerners led the party that came to dominate in the village, the SDP of Kyrgyzstan. It was through this party that the village's long-standing patron, Rahim, sought election to parliament. This provided the setting for the dynamics of political contestation in the village.

In this chapter, I first provide more detail of the specific kinds of symbols that the patron shared with his community (and specifically Bulak villagers) during the elections and also the emotional bond he forged with his people and followers. The most important symbol on which he drew was the symbol of the native son, which presumed both hierarchy and common identity. A native son is expected to protect his community in times of need and to represent it in a political arena. Rahim used this symbol to justify his exercise of power over the community and to legitimize his authority and decision-making.

I also propose a second argument in this chapter, which is that the events of Election Day represent the localization of democracy and an effort towards democratic reform through local practices. In this respect I employ Spencer's (2007) notion of the political domain and apply it in the context of Kyrgyz elections. Also, following Comaroff and Comaroff (1997, 123), I try to better understand the local processes of building democracy in rural Kyrgyzstan and what "democracy" actually means in rural post-Soviet Kyrgyzstan.

The Election in the Village

In the autumn of 2007, the announcement of early parliamentary elections ruptured the everyday routines of the village. People began to hold lively discussions about the party system, expressing their desire to reconstitute "normal" (R. *normalnyi*) politics after many years of political instability. As one of my informants noted: "At election time men stop their normal working activities. Instead, they talk only about politics and read a lot of newspapers. But the good thing this year is that the election is in the winter and not at harvest time."

During previous political campaigns, politicians had typically shown up in the village for short meetings and public speeches before disappearing again. In anticipation of this, and after extensive meetings, the elders decided to demand "useful items" (*kerektüü nerse*) for the village from politicians during the party campaign, such as a yurt, cattle, or a mill. This signaled a more ambitious request than the bags of flour that had already been distributed to select villagers in return for party loyalty. People anticipated the arrival of the same old politicians that they were used to seeing and listening to the same old speeches as before. However, this time, they were prepared to make new demands, such as a request that the politicians buy an old store in the village and turn it into a café, which could then be used for ceremonies on the occasion of life cycle events.

For the people of Bulak the election campaign thus constituted a short period during which people's concerns could be heard, taken into consideration, and realized in practice. This could also be a divisive time, however, during which the fabric of the village could split as people's loyalties were divided and commitments came into conflict. There were even reports of fights between husbands and wives as a result of politics, with some even ending in divorce.[1] As Spencer (2007, 85) found in Sri Lanka, politics had "provided a new idiom in which villagers could express the kinds of division that had long existed." In other words, social cleavages that existed before came to be animated in new ways.

For all the expectations that this would be a time to make material demands of visiting politicians, the village was in fact visited little by politicians during the election campaign. Bulak village was promoting its *öz bala* (native son), Rahim, in the political arena. He was a member of SDP and was poised to become the party's next leader. In the previous election two years earlier, he had not received enough votes to become a member of parliament, but his new stature made his success almost certain. Other candidates therefore saw no point in coming to the village, because it was assumed that the villagers would vote for their native son. They turned their attention and largesse elsewhere, and the elders' hope for a new café was consequently frustrated.

Rahim secured the loyalty of the whole community by promising both economic security and reinforcing social values (respect, honor, loyalty). These values were integrated into the overarching ideology of kinship *tuugan* (relatives), which served to justify and legitimize both the system and how it operated.

I arrived in Bulak on December 16, 2007—Parliamentary Election Day—at around six o'clock in the morning, to observe the election in its entirety in the village. My position was that of an international observer. I had traveled from the village of Orlovka, my first site of field research, reaching Bulak within an hour by car. The day before the election, I attended a training conducted by the International Center InterBilim, where I had been taught how to observe an election for irregularities and to write a protocol. At that training I had been asked to arrive in the village before members of the electoral commission arrived at the village club to open the sealed packages containing the ballot papers.[2] When I arrived, the temporary election office was still closed. After two and a half hours, the commission members began to arrive at the polling station.

At first sight the differences between Bulak and Orlovka are striking. In Orlovka diverse ethnic groups living in the village had built different types of house, whereas the housing in Bulak was largely uniform in style and unrenovated. What made me want to observe the elections in this village, rather than in Orlovka, was this village was nominating its native son for the election. However, this same fact provided both the representative of the electoral commission, as well as the community itself, with a challenge: the village administration was supposed to support the pro-presidential party, Ak-Jol, whereas the villagers were supporting SDP. I was interested to see how these social actors negotiated the rules of the election and how they bargained with the state. The state representative (or village administration) in this case was a widow named Ainura, who at the time of the election was working as the chairperson of the electoral commission.

I introduced myself to the commission members (village administrators, local teachers, and young brides of the village) at the polling station as an independent observer. There were several other observers present, each representing either Ak-Jol or SDP, these being the better represented of the twelve political parties running in the election. My primary aim was to observe the activities of the commission members: how they counted, compared, and labeled the ballots. The commission consisted mainly of women. They compared the number of eligible voters (just over one thousand) with the number of ballots that had actually been cast. They had been struggling to keep count and label the ballots. Two local police officers stood outside the polling station, which was the village's former house of culture, to manage the crowds at the door. Upon entering the polling station, two other men checked ID and marked people's thumbs with indelible ink (and checked voters' fingers for traces of ink) to prevent multiple voting. Eki, a brother of the Rahim and a village political leader, voted first and complained that the pen for writing on the ballot papers was not working properly. Eki was anxious to make sure that everything inside the polling station was accurate and properly prepared.

I spent the first three or four hours sitting in the cold polling station, watching to see what would happen. As villagers entered, they greeted one another and the commission using kinship terminology, as *eje* (older sister) or *aga* (older brother), *singdi* (younger sister) or *ini* (brother), respectively. The young, newly married women of the village who served on the commission had little authority. Although their role was to direct and regulate the voting process (including prohibiting villagers from voting if they failed to produce the necessary documents), as *kelinder* (daughters-in-law) they were structurally subordinate to the majority of villagers who were coming to vote. They had been allocated their role by elders of the village's council of internal affairs and were confronted with something of a dilemma when faced with elderly people who had not presented the right documents to vote. Asymmetrical expectations of honor and respect were often in tension with the demands of electoral law: should they insist that an elderly person return home and bring the requisite identification, or allow them to vote without his or her ID? It seems that young women may have been deliberately appointed by the commission to regulate the election process as a way of making sure people could still vote even without the right documents. Changes in Kyrgyzstan's many bureaucracies meant that many villagers were not in possession of the military record, pension book, or passport they needed to document their identity. Others who considered themselves to be village residents found that they were not on the list of voters because they were not registered as owners of assets such as land or a house. Those who could not vote were angry, shaking their heads, debating their mistakes. They often quickly went home and brought back different documents to make sure that they could still vote.

During this intensive phrase of voting, I met with various people who had come to vote. As we chatted about their thoughts and expectations outside the club, I saw that Oroz, a very close friend and distant relative of Rahim who worked on the farm in Orlovka, was greeting voters before they entered the polling stations by shaking their hands. Oroz work responsibilities included managing Rahim's business but also campaigning for him during the election. Oroz was wearing a blue cloth cap and a scarf with the SDP emblem. He asked the villagers to vote for a candidate that they believed in, but also made rhetorical appeals to solidarity and unity, insisting that *köngülübüz tüz* (we understand each other); *kaaloobyz bir* (we have one aim); and *tilegibiz ak* (we have the same good purpose).

Voters and their families approached the club, dressed in their best outfits, congratulating one another on the holiday with the expression *mairamingar menen* (happy holiday). Whereas women and their children quickly returned home after voting, men remained near the polling station to discuss politics, the president and his programs, and the probable outcomes of this election. There was a celebratory atmosphere in the village with many people gathering on the streets to drink and talk politics.

Oroz stopped voters on their way home, too, asking them to remind those who had not yet voted to come to the club to cast their ballot. Meanwhile Oroz's family had prepared some food and drinks for the commission members and election observers. While we were having our lunch, he called university students from the capital, sixty kilometers away, to ask them to return to their village to vote, promising to reimburse the cost of their transport. He also tried to contact those who could not reach the polling station for health reasons, quickly mobilizing young men from the village to bring elderly or disabled people with them in their private cars. His ability to administer people in this way increased the number of votes and exerted some control over the election process. Those who were unable to reach the station were meant to state in advance and request a special mobile ballot box so as to cast their ballot from home. But many villagers had not known how or where to do this. So Oroz asked young men to bring people to the polling station, dividing them according to the lineage of the village: first Ak Jol, then Karasakal, and so on.

After the election, Oroz told me that he had been so worried about the election that he had forgotten to eat all day. His informal negotiations with Ainura, the chair of the electoral commission in the village, had made it possible for the election process to run "smoothly" for the Bulak villagers. First of all, he had persuaded Ainura—by giving her some money—to provide him with a list of those who were eligible to vote but did not have the necessary documents. Ainura then permitted such people to vote using other kinds of documents including library cards. Ainura admitted to facilitating the irregularity; she said she had "closed her eyes" (*köz jumup koidu*).

Ainura, however, was personally in a difficult position. Her representative mother was a sister of the village headman who supported the pro-presidential party; Ainura was therefore also expected to support Ak-Jol against SDP. Rumors circulating during the election also alleged that Ainura had once received a plot of land from the village headman for her two young married children and that she was particularly obliged to repay this gift by voting for the presidential party.[3] Moreover, Ainura had married into Bulak; her father was head of her natal village, and also an Ak-Jol supporter. There were thus multiple pressures on Ainura to vote for the presidential party. Indeed, it is very likely that precisely this presumed party loyalty was the reason why she had been appointed by the state to chair the electoral commission in the village.

In the end Ainura and her family voted for Ak-Jol. But, she helped SDP by "closing her eyes" and by allocating to them fifty unused ballots at the end of voting, a phenomenon to which I return below. Ainura's case illustrates vividly how different kinds of commitments shaped her behavior on electoral day, but also how others assessed her navigation of these competing obligations. For Oroz, Ainura was "doing nothing but making money all the same" (R. *ona nichego ne delaet, no po khodu p'esy babki delaet*), suggesting that the job of the chairperson is easy and profitable because many party members sought to bribe her.

The outcome of the election at a national level was assumed by most of my informants to be a foregone conclusion: the party supporting the president would take the majority of seats in parliament. This was deemed obvious because the Ak-Jol Party was forcing state officials to vote for it at the risk of losing their positions. One policeman, for instance, an SDP supporter, told me that fifteen thousand policemen had been told to vote for Ak-Jol. At a village level, however, the actions of Oroz and others were important not only because they increased voter turnout but also because they persuaded the majority of local voters to choose SDP and demonstrate their support for their native son. Such pressures could be considerable. When a community member called Baktybek, for instance, wanted to start campaigning for the Ak-Jol Party, he was asked to stop and was demonstratively not invited to the life cycle event of one of the community members. Consequently local villagers did not distribute pro-presidential Ak-Jol Party posters to community members, instead hanging caps, scarves, posters, and calendars with SDP slogans in every house. People would try to get as many caps and scarves as they could to wear them in the street (see Figure 6.1).

As Coles (2004, 554) states, "Election day, as a ritual and viewed as 'signifying practice,' might be thought to symbolize the changing values of democracy." In this line, for people in Bulak, Election Day was seen as a positive event that signaled hopes for change in the country's political fortunes. Their main concern was for their village son to get a seat in the parliament.

If Election Day was celebratory, the business of preparing for it was also an important education in "doing" democracy. Elders would tell each other for hours about changes to electoral politics, rules, codes, and procedures learned from newspapers or Radio Free Europe. They would constantly switch their conversations from election techniques to the political agenda, the future perspectives of the SDP, and the promise of democracy. At a meeting I attended, one of the elders of the community read out the booklet of the party system in Kyrgyzstan in general to the audience in a loud voice: "The party system was designed to

Figure 6.1. Elders' supporting their native son.
Photo: A. Ismailbekova.

avoid kinship division and regionalism in the country; instead it should decrease the price of bread and electricity, and increase people's salaries and pensions."

Elderly people—the *aksakal*s of the village—were also actively involved in mobilizing people and getting them to vote by ordering the younger generation to be more proactive in their community. The campaigners asked people to vote for *öz kökürök kychgybyz* (our son, our brother, our dignity, and our foal); someone who was better than any outsider, and *eldik kishida, eldin kishisi* (a man of the people). Private farmworkers also worked hard to get people to vote. Some of these employees were election observers themselves, who monitored and managed the voting situation in other parts of the region at the district (*raion*) polling stations. These followers returned to their own polling station to vote, arriving in their village at 7:30 p.m., before the polls officially closed.

One of Bulak's private farmworkers, Maria, who went to observe the election in the neighboring village of Orlovka, complained to me that the people of Orlovka were ungrateful. Rahim had supported them by buying their bankrupt kolkhoz and repairing their schools and hospital. And yet Orlovka had voted for another party all the same! Maria also told me of her nervousness: nobody had slept properly that day, she told me, because some of the voters followed the car with the used ballots in it to the capital in order to be sure that the car arrived safely. Others had been calling each other and asking about the results, concerned about possible falsification of the results in Bishkek.

By the end of the day, hundreds of men had gathered outside the polling station to observe the counting of the votes. The windows of the polling station had been covered with material brought by Ainura, perhaps to prevent prying eyes. As chairperson, Ainura asked observers to monitor the counting procedure but not to touch the ballots. She proceeded to give a formal speech, thanking those who participated in the election and announcing to the audience that 700 out of a total of 1,007 people had voted, leaving 307 unused ballots. She said that the remaining ballots should now be ceremoniously destroyed in front of the audience. Suddenly her speech was interrupted by Oroz, who instead asked her to distribute the unused ballots between the party members present. Ainura immediately agreed as if she had been expecting this request. She then went on to give a speech in which she stated that she would accept the request on the condition that she, too, be allotted an extra fifty ballots for herself. None of the other commission members opposed Ainura's conduct because they owed her respectful deference and because she was responsible for distributing their pay for the day's work.

After thirty minutes of discussion, Ainura finally handed her additional fifty ballots, with which she voted for the Socialist Party (instead of Ak-Jol or SDP). Ainura told me that while she had been appointed to the position of chair because of her loyalties to Ak-Jol, she had also received money from the Socialist Party. In this way, she enacted her own complicated interpretation of party loyalty. The party observers filled in the remaining unused ballots, voting for their respective parties (Ak-Jol and SDP). In the end, almost 90 percent of the local population had voted for number six on the voting list: the SDP, in the person of Rahim. Every ballot was counted to ensure that the total number of ballots matched the number of registered voters. The package containing the ballots was then sealed, stamped, signed, and sent to the district headquarters.

During this procedure there was some discussion as to whether I, as an "outside observer," should be given fifty of the unused ballots, too. Instead of deciding myself (and ignoring the fact that I was officially an "international observer" for an organization committed to reducing electoral fraud), Oroz decided for me by claiming that I belonged to the village. I was *svoi*, he said, using a Russian term to express my belonging rather than a Kyrgyz kin term, and that I therefore supported this village's candidate. I told them that I was not interested in any ballots, and after a long discussion, I was not given a vote. My role here was quite different from that of the other "observers," who, since they were observing on behalf of a particular party, were each eager to take unused ballots to mark for their desired candidate. My observations of this process of collective ballot stuffing posed a tension between my role as outside observer and insider-fieldworker. For

Figure 6.2. The author's membership in SDP.
Photo: R. Sultanaliev.

although I was in the village as a representative of Interbilim, the very fact that I was given access to this process of allocating unused ballots reflected the fact that I was seen by many in the village as an "insider" and unthreatening.

This had not always been the case: when I had first arrived in the village before the distribution of party posters some in Bulak were quite suspicious of my presence. I heard later that people thought that I had come to the village to inspect whether Ak-Jol Party calendars and newspapers had been properly distributed. Indeed, whenever I wanted to take a picture of Ak-Jol newspapers that had been scattered and about to be burned, I was not given permission. Party membership, in this polarized field, thus became crucial to acceptance in the village. I later returned to the village from Bishkek with a registration document attesting to my membership in SDP and I was welcomed quite differently. People addressed me as "a member of their community" and recounted their hopes and expectations. Although my position as a woman and a researcher meant that I was never admitted to the inner circle of political discussion, my notional party membership meant that I came to be treated as a village "insider" during the election period (see Figure 6.2).

Part of the reason for this politicization of life was that the stakes were high. One of the village leaders of SDP told me that if they did not get a single seat in parliament, his people were prepared to express their dissatisfaction publicly, taking their cause to the streets. His reference point here was the flawed parliamentary election of 2005, which had been a crucial catalyst for the eventual overthrow of President Akayev in the spring of that year. Spontaneous demonstrations in the months leading up to the revolutionary ousting of Akayev consumed the main streets of the capital, and protestors had blocked the main road between Bishkek and Issyk-Kul. For my interlocutor, this had been a struggle over justice, community, and political rights. Therefore the 2007 parliamentary election was seen as crucial in sustaining those principles in the face of an increasingly authoritarian presidency.

We learned the next day that the village candidate had come top of the list in the local electoral district, and was to receive a place in parliament. SDP had received 6 percent of the national vote and eleven seats in parliament; however the pro-presidential Ak-Jol Party gained seventy-two seats, giving it an overwhelming majority. It had ninety seats in total. As with many Kyrgyz elections there was a distinct regional pattern to the voting. The majority of the votes for SDP had been cast in the Kemin region, a cluster of twenty villages in the northern Chüi oblast,' as well as in the Chüi Valley, Naryn, and Issyk-Kul regions. There was very little that was "private" about the elections. Villagers knew who had voted for whom, and how many ballots had been distributed, to whom, and why. Everyone knew, for instance, the one person who had voted for the Socialist Party, the same party that Ainura had voted for when allocated her extra fifty ballots. They were tolerant of his actions, claiming that his brother was a member of the party in a different district. However, there were ten votes for the Ak-Jol Party, excluding the additional fifty votes that had been allotted to it, producing much discussion of who the ten "traitors" might be. It was only later confirmed that indeed Ainura and her family had voted for Ak-Jol, as suspected, and many people said that Ainura herself had not only voted because of kinship loyalties, but because she had been against SDP from the very beginning.

What is striking is that while people were aware of the distribution of extra ballots at the end of the election, the act was not morally categorized as "fraud." In part, the morality of the act was linked to the identity of its initiator; Oroz was Rahim's right-hand man. It was also described as legitimate through a creative appeal to the principles of democracy: this had been a "fair" distribution of the extra votes, one that had allowed each of the election observers to cast an extra fifty ballots for the candidate of their choice (see Figure 6.3).

Speculation over who voted for whom lasted for about a week until Rahim's inauguration, guaranteeing their deputy obtained a stable position in the parliament. From the perspective of people in Bulak their efforts had paid off: they had

Figure 6.3. Supporters of SDP.
Photo: A. Ismailbekova.

refused to be "bought" by other candidates in the form of money, sugar, vodka, or tea, all regularly distributed at election time. They had instead opted for long-term gain with a view to the resources that were perceived to accrue from having their son in parliament. This was also seen as a victory for their region in a context where the president was identified as a "southerner." Soon after Election Day, the SDP's local victory was marked with the slaughtering of a sheep, inviting only the elders of the community. Two months later, the patron whom they had supported sponsored a feast at a café in the town of Tokmok to which more than a thousand people were invited and a special toastmaster was appointed to say toasts to the community and to the SDP (see Chapter 7).

Rahim's Contribution to the Village before the Elections

Prior to the elections, Rahim's sponsorship in the village was strongly felt. On Election Day, he had provided food and drinks, and in the months before he was also deeply involved with local practices—he prayed for ancestors and slaughtered sheep for the village elders. His construction of a mosque, assistance with schooling, and organization of festivals was only the tip of the iceberg. He was a son who respected his elders, knew his place and role, and had even bought a yurt for the village's life cycle events.

The native son had:

- Sponsored the building of a hippodrome and organized the traditional horse festival, *At Chabysh* (endurance).[4]
- Following a request by the *aksakal* court, he had purchased a big yurt for life cycle events.
- Bought a horse for the village to use for common needs.
- Sold his fattest cows to villagers at half price, or given them in exchange for farm labor.
- Provided for potential voters by, for example, distributing money for food and vodka (*eldi arak sharak menen syilap tyrat*).
- Offered to help vulnerable members of the community; he supported poor women with many children by giving them livestock, helping them get their passports, negotiating with doctors in hospitals, and supplying them with tractors and other machinery for spring sowing and harvesting.
- Bought a young sponsor a ticket to Moscow, and helped a small child pay for heart surgery.
- Bought people's milk for a high price; first milk netted eighteen som per liter (and resold in Kazakhstan for thirty-six som).
- Hired many villagers to work on his private farm, in his office, and in his other business centers. He also helped local villagers to obtain loans with low interest from the entrepreneurship fund when he was the director of the fund In addition, he provided villagers with several combines during harvesttime. In the future, he promised to open a small factory in cooperation with a Korean company to make tomato juice.
- Congratulated the village elders during Victory Day and Elderly Day by distributing special gifts and organizing special parties in their honor.

Thus the native son fulfilled the needs of the community before the election: providing a stadium, a traditional yurt, and a horse. The villagers had made many informal proposals (including for a café), but Rahim supported those which were suitable for his purposes. He spread his support across different social categories: the stadium was provided for the younger generation, a life cycle event yurt for the elderly people, and the horse was mostly a donation to the poorer people. In return for such support, the native son was entitled to the local community's loyalty and deference, especially that of young people, the elderly, and the poor. His initiatives provided support to the whole community, yet closer bonds of kinship were also respected; those who looked after the yurt, horse, and stadium, for example, were people close to Rahim.

People called Rahim their "native son," "own foal," "dignity," and "pride" because he fulfilled their basic needs. In this sense, people were rational enough to evaluate what was the best for them. Nevertheless, his position as son of the village was glorified when he became a member of parliament. People were especially proud of him because he had fulfilled their basic needs and expectations within the boundaries of kinship. As one woman in her sixties, called Anara, said, "The state does not think about the village, deputies think only about their own pockets, no one thinks about us. Deputies have thick pockets, one day they spend, the next day they earn. Here we cannot get even our pensions. The reason why we vote for Rahim is because at least he helps us by buying our milk and provides additional support for the poor." Rahim, of course, shared some common ancestors and existing family interests with other villagers. But the question remains, why did he use the preexisting notions "son and community," and highlight the importance of his relatives and ancestors before the election? The reason for this was obvious to locals—to prove in action that he belonged to the community despite having been absent for many years. As with so many dimensions of patronage, local ideology provided a way to naturalize Rahim's "return."

In general, ethnic Kyrgyz value the place of their birth. They say the birthplace's soil is golden (*öskön jerdin topuragi altyn*). Young men are expected to feel especially attached to their birthplace, and to seek to return to it after the temporary absences required of them. If he does not return earlier, then upon retirement a Kyrgyz man is obliged to return to his own place of birth; he should be buried in his birthplace, and be prayed for by his children at that place. What actually motivated Rahim's return to Bulak was therefore of relatively little concern to villagers. They were concerned that he behave properly while he was there, and always encouraged him to pray more for his ancestors, read the Qur'an more often, and participate in life cycle events.

To fulfill his duties as a Kyrgyz man and as a villager before the election, the native son began to participate in life cycle events, especially funerals. In Kyrgyz villages a person fulfills his duty to the community by praying to God, and by honoring and remembering his ancestors (*öz mildetin atkaruu*) (to do one's duty such as to worship). The person who undertakes such worship, usually a man, has a special identity as a protector of the community. Thus, a man is not singular, nor separate from his community, but linked to it through his genealogy and ancestors. Before the elections, Rahim became such a person. He took up reading the Qur'an in the name of his deceased ancestors. He prayed for his own ancestors. And he invited people within his lineage to sacrifice with him a sheep in commemoration of his ancestors and the spirits (*arbaktarga kyran okytyy*) of his deceased father, uncle, grandfather, and other respected elderly people from his lineage.

Corruption or Native Son?

For international organizations, the election as it was conducted in Bulak is symptomatic of a democratic "failure" of the principle of one person, one vote. This had, after all, been an Election Day characterized by bribery, fraud, and ballot stuffing. The Organization for Security and Cooperation in Europe noted numerous voting irregularities and other international organizations slammed the election as flawed and corrupt, noting the falsification of votes and the role of bribes (Human Rights Watch 2009; UNHCR 2012). Since the 1990s international organizations have dedicated considerable resources to anticorruption campaigns in Kyrgyzstan, including the International Center Interbilim, which trained me as an international observer. Reports on electoral irregularities in Kyrgyzstan have become common following parliamentary and presidential elections, bolstering a broader narrative of Kyrgyzstan's weakness as a state.

Anthropological perspectives show how such accounts often ignore the complexity of social life and the mutual obligations it entails. State "weakness," from an anthropological perspective, is symptomatic of broader social relations that cannot be easily changed through legislative reform or enforcement. Cynthia Werner (2002) notes how corruption has been deemed a serious threat to political stability and economic prosperity in Kazakhstan, even as ethnographic research highlights the "security of mutual indebtedness" between rural households at a time of economic shortage. Gupta (1995, 377) has shown in an Indian context that corruption is not understood locally to be antipolitical but instead "seen as simply a different, and no less functional, mode of political action." Smith (2001, 345; 2008) likewise shows how people socially reproduce the patterns of corruption for which Nigeria is notorious. For example, people approach their distant relatives to find them jobs, thereby undercutting competition and the possibility of an equal chance of obtaining jobs.

In Kyrgyzstan diagnoses of corruption fail to account for the complexity of social life, and the degree to which it is structured by mutual obligations, exchanges, and the demands of community membership. Perhaps more important, such diagnoses fail to explore what elections mean from the actors' own perspective: why it is that people still vote for "corrupt" state officials and protective patrons. My analysis has shown how the social roles, status, and hierarchies that are conferred as part of the kinship system matter in the election process. "Democracy" was not merely a cover or an empty claim in this process. The election mobilized a particular local idiom of democracy as fairness (every interested party should be given the same number of ballots at the end), loyalty (elderly men should not denied the right to vote even if they cannot formally document their identity), and solidarity (we are proud to support "our son"). Moreover, this performance of democracy derives from a significantly different notion of "representation" than that espoused in western democratic theory. For the people of Bulak, citizens are not represented in the form of their individual personhood, via an elected deputy who is answerable to them as individuals. "Our son" is seen as representing the village as a whole, rather than a constituency of individuals who share a similar set of interests. Villagers ensure representation not by legally "pure" votes but by ensuring that their patron is able to engage with the centers of power through a parliamentary position. In this context, anticorruption measures at the local level risk undermining relations of patronage that function as a crucial mechanism of social protection.

Potential politicians are aware of the fact that an honest person cannot enter into politics, and therefore create their own strategies by involving themselves in "fraud." They do this to enter into the "corrupt" system of politics with the hope of having access to resources and a better life. Rahim's known illegal actions (for example, giving money to state authorities, starting the campaign process earlier than permissible) strengthened his position in public life because they mark his ability to deal with the corrupt system of the state. In this case, it is not only donor organizations that claim that Kyrgyz politics are corrupt but ordinary people, too. In this rhetorical move, however, it is always "others" who are (morally) corrupt.

People perpetuate corruption, but they do not consider actions undertaken by common people to be "corrupt." Olivier de Sardan (1999, 34) argues, "The real borderline between what corruption is and what is not fluctuates, and depends on the context and on the position of the actors involved." Thus, the Bulak voters did not view the election in their village as corrupt. Rather, people found ways to justify their actions and legitimate their behavior through social networks of reciprocity and out of obligation and loyalty to their son, and as a result of community cohesion. This is reflected in proverbs that served to moralize their action, which circulated widely at the time, such as öz bala küiöt (our native son will always be with us). In this context, patronage was viewed as a coping strategy, constituted through interpersonal trust and profoundly important to the exchange of goods and services. People in Bulak were committed to supporting Rahim because, in the contemporary Kyrgyz context, their patron offered political protection, the chance of greater investment in the future, and someone who could mediate their interests before the government.

To note this is not to suggest that people were oblivious to the technical violations that were occurring. People in Bulak knew the boundaries between legal and illegal were blurred in relation to state bureaucracy, just as Rasanayagam's (2011) Uzbek interlocutors did. For example, people knew that it was not possible to vote without proper identity documents. But they also knew that it would be possible to bribe the chairperson, or to negotiate with her subordinates to be able to vote nonetheless. People knew that it was not legal to buy votes, accept bribes, and otherwise ignore the rules of the election. When "others" undertook such actions themselves, villagers identified them as being "corrupt." There was general recognition of the vote as fraudulent (*jazalgan*). This was moralized locally, however, as being the only way they *could* vote. People noted the need for "constant negotiation with state officials" and the need to "speak their language." Similarly, in a context of economic volatility, having a "son" in parliament who would protect their interests alongside his own was seen as the best guarantee, not just of economic development but of political voice and ultimately, of political integrity.

Was the electoral cycle that culminated in the parliamentary elections I described above merely an exercise in collective political pragmatism or a cynical enactment of a ritual in whose authenticity no one really believed? No. The villagers saw the promotion of Rahim as a sincere demonstration of political participation and democratic intent. For all the procedural violations, people saw themselves as performing a localized version of democracy: the intense discussion of electoral rules. The active process of campaigning and distributing merchandise; the act of dressing up to participate in the election—all these were sincere gestures of political commitment, a belief in the significance of this event and of the voters' role in shaping the outcome. Second, and equally significantly for thinking about the performance of politics in Central Asia, is the way in which, through such performative actions, villagers also upheld a normative image of the state as the proper locus of moral authority: a source of order and stability as well as a guarantor of basic economic protection. In this context—a context, as Humphrey (1998) notes, in which party, state and people are understood as properly fused in ways that might be considered problematic in the liberal imagination—participating in an election can also be read as a hopeful act: a reassertion of the authority of the state as such in a context where statehood had been dramatically undone by two years of revolutionary upheaval.

The Two-Dimensional Man: "Native Son" and Parliamentarian

In the Kyrgyz context, kinship forms the basis of the interplay between power and the symbolic order (Cohen 1974). As already described, Rahim's party gained the vote of his native village (and others in the region) largely because he had performed the role of "native son" particularly well in the months leading up to the elections. He had demonstrated many of the qualities most admired by ethnic Kyrgyz in the politically ambitious: generosity, hospitality, modesty, deference to elders, and some religiosity (Shahrani 1986, 264). In this section, I want to examine how the local population came to believe that the best political party to represent their interests as citizens was the one in which their native son was rapidly becoming powerful and influential.

By selectively distributing goods and services, Rahim strategically established a strong link between himself and members of his community. The patron did indeed behave as a "native son," and lived up to this title by respecting elders, and inviting people to celebrate Victory Day and the Nooruz holidays, displaying hospitality, helping close kinsmen, representing them in a political arena, and generating discourse. It was not only his rhetorical skills that mattered but also his actions, which were carefully judged.

As already described in earlier chapters, Rahim (and his village clients) used the role of the native son to broker an exchange (balanced, but unequal) of economic and political interests. But the image of the native son was also imbued with the emotional ties of the father-son relationship; obligations to protect and to care for (that are reversed over time); and the ideas and practices that link subordination to protection and care (both between individuals and of the individual to a larger collective). By performing the role of the native son, Rahim also conveyed the following message: I am the only son who is their own who will protect the people no matter what and they accept this because they share the same blood and belong to the same lineage and share the same ancestor.

The metaphor of the native son is associated with the father-son tie. It conveys the importance of lineage and of protecting or living up to the name of one's ancestor, which entails honoring and taking responsibility for the whole community. Even though the native son was of instrumental use, for members of the community, the relationship between the native son and the community was an emotionally bounded one. People expressed their opinions of Rahim as "good" (*jakshy*); they often stated that "we like him so much." (*biz any jakshy köröbuz*). Like a real father and son, a native son and his community are united in the face of difficulty. From this perspective, the reason that Rahim was able to win people's votes was not because he was a particularly good native son, but because they had been convinced to see the state in kinship terms: who else but a native son would protect the community? Or, as villagers put it, *bizdin bala jardam berbegende kim beret* (who will help if not our own son)?

The position of native son is organized according to the social hierarchical system of the Kyrgyz, which relies on customs, habits, and routines, allowing people to distinguish between "insider" and "outsider" (native and nonnative) and providing community stability. Thus, the native son is seen as a protector of his own community and a defender of them from outside forces. Patrilineal descent serves as a metaphor for the transformation of the father-son relationship into a community-native son tie, in which the community can also be perceived or understood as the land of fathers and patrilineal group.

Within the community setting, the behavior and prospects of all young men (as community sons) are monitored, supported, and celebrated as the success, future, and honor of the whole community. By extension, the election of a native son to parliament gives the community a sense of belonging in the national community. Its responsible son, through his visible actions and his support for poor people, promises them better future lives and well-being. SDP's success in and around Bulak was also reflective of the fact that Rahim was more widely considered the native son at the provincial level. Rahim's hope was to expand his symbolic role of son across an even broader swath of northern Kyrgyzstan. He could hope for such success because, according to my informants, all villages and provinces hope and believe that a native son will represent them in parliament; the ambition of all communities is to see "the native son from the village rise within the state."

In the northern part of the Kyrgyzstan, Pétric (2005) similarly demonstrates how networks of solidarity function during election time. He states that politicians must have an important local stronghold to ensure popular support (325). Petric argues that "politicians are not devoid of social legitimacy and, where political competition exists, they must build their political legitimacy by distributing their wealth" (ibid.). Borbieva (2008) also demonstrates that people vote for politicians who distribute their wealth because they feel guilty if they do not show their gratitude. These findings are true, but in Bulak Village, people did not vote just for those who gave them money. Sometimes they did, but not always. Sometimes, villagers admitted, "We take money from one politician, but vote for another—for the one who shares our concerns." Whether or not they voted for money, people preferred to vote for a candidate who offered them more than material gain. Their collective vote for a native son was also for a person who displayed a readiness to protect them.

The symbolic legitimization of a native son is a difficult and slow process— he is not simply accepted in one day. Politicians who would-be native sons have to be accepted by a community by playing their unique lineage card, rather than simply distributing their wealth. People develop emotional ties with their native son, which they feel justify open involvement in bribery and fraud. Simple distributions of money only buy votes and situational alliances.

Patronage: Myth or Reality?

The ideology of the native son is an appealing one. It provides a moral account of what international political observers identify as endemic corruption in Kyrgyz political life. But, how should native sons themselves be evaluated? Are they really the ideal persons that they are depicted as? Or does the mask of the native son disguise the sole pursuit of self-interest and a wholesale manipulation of kinship ideology and relations in the service of political patronage?

Silverman (1977, 11) writes that the myth of patronage is based on rhetoric and promises rather than real exchange. Thus Silverman's statement challenges the image of Rahim that villagers described to me: an ideal native son who merited their sympathy and support. During the elections, most villagers had managed to forget (at least temporarily) Rahim's shortcomings: he had broken some promises, he did not cover all the expenses that people requested of him, and he certainly had not provide for people's basic needs thoroughly or equally. Similarly, villagers could have expected that Rahim would benefit more from their support in politics than they would benefit from his role of parliamentarian. Surely they knew that the role appealed to him primarily because it would enable him to secure his business interests. In their insistence on voting for a native son, people also revealed their extreme hope for a better life. Such hope gives rise to an exaggerated (and yet sincere) impression of the benefits a native son can bring.

The appeal of the native son in Kyrgyz politics has deeper roots than those of post-Soviet economic hardship. The image also calls to mind historical associations that became very important as a result of the nation building and re-ethnicization of Kyrgyz politics in the post-Soviet context. In the past, as my elderly informants reminded me, native sons were not just political leaders; they quite literally defended the community from outside force (*er jigit el chitende joo betinde*). Numerous proverbs refer to the specificities of the role. Some emphasize the difficulty of the role: for example, "It requires respect to be a son of the father, but it is very hard to be a son of the community." Others comment on the community's preference for a native son's leadership and protection: "A native son is better than an outsider."

A Local Perspective

Much academic and policy analysis in recent years has been dedicated to diagnosing the failures of political institutions in Central Asia; the destabilizing effects of regional or kinship loyalties (Collins 2002; Schatz 2004), or the "temptations of tyranny" (Lewis 2008). In this chapter, I have sought to explore what electoral democracy means in rural Kyrgyzstan through a focus on the performance of one particular ritual of contemporary Kyrgyz politics: the parliamentary election. By this way, I looked at the local understanding and meaning of the local elections, circulating political discourses, a set of negotiations between local community and state administration (Paley 2002). Following Comaroff and Comaroff's (1997) call to pluralize the study of democracy, I have argued that we need to understand democracy in Kyrgyzstan as a situated local practice, one that is both molded by, and in turn serves to shape, understandings of community, obligation, and respect. Elections, seen as a ritual, are crucial to performing the state and bringing it into being in rural Kyrgyzstan.

From a local perspective, corruption in politics is unavoidable, but real democracy can nevertheless exist if and when people have the opportunity to voice their collective political claims. Villagers are less concerned with expressing their individual political preferences and more concerned with propelling the community's "son" into parliament. This is the best guarantee that local demands will be heard in the halls of power. Much of the anticorruption rhetoric in Kyrgyzstan subsumes the vertical patronage networks established between parliamentarians and local regions to be a sign of corruption in itself. Little effort has been made to understand why voters themselves prefer such relations when, as indicated by the lively debates in the weeks leading up to the elections, knowledge about electoral politics and procedures is widespread. The decision of villagers in Bulak to forego the foodstuffs offered by other parties in return for political loyalty, and the acceptance of some individuals' decisions to vote according to personal conscience, complicate assessments of political patronage as based on the benefits of short-term material exchanges (for example, Pétric 2005; Borbieva 2008).

Another important issue to tackle here is kinship loyalty in the electoral politics. Rather than seeing "traditionalism" or kinship loyalty as an essential trait or obstacle to western-style electoral democracy (Juraev 2008; Khamidov 2006b), it is necessary to ask how regional or kinship loyalties are hypostatized by the fact of electoral politics. How are they turned from a relatively fluid and situational aspect of village life into a dramatic line of demarcation: Are you with us or against us? Are you for Ak Jol or the SDP?

In this respect examples like Ainura are critical. Ainura faced a dilemma in voting in an electoral system that requires a choice for a single party because of her multiple obligations based on ties of kinship, marriage, and work. Ainura's solution to meeting all of her obligations was to demonstrate loyalty through alternative modes of political support. Kinship ties plus electoral rules forced her to pursue behaviors normally identified as "corruption."

In Chapter 7 I address the consequences of marrying Western-style electoral politics with systems of regional and kinship loyalties. The speeches given at Rahim's victory party demonstrate the extent to which political divisions across Kyrgyzstan had become assimilated with regional differences, with a rapid intensification of a north-south division that was largely devoid of actual "issues." Politics is rapidly becoming "kinship politics," but as this chapter and the next demonstrate, the prominence of "kinship" is not corrupting a "purer" form of democracy. Kinship politics are actively constituting what democracy is and can be. As Jonathan Spencer found in the Sri Lanka of the 1980s, party politics "had become braided into the very fabric of local sociality" (2007, 33) such that local disputes came to be articulated in the language of party political difference. So, too, it seems to be rapidly becoming in Kyrgyzstan.

Notes

1. Disputes between husbands and wives were likely to emerge particularly when the wife's natal village supported a different candidate from her husband's village. As a result there was often a debate between the side of the in-laws (*kuda jak*) and that of one's own kin (öz jak); a woman is expected to show respect toward her in-laws by taking their side at election time.

2. Interbilim International Center is a nongovernmental organization with a mission to strengthen civil society in Kyrgyzstan. The electoral commission is an independent agency charged with regulating the electoral process.

3 The village headman was appointed by the state. He was usually responsible for all the village lands. The village headman, using his authority to distribute lands for Bulak, encouraged those who did not have land to vote for Ak-Jol; otherwise, he claimed their land would be distributed among his own followers. By law the head of the village has the right to distribute land to young married couples, but not to distribute the land belonging to the National Land Fund (FPS) (see www.gosreg.kg/index.php?option=com_content&view=article&id=89).

4. In a Kyrgyz context, the horse stadium is not like in Europe. Rather the stadium in the village is fenced.

7 Rahim's Victory Feast

Political Patronage and Kinship in Solidarity

Rᴀʜɪᴍ ᴜsᴇᴅ ʜɪs unique aristocratic Ak-Jol lineage to legitimize his authority in the political competition and claimed to represent his community in parliament as its native son. Rahim was supported by his local networks during the elections, as a result of which he was elected a parliamentarian. To celebrate his political victory, Rahim organized a large-scale banquet, a known cultural format for sharing public news. Through the feast, Rahim sought to reestablish himself as the successful son of a widely defined "lineage" and to consolidate his newly gained political power.

In this chapter, I focus on identity politics, showing how Rahim, as a patron, newly elected parliamentarian, and leader of the SDP, used and adapted the form and rules of the traditional feast (*toi*) to turn it into a political mechanism, with the aim of shaping and strengthening provincial loyalty and encouraging people to accept his authority as the native son. In this way the patron sought to build loyalty to him within a wide provincial network. Rahim was not alone; the *toi* of other victorious politicians were broadcast by the television channel Sobitia Dnya on January 23, 2008.

This is a the story of postelection solidarity culminated in Rahim's victory feast, attended by more than one thousand people, specific rules and norms of the ideal feast (*toi*) in Kyrgyzstan, and the dynamics of gift exchange. Of particular interest is the role of the *tamada* in making guests feel welcome and at ease, providing entertainment through jokes and witty banter, ensuring the smooth progression of the feast through its various stages, preventing the emergence of conflict between guests, and enhancing the host's honor. The word *tamada* is Georgian in origin, but it has been widely adopted throughout the former Soviet Union to describe the specific activities of "toastmasters" in local traditions (Mühlfried 2005, 2006). At this feast, the *tamada* had the task of advancing Rahim's political agenda while convincing guests that they were participating in a "traditional" feast organized along kinship principles. The current political organization of the SDP consisted of the various government officials who were invited to the feast based on kinship solidarity, and the feast's influence on politics and the struggle for power—in particular in relation to the SDP's struggle against its main opposition, the Ak-Jol Party. In this way, I provide an example of the interconnectedness of identity and power politics.

This feast provides an excellent example of Kyrgyz social poetics in the domains of kinship, politics, and feasting. The patron and his kinsmen creatively tested and reformed the norms of the *toi* in an acceptable way. This led to the emergence of a new type of feast, one that took into account the needs and expectations of guests but was also organized slightly differently from a conventional feast. In other words, these skilled actors deformed the structure of *toi*, and thus succeeded in incrementally changing the larger value structure. This was an acceptable and subtle means of change since the feast and performance of patronage has poetic effects.

Hospitality as Exchange and Acceptance

In contemporary Kyrgyzstan, close kinsmen and friends are invited to feasts to partake in either a family's happiness or grief. Feasts are held at weddings, circumcision, celebrations of the building of a new house, and the birth of children (*beshik toi*). Feasts on the occasion of life cycle events serve to mark a change in status of host group and to legitimize the claims of the members of this group to occupy a new status position.

Each member of an extended family is expected to contribute a certain amount of money to a celebration, from five hundred som (seven euros) upward. At these feasts, the *tamada* is responsible for leading the activities of the invited guests. Speeches are given to wish the hosts happiness and long life. Sheep and cattle are slaughtered for meat, which is distributed according to the rules of the feast (meat is first given to an elder). Depending on the customs of the province, the *bash* (head) is presented to the eldest or youngest male who, in turn, cuts pieces from the head (eyeballs, tongue, jowls, ears) and distributes them within the group. The hip bone or pelvis (*jambash*) of the animal is given to the oldest and most respected men and women in the group. As Light (2015, 55) states, distribution of meat and other foods in a feast context provides people with positive feelings, recognizes the personal value of the host, and contributes to maintaining social ties.

Meanwhile, the behavior of the guests must be similar to that described by a famous proverb: "guests must be quieter than sheep" (*konok koidon josh*). Guests should be passive and demonstrate subordination under the host's roof; they should not demand things that are not offered; they should be quiet, even to the point of shyness. As a result, the host and *tamada* must encourage people to eat. Yet in being so inactive and acquiescent, guests are able to judge the host's performance since the host is expected to actively demonstrate his or her hospitality.

Although "the host" is described and evaluated as if a single individual, in reality married couples work together to provide guests with hospitality. Additionally, the guests must remain in their seats so as not to interfere with the "sphere" of the host. The space between the host and the guest—the boundaries between them—are clearly drawn.

The basic function of hospitality as well as the building of social relationships is facilitated by the exchange of symbolic and material goods and services during the feast (Herzfeld 1987; Pitt-Rivers 1968; Selwyn 2002; Werner 1997, 246). Hospitality is seen as an expression of support, gratitude, and kindness. The Kyrgyz hold the idea that hospitality is directly or indirectly to be repaid one day, and apply general rules of gift exchange—that is, hospitality places guests in debt to their host. Kyrgyz sayings convey as much: "a guest is the house's prosperity" (*konok üidün kutu*),[1] or a "guest is like God" (*kudai konok*). In the exchange of hospitality, the host provides food and shelter, while the guest blesses the host and provides him with good luck. The guest's blessing (*bata*) provides the host with a deep sense of comfort, care and guidance of elders, and well wishes of ancestors (Dubuisson 2017).

Many similarities exist between the hospitality rituals of Kyrgyzstan, Kazakhstan, and Uzbekistan (for example, Michaels 2007; Werner 1997), and in each case hospitality is associated with ethnic and national identity. By being hospitable, Kyrgyz consciously distinguish themselves from Russians in both ethnic and national terms.

Invitations to a feast are made therefore within the confines of a Kyrgyz moral and social framework on at least three levels: local, ethnic, and national. In all cases, the obligation to exchange and to reciprocate in return for hospitality is culturally respected. Thus, the obligation to return a gift means that relations remain unbalanced until a guest reciprocates his host's generosity. Since reciprocity is required to balance the relationship between two actors, the relationship between a guest and a host remains unfulfilled until a return is made. In the social context of this expectation, an unfulfilled relationship between a guest and a host is remembered, and it is hard to escape until the debt is met. Basing a relationship on the principle of reciprocity, the patron emphasizes that he honors (*syilap koi*) his guests and obligates them to honor him in return. In arguing about the political efficacy of the feast, there are many parallels to draw with the symbolic aspects of hospitality elsewhere in terms of gender, honor, and national "obligations" (for example, Cash 2012; Herzfeld 1987; Shryock 2012).

Kyrgyz people mark their ethnic identity through displays of hospitality. Feasts and other demonstrations of "traditional attitudes" are important for mutual acceptance among ethnic Kyrgyz. According to custom, as among Kazaks in Kazakhstan, "social status and power is achieved largely through displays of hospitality and generosity" (Werner 1997, 247). With his victory feast, Rahim used hospitality to transform himself from a patron into a "big" (*chong*) man, a government official.

Rahim's Feast

After Rahim's election to parliament, a celebratory feast was held in a café in the heart of Chüi Province. The Nur Ata Café was deliberately chosen for its symbolic location in Tokmok, in the middle of the province. The owner of the café came from Rahim's native village. The feast was organized by Rahim's relatives, colleagues, and friends, and attended by selected residents throughout the province. Invitations were delivered orally, through social networks, specifying the date and time of the occasion. Since so many people had been invited, several assistants had been recruited to help out on the day of the feast.

Thus far, with the exception of being held in a café instead of the host's home, the event's organization modeled a traditional *toi*. As the proceedings unfurled, however, a number of alterations to make the feast more political became clear. For example, many of the assistants recruited for serving were Rahim's distant kinsmen. In traditional *toi*, female relatives and friends would be responsible for serving guests. Here, male relatives took on the role of service, under the firm direction of Rahim's wife.

Government officials (guests of the feast) can be described as the following: (a) officials of ministerial rank, as well as some members of parliament, provincial governors, rayon-level government officials (*akim*), and the city mayor;[2] (b) village headmen; and (c) local schoolteachers, doctors, and police officers. Normally, close relatives would be invited to a feast as the most honored guests, and they would bring a cash gift. In this case, government officials were the most honored and highest-status guests, but they brought no cash gifts. I use an emic notion of high status, which mostly refers to the government officials (*chong*) but not the rich new businessmen.

Prior to the feast, there was much preparation, during which Rahim's clients took leading roles. Their tasks (providing services and cooking) were divided among them according to their age and gender. Younger assistants were responsible for serving the guests; delivering and clearing dishes of food; cleaning dirty dishes; and pouring tea. Almaz and Zakir, private farmworkers, slaughtered seven sheep and one bull before the feast to distribute to the guests. The average gift of meat is one bone with some meat (*ustukan*). Older assistants were responsible for showing younger men how to slaughter cattle for the feast and how to cook the meat by checking the quantity of salt and water in the main dish. Generally four distinct groups were involved in the event—Rahim's close relatives, clients, assistants, and friends—and their obligations were to serve guests and otherwise help the hosts.

The café was large and wide because it had been built specially to accommodate life cycle celebrations. The walls were decorated with traditional paintings of a yurt, horses, and a Kyrgyz family. The building was also fully furnished with modern furniture (tables, sofa, and chairs). The guests, mostly of rural background, were stunned by the café's modern appearance. The guests were asked to sit down at particular tables with close friends and acquaintances, with the aim of making the event interesting and cozy for everyone. Rahim greeted his guests outside the café and accompanied them inside. Rahim's assistants were aware of Kyrgyz etiquette and norms, and not only acted as waiters but were also careful to treat each guest according to Kyrgyz custom, taking into account their age, gender, and status.[3] They treated the guests well by constantly encouraging them to eat and drink; they filled guests' glasses with vodka, offered food, and refilled plates. The organizers also continually provided the assistants with instruction to fine-tune their treatment of particular guests.

The café could accommodate almost 500 people, but by the beginning of the event at six o'clock in the evening, approximately 750 guests were in attendance, and more continued to arrive. However, the organizers expected this and welcomed every guest with respect. As the numbers mounted, the hosts divided the guests into two groups: those who were considered "important" and those "less important." The important people included elders, state officials, and businessmen. The less important people included younger guests, and also me. The most important guests were asked to remain in their seats, while the younger guests were asked to move to a second café. The toastmaster assured us younger guests that Rahim's "brother" had three more cafés in town, so guests should not worry about being moved to other cafés. But of course the quality would not be the same as the main café. I knew that the younger people would be provided with music and food, and would be encouraged to have a good time, but they would not have a *tamada* (toastmaster). The most interesting part of the feasts would take place in the first café with the elders and state officials, so I asked permission to stay and observe the main feast. I was given a small chair, and allowed to stay as a "special young guest." As described in Chapter 6, I had become a member of the SDP before the elections to be better accepted within the community, and the organizers who granted my special status took this into account. Attention was lavished on the state officials: they were given the best tables and were honored with gifts of meat.

The seating arrangements in the two cafés explain the relative importance of each guest. The main table was in fact made up of two long tables arranged in parallel. These tables were set apart from the other tables and positioned toward the back (*tördö*) of the café, opposite the door, so that the most honored guests would not be disturbed by passing visitors and food (see Figure 7.1). The stage for giving toasts was located near the door. The tables were decorated with balloons

Figure 7.1. The table of the state officials.
Photo: A. Ismailbekova.

and flowers. As guests appeared, the *tamada* directed them to specific tables according to a prearranged seating pattern. One side of the head table was reserved for influential guests, such as the rayon-level government officials of the Chüi Province (mayors, vice mayors of the rayons), and the village headmen from several different rayons. On the other side of the head table, important co-villagers, elders, and members of the election commission were seated. At other tables, in order of precedence, sat together the representatives of the surrounding several districts. Guests were also seated according to age and status to satisfy their expectations and requirements. Representatives of ethnic minorities such as the Dungan and Turks were also invited. Regardless of their age, status, and gender, the minorities were given the most honored seats, which were on the front tables near Rahim, because of their support for him during the elections.

When the waiters were distributing the gifts of meat, including the meat bones called *ustukan* that guests take home; Rahim's wife ordered the heads of all the sheep to be given to the rayon government officials. This was the second significant change in the structure of the event. Normally the head should be given to the village elders. Elders are also served all food and drink first because they are the most important and respected members of the community. Everyone attending the banquet can see who is served first, a public display of proper respect from host to guest. However, in this case, the venerated role of elders was assumed by government officials, a move that shifted the dynamics of the entire event from a community celebration to one of a specifically political character. One might have expected older community members to become offended, but surprisingly they told me that their displacement was necessary because Rahim needed to attract younger followers.

At the same time the honoring of officials made the event a political one, the courtesies that Rahim extended to the officials also domesticated the political arena. Rahim treated the government officials as if they were in their "own home" to make sure that everything was comfortable for them. They received special treatment and waitstaff members were sent over to them several times during the feast to check that they had enough food and vodka. Yet Rahim also made sure that the "house" of the event did not really come under the control of his guests' wishes. Just as Shryock (2012, 24) writes that the proclamation of Bedouin hospitality that "my house is your house," does not really extend to the entire house, so, too, did Rahim's guests find that they could only go through the parts of the house where their host led them.

As soon as the guests were seated, they were served tea and alcohol, and hosts encouraged them to eat. The tables were preset with bread (traditional *borsok*); drinks (tea, soft drinks, and alcoholic drinks); three kinds of salads; and sweets (candies and cookies). The first of the hot dishes was then presented immediately after being seated. As in a typical feast, the first course was *shorpo*, a soup made

Figure 7.2. Distribution of meat.
Photo: A. Ismailbekova.

with mutton, carrots, onions, potatoes, and greens, and *kesme*, a meat and vegetable noodle soup. After the soup, the guests continued to drink tea, nibble on sweets, fruit, or bread, or just talk, while waiting for the second course. The second course consisted of rice with fried meat (*gulash*). The third course, served as a soup, was prepared by the men and consisted of sheep's carcass stripped of the remaining meat and mixed with noodles and herbs. This was a traditional dish (*beshbarmak*) (see Figure 7.2). It took almost six hours to serve all these courses.

While guests were eating, Rahim circulated among the tables. When he visited my table, he drank a glass of water. He left some in the glass when he walked away, and a lady next to me told me to drink it to get some of Rahim's "holiness" (*yrysky*).[4] She also gave me some bread (*borsok*) and candies for my son, so that in the future he would also be famous (*ataktuu*), rich (*bai*), and influential (*barktuu*). The food, she said, was already made "sacred" (*yiyk*) by Rahim's generous distribution of it. Other guests also took leftover food and drink as a gift (*geshik*) to eat later or give to others who had been unable to attend. The *geshik* plays a crucial role in uniting people who cannot attend an event. And in this case, women were specifically asked to take food for their children as a sign of success (*yrym*).

From my vantage point at the last table, I could see that the bones of meat were distributed differently: to the government officials, whose tables were first, big parts of bones with meat were given; small parts of bones with meat were given to the less important individuals.

At all tables, however, the meat was distributed cold but cooked, as it is characteristic to do in Chüi Province. In other provinces (for example, Issyk-Kul and Naryn) hot meat is distributed. Guests noted Rahim's adherence to this local tradition, and other differences in the quantity of meat distributed (in Osh Province only half the meat is distributed), and the destination of particular pieces, such as the fatty tail (*jambash*), to guests according to age and status. Guests noticed Rahim's "northern" generosity (in contrast to the southern Osh traditions), and deemed him to be adequately being *Chüilük* (following Chüi ways).

Hospitality of the Native Son

Rahim's victory feast was between convention and invention. He succeeded in making this *toi* a political one, as will become especially clear from the speech of the *tamada* to be described below. Yet the political dimensions were cast within the conventions of hospitality.

During the feast, the conventional rules were applied as in any typical life cycle event, but the way in which the seating was arranged, the food was distributed, and the guests were treated was tailored to the needs of specific people: (a) the state officials, (b) heads of the villages, (c) teachers and doctors. People accepted the alterations and did not become offended. Interestingly, Rahim turned his direct kinsmen (both close and distant) into waiters; those who should have been among the most honored guests turned their efforts to honoring others.

Thus the hospitality of the native son reflected his wider role as one who was responsible for constructing Chüi Province as an "imagined political community" (Anderson 1999). At one level the feast operated as a means through which to perform hospitality, and to stress the cultural specificity and importance of Rahim's lineage, village, and province; at another level the patron and his kinsmen used the feast to construct an image of the province's overall unity. The event might well be considered as contributing to nation building, but it was privately funded and directed by the patron himself rather than the state.

Rahim used the obligation of "giving the *toi*" (*toi berish kerek*) and performing hospitality strategically. If we follow the logic of gift exchange (Mauss 2000), guests must repay the honor bestowed on them at some point in the future—but they do not know when or how. The logic of hospitality leaves the initial exchange unfulfilled and indebts the guest. As long as the exchange is unreturned, the relationship remains unbalanced with the patron in a superior position to his guests. In general, hospitality in Kyrgyzstan should be repaid in kind. Hospitality received indebts the guest to receive his host on a later occasion.

In fact, for many of the guests the imbalance was likely to continue indefinitely, as it was unlikely that Rahim would attend feasts of similar opulence hosted by the majority of his guests. This raised a problem of reciprocity. This was not an exchange of tangible (food) for intangible (authority) assets. Rather, it was an exchange of intangible assets—for his hospitality, Rahim received the of guests' recognition of his symbolic capital and their social obligation to reciprocate his generosity. The feast was, moreover, one point of exchange in a longer chain of exchange: the feast was given because the guests had elected Rahim, and the guests also brought many gifts for Rahim to his victory feast to symbolize and strengthen their relationship (see Figure 7.3).

Even if most of his guests did not succeed in repaying their debt to Rahim through hospitality, Rahim stood to gain much from throwing the feast. At one level, Rahim stood to be accepted (*kabil alyy*) as a native son by large swathes of the region's population. His claim to this status needed to be validated across Chüi Province, so he invited the most respected men and women in the province to his feast. The feast served as a public announcement by the patron who sought to achieve recognition as the representative of the province and to be seen as autonomous with state officials. People's attendance of his feast served as a blessing and legitimized his status. Rahim's acceptance was not guaranteed by the mere attendance of guests. He also needed people to talk about him; claim him as their leader; and begin to invite him to their own public *toi*. If they did not accept his claims, people would not invite Rahim to various events or offer their support, and they would ignore him in public. This politicized feast, in contrast to the nonpoliticized feasts discussed in other parts of Kyrgyzstan (Light 2015), produced political power, authority, and acceptance.

Acceptance as the region's native son would strengthen Rahim's status vis-à-vis both unelected government officials (that is, provincial bureaucrats) and political competition. State officials and simple people of the province would honor and support him at election time, and their acceptance made him "strong" (*küchtüü*) in facing future challenges. People's acceptance also enabled him to build social networks and establish his own followers within national politics. Without any followers or acceptance, he would not be strong enough to compete against southern politicians.

The Toastmaster and the Toasts

In most life cycle events in Kyrgyzstan, a *tamada* is appointed as a mediator between guests and hosts. The *tamada* as a decision maker manipulates the rules of the feast without breaking them. He stresses the most important aspects of the

Figure 7.3. Gift giving.
Photo: A. Ismailbekova.

event and gives the event political significance as a result of his ostensibly neutral position. His responsibilities include managing the occasion, treating the guests according to their status and authority, making sure that no one is offended, and proposing toasts on behalf of the speakers. In between toasts, the *tamada* usually encourages guests to drink, eat, and dance. This feast was no exception. However, on this occasion, to satisfy the aim of the feast, the *tamada* was expected to know which guests he should approach, when, and how. He did this by capturing people's attention, involving people into political discussions, and highlighting the importance of the event. The *tamada* enabled Rahim to underscore the feast's political relevance.

The *tamada* had the additional responsibility of smoothing conflict between political parties and of creating regional unity. The Chüi Province officials were in a dilemma. On the one hand, they had a strong affiliation with their lineage system and thus also a strong provincial and party affiliation with Rahim. On the other hand, as state officials, they were subordinate to the president's administration and had a professional duty to support Ak-Jol, the president's party. Some of the invited guests did not even come because they had supported Ak-Jol to secure their positions. In this setting, the *tamada* had to work both forward and backward; the feast had to be celebrated as one of kinship, even as political aims were advanced. A political *toi* had to regenerate a real community based on kinship.

The *tamada*'s speeches, such as this one delivered at the beginning of the feast, were essential:

> *Tamada*: We should probably start our feast. We are late as usual. But it is acceptable because we are Kyrgyz. Today we are celebrating a unique occasion in the town of Tokmok. Probably this celebration is the first of its kind. We have been participating in various feasts (weddings), but today we are celebrating a special event—our son's election victory. As you may know, the guests for this feast were invited from several districts, from the Kemin Rayon to the Jaiyl Rayon. As you probably remember, in 2005, 2006, and 2007, we experienced some unusual elections. Now we have three parties in the parliament: Ak-Jol, SDP, and the Communist Party. Our son Rahim is from SDP, as a result of which he became a parliamentarian of the Kyrgyz Republic. This feast was organized with the purpose of uniting you all—as representatives of Chüi Province, to thank you for your support during the election, and to introduce you to one another. The population of Chüi Province supported Rahim, because for some Rahim is a younger brother. For others, Rahim is an elder brother. But for many of us, Rahim is our son since we share the same ancestor (*ata babalarybyz bir*).
>
> As you know, two years ago, Rahim also ran for the position of parliamentarian. At that time, however, he came second, and consequently could not represent us in parliament. Thank God, today we are celebrating our victory! Now, I think we should start giving speeches to our honored and most respected guests. We are descendants of Ak-Jol, a founder of *uruu*; let us step on

Ak-Jol Party (*Biz Akjolbuz Ak-Joldun ystynon basaly*). As you probably know, the leader of SDP is a former prime minister, Almazbek Atambaev. Tuigunaly, who was also part of SDP from the very beginning, and is our representative and friend, has been supporting Rahim as an elder brother, representative father, and a teacher (*shakirt*). The first speech will be given to Tuigunaly.

Tuigunaly (Rahim's representative father): Dear people, Happy New Year! As you probably remember, in 2005 we were sitting in this café, but we were unhappy because the state used its power to block us. Despite the pressure this time, we have been able to progress further and make Rahim our representative in parliament. You [*addressing Rahim*] are young and energetic. You have to win the trust of the people; therefore, I wish you strength, patience, and success. I think we should support our younger generations in their growth and development. Only mutual support can lead us to prosperity. If you want to join me in wishing Rahim a good future, then please drink what you have in your cups.

Tamada: Let us stand up and drink to Rahim, who is part of the Ak-Jol lineage, to go on the white road, and achieve success. Rahim is for the people!

At the *tamada*'s command, music played and the guests stood to drink a toast to Rahim.

With almost every speech that is given during a feast, the *tamada* speaks both before and after the person who gives the toast. In this way the *tamada* literally frames what is said—he can suggest a new topic to consider, rephrase what has been said to be more acceptable, or make a joke. In this case, the toast was apparently acceptable, and the *tamada* enjoined the other guests to make the requested toast.

More significant is how the *tamada* rhetorically framed the opposition between the president's Ak-Jol Party and the Ak-Jol lineage shared by Rahim and his guests. Throughout his speech, he inserted several short anecdotes that refer to the north-south division in Kyrgyzstan. Translated into English, the word *Ak-Jol* means "bright way" (or "genial way"), and is interpreted as "fortunate path." People in Bulak and Orlovka would say that "our lineage is Ak Jol, and we are on the 'bright way' and will achieve success." The *tamada* punned: for the Ak-Jol lineage to achieve success in politics, they first had to "trample" the Ak-Jol Party. The "bright path" of the Ak-Jol lineage has thus been figuratively paved with the (tomb)stones of the Ak-Jol Party.

The *tamada*'s pun thus subtly encouraged local villagers to equate their own "bright" identity with the rejection and destruction of the Ak-Jol Party. He tried to reframe the rejection of the president's party as a local and moral response to domination by the corrupt Kyrgyz state. In this case, Rahim, as the native son, served a defensive posture vis-à-vis the Kyrgyz state; by supporting their own son, people were proactive in promoting local cultural and moral autonomy.

This *tamada* had excellent rhetorical skills; he was fluent in both Russian and Kyrgyz and knew the languages of humor and honor. He thus spoke rhetorically using Kyrgyz proverbs relating to identity, personality, and politics. Furthermore, he was able to combine both honor and humor, which was a great advantage. His extensive knowledge and understanding of politics enabled him to contextualize and appropriately deliver his speeches, supervise the proceedings, and gave him the necessary authority to satisfy the aims of the event. While entertaining, the *tamada* was mainly responsible for addressing the guests in a way that stressed certain political topics and Chüi provincialism at every possible opportunity. By using the expressions "as you probably remember" (*biz estegen*, and "as we know" (*biz bilgen*), the *tamada* sought to activate individual and social memory. Linking the past with the future, and emphasizing the political process and the evident progress, the *tamada* touched on past issues and related them to the present situation.

When the *tamada* had finished asking for a toast, he asked people to bless Rahim by clasping their hands together in front of them, palms facing upward, and bringing their hands down over their faces while saying Islamic invocation "Oomiyn" (Amen).

Between speeches the *tamada* attended to guests. He asked whether someone had enough food. In cases where there were no spare seats, the *tamada* would ask a younger guest to stand up, so that he could give their seat to someone more important. On occasions, using a microphone, the *tamada* would order an assistant to deliver or take away plates, food, or glasses from the tables. In other words, the *tamada* reassured the guests that they had his attention and were under his constant supervision. In this way, the *tamada* demonstrated his ability to control the situation with his "neutral" position. Additionally, people carefully listened to the *tamada*. In fact, they were compelled to listen to him since interrupting the *tamada* was considered impolite and improper. Several times the *tamada* asked guests to stand for Rahim, drink for Rahim, and present their gifts to Rahim. At each occasion, he stressed that Rahim deserved the honor because he was the only one who represented the "real" (*daana*) Chüi Province.

The *tamada* was neither part of the community nor outside of it. Under these circumstances, he was not fully obliged to follow the rules of the community imposed on him; he enjoyed his freedom and joked and imposed his own authority on the event. He did not venture outside "community issues," nor was he constrained by its rules. When guests challenged him, he would claim that his comment had been a joke. The *tamada* was in a position to violate the rules of the situation; people took his comments seriously and saw him as a source of truth. While his conduct followed an established procedure, equally important was his ability to improvise and propose toasts in an original and personalized way. The *tamada* mediated the process of the feast, because he was considered *ob'ektivny*

(R. objective, neutral) who facilitated the guests' political discussions within the framework of the feast.

Sometimes the *tamada* might intentionally take the side of the guests as opposed to that of the host, and vice versa. He was not quite an insider, but neither was he a clear outsider. Moreover, his behavior did not quite *relate* to an ideal standard or model but was sufficiently close to the norm to command acceptance. His neutrality conformed to Herzfeld's concept of "social conventions." In this case, the *tamada* was able to deploy what Herzfeld suggests is "the necessary ambiguity of social interactions for the enhancement of [one's] own goals" (2005, 197). Herzfeld describes a situation when each man performs for himself, but the *tamada* advances the host's goals, even as he is "neutral." The poetics of the commonplace is thus ultimately an exploration of how members of the social group fashion and refashion their imagined iconicity. As Herzfeld puts it, "Regularities, which seem to be embedded, are subject to negotiation. But this is not free play: the deformation of norms requires a skilled appreciation of what others consider the norms to be. And there are limits to invention as well as traps for those who cannot back up their eccentricities" (198). In this case, the *tamada* deformed the norms of the feasting by granting the rights to speak to the government officials instead of the elders of the community, and this action was accepted by the elders and other guests as how things should be in a political feast.

This *tamada* made jokes about sexual relationships that came close to violating social norms. He compared the affairs of political parties to those of men and women, and he poked fun of the president's several lovers. The criticisms that he leveled at the south (metonymically equated with the Ak-Jol Party and the state) and mockery of the president's private life, however, seemed to satisfy the demands of the guests. They laughed and clapped their hands. As he "entertained" the guests, the *tamada* also slowly advanced the host's interests. His rhetorical strategies were selected and deployed to successfully gain the audience's support for a political discourse that distinguished north from south and united the north behind Rahim. Yet guests continued to believe that the *tamada* himself was neutral. Indeed, he involved people in the debate concerning the "south and north division," so that the guests themselves became the authors of the evening's political discourse.

One of the main roles of the *tamada* is thus to situate people within a framework in which they can act.

An Analysis of the Toast—*kaaloo tilek*

The *tamada* clearly states the aims and expectations of the feast and thus provides the framework for any conversation, whether in a joking or serious manner. The *tamada* is the vocal representative of the host, and as guests should receive hospitality passively, so, too, do guests at a celebration allow themselves and their own contributions to be completely guided by the *tamada*. If there is a mistake in his speech, the *tamada* is responsible, answerable to the host. The guests are expected to act within this framework and to satisfy the demands of the *tamada*, thus fulfilling the expectations of the host. This section analyzes the toasts (*kaaloo tilek*) given in response to the speech described above, and how they fit into the framework of the feast.

Guests' speeches and their good wishes are as crucial to a Kyrgyz feast as is the distribution of meat and eating. The Kyrgyz give short toasts at small and intimate gatherings. At feasts people call for *kaaloo tilek*—defined as a way of desiring people to be united for the same purpose.

The longer the speech, the more likely the speaker is able to list all his wishes in one speech. A shorter toast would mean that the person did not respect the host. For this specific event, the guests also composed short poems in which they compared the host to various heroes like Manas (the national hero of Kyrgyzstan) and Bakai, and invoked other sites associated with supernatural powers such as Ala-Too Mountain and Issyk-Kul. This was unusual, since the language of toasts is usually very realistic. The toasts were also unusual in that speeches commented extensively on contemporary difficulties, a theme usually avoided. But Rahim's guests were careful to design their speeches in such a way that they did not offend their host. It was crucial that guests performed their *kaaloo tilek* well, since it is an important way of obtaining acceptance, displaying honor, and getting support from others.

Speeches must be given in the correct order to appropriately honor both the speaker and the host. The *tamada* asks the eldest people and most honored guests to speak as representatives of their larger groups or provinces. Such speech giving enables the speaker to build a good alliance with the host, and also for others lower in the hierarchy to honor the speaker during their own turn.

The guests were invited to give their speeches in a particular sequence. Tuigunaly was asked to give the first speech—as an elder brother of Rahim, representative father, and Rahim's patron and colleague. The paternal grandparents of the host were asked to give the last speech, to close the ceremony by giving their blessing with "Oomiyn" (Amen). However, between these two speeches, various representatives of Chüi Province were invited to the stage to offer their words.

While the elder guests gave the toasts, the younger guests were expected to carefully listen to the speeches. In addition, younger guests were forbidden to drink alcohol in front of their elders the whole time, and had to remain in their seats as the elder guests mounted the stage and performed in front of the audience. Onstage, the elders gave their speeches and also offered gifts and sang (see Figure 7.4).

Figure 7.4. The blessing of elders (*bata*).
Photo: A. Ismailbekova.

Representatives from each rayon were asked by the *tamada* to come to the stage and give their speech. The speeches were accompanied by music and hearty applause from the audience. Under the direction of the *tamada*, the first speeches were given by the guests from the rayons of Chüi Province: Jaiyl, Moskovskyi, Sokulukskyi, Panfilov, Alamedin, Kemin, Chüi, and Issyk-Ata districts. As the rayon officials mounted the stage, the toastmaster emphasized their courage in fighting against the pressure of the pro-presidential party and in supporting their candidate from Chüi Province. Thus, guests were carefully selected and speakers were grouped in advance to meet the expectation and the aims of the patron.

In the following paragraphs, I have recorded the speeches from the representatives of the different districts. After the every speech, the guests presented their gifts to Rahim.

Jaiyl rayon (eight people stood to give this speech):

We proved to ourselves that we can make it by supporting our son Rahim during the election. Our faces are open (*jyzybyz jarygyrak*). Of course, it would be great to have more of our sons in parliament; life would be easier for the people of Chüi and the whole of Kyrgyzstan. However, unfortunately many of the northerners were not accepted. Despite this, we still have Rahim. Rahim is young and full of enthusiasm to work for his people. This party system remains uncertain; we did not have enough time to learn this system. The situation in Kyrgyzstan becomes more and more unstable. This time we were not prepared for the quick changes and unexpected elections. However we should be ready for the next elections. Meanwhile, we need to work together as a team and continue to support our "own son."

Moskovskyi rayon (ten people stood to give this speech):

We are the representatives of the Moskovskyi rayon district. However much you honor and respect Rahim, we honor and respect Rahim in exactly the same way as you because we share the same blood (*kan*) and bones (*söök*)—we are kinsmen through fathers (*atalash tuugandar*). Be always with your people. We are proud of you. You are the leader of Chüi Province; therefore you have to work very hard. Then we will be together with you, always. We are all relatives. A long life for Rahim, *Uraa!*[5]

Sokulukskyi rayon (five people stood to give this speech):

We are SDP members. We got only eleven seats in parliament. Unfortunately, I was not included on the list. Of course, it is not the wish of God; instead it is the act of the cunning president. "Politics is dirty business"! The general situation in Kyrgyzstan is difficult. Sokuluk rayon is the heart of SDP. However, today the heart of SDP is the Issyk-Ata rayon. You are not alone, because people will support you, and the party is behind you, so be strong and confident in facing the challenges. Thanks to our brother leaders of SDP, Almazbek Atambaev and your brother Tuigunaly, who have given your life direction and provided their support in times of urgent need.[6] Let SDP live longer with its Chüi leaders.

Alamedin rayon (seven people stood to give this speech):

Dear kinsmen and brothers (*agaiym tuugandar*), this year's election was competitive and tough. With dignity, we were able to support Rahim in the race. Thank you all. First, we should not divide ourselves. Second, I met Rahim during the election campaign. I was glad to meet him, not only because he is a charismatic leader (*tatyyktyy jigit*), but also I met my younger brother (*atalash ini*) because my lineage Suu Murun can be traced back to the village of Bulak, where my grandfather was born. Now we have become brothers. What I wish for you is good health, wealth, and success, but I also want you to learn how to be cunning (*kuu*). It is otherwise quite difficult to survive in life without these important qualities. Soon there will be elections again; there you have to be a teacher to your younger brothers and be their backbone. Now I sit with your kinsmen and friends at the same table—indeed you have excellent followers (*jigitering*). Last, I want you to be very careful and attentive (*ekiatbol*): you are ambitious; some politicians might not like your personal qualities—in which case, you have to be wise, smart, and cunning. I remember how my grandfather always recalled several songs about your village. Therefore, in honor of your paternal grandmother and your villagers, I would like to present this song.

Kemin rayon (eight persons stood to give this speech):

Dear kinsmen and *Chüilüktör*—we congratulate Rahim with his mandate as a parliamentarian. According to the Kyrgyz saying, the best leaders as well as the best horses come from Chüi. Follow your brothers (*aga*) such as Tuigunaly, Almazbek—you became the parliamentarian of the parliament (*Jogorku Kenesh*).

Archadai yzyn jashtyk bersin	May you be given as long life as a juniper
Ala Toodoi byiyktik bersin	Be as high as Kyrgyz Ala Too Mountains
Asmaning achik bolsun	May your sky be always open
Kok asmandai kenen bol	Be as wide as the blue sky
Yssyk-Koldoi tereng bol	Be as deep as the lake of Yssyk-Kol
Manas atangdai uluk bol	Be as great as your Manas father
Bakai atangdai silik bol	Be as polite and respectful as your Bakai father

Dear Sary Özön Chüi,[7] here are the representatives of several districts from the west to the east of Chüi Province. Our land had many khan and leaders. As our Kalygyl *ata* said,[8] the *bii* (khan) is not part of the Sary Bagysh lineage, instead it is part of the Sary Özön Chüi. This year you are a parliamentarian. Next time you will be president of Kyrgyzstan. If you should become a *khan*, then your wife will be a *khanisha*. May the souls of our ancestors always support you (*ata babalardyn arbagy daiyim koldop jürsün*)!

The sixth speech, from the Chüi rayon (nine persons stood to give this speech):

Rahim, Thank for being with us! As you told us that you would serve for your people, we have been supporting you since the first day. You should then defend our dignity and honor in parliament. I wish that you are strong and healthy. Always be with your family and your people. I should address you with "*Siz*."[9] We are all from Chüi, and share the same ancestor. My body belongs to Sokuluk, but I myself belong to this area.

Kish mezgilindei tazalik	Be as pure as winter
Jaz mezgilindei suluuluk	Be as beautiful as spring
Jai mezgilindei jilyylyk	Be as warm as summer
Kyz mezgilindei molchuluk	Be as wealthy as fall
Biz sen menenbiz Rahimchik!	We are always with you, Rahimchik!

The seventh speech was from the Issyk-Ata rayon, and was given by the village elder of Bulak (an expert on genealogy). He simply called to the assembled guests, "Let us bless our son (*bata bereli balabizga*)," and concluded, "We belong to Solto and Nurmanbet (Suu Murun), we are proud to have our son from Nurmanbet (Suu Murun) in parliament" (see Figure 7.5)

After the speeches, people continued eating, drinking, singing, and dancing. The elders of the community and the parental grandmother of Rahim gave the final speeches. Rahim thanked all of these guests and the whole feast drew to a close around 11:00 p.m.

Cultivating Loyalty (and Betrayal) in Chüi Province

Despite their differences, each speech was structured similarly. After a creative opening, the speaker shifted to an invocation in which he blessed Rahim but also called on him to do specific things. Other common themes include the following: (a) wishes and comments on the health, well-being, and prosperity of the patron; (b) claims of provincial unity and identity; (c) a report on the region's or the SDP's "victimization by the northerners"; and (d) an expressed desire to see northerners represented in parliament. In the following section I want to draw attention to how these *kaaloo tilek* facilitated the collective identification of the guests as northerners who had been politically excluded. Through the speeches, collective identity is shaped and then made manifest in one person. In this process, people's political victimization became a shared challenge rooted in and strengthened by a Chüi provincial identity. The solution to this victimization was also presented through the construction of Rahim as the native son who would give people access to national resources as a parliamentarian.

In the *kaaloo tilek*, the beauty of the golden Chüi Province (*Sary Özön*) was expressed in a description of its strong and talented people (*Kalygul*), and the fertility of the Chüi Valley. In daily life and other festive contexts each province and village would claim their differences, but in this particular context, people expressed their sense of unity through common kinship, political party, and provincial criteria. Stories, proverbs, and sayings were incorporated into *kaaloo tilek* with the aim of reinforcing the uniqueness of Chüi. The *kaaloo tilek* asked those who live in Chüi Province not to divide themselves according to rayon or village, but to be united as Chüilük since they share common blood, the same ancestor, and the SDP.

The guests not only celebrated Rahim's victory but also honored and praised him. They were witness to the power he held in his hand and legitimized this power. The patron was perceived as the representative of the northerners who had been victimized politically by southerners. Consequently, their *kaaloo tilek*

Figure 7.5. The guests giving speech.
Photo: A. Ismailbekova.

combined several elements—happiness in celebrating a political victory, the importance of widening groups under the umbrella of Chüilük, and the need for the support of an individual in a political arena—which led to the facilitation and reinforcement of the alliance between different groups, created a network of connections, and strengthened Chüi provincialism.

Hence, being blessed and accepted by people gave Rahim power. In the context of both "traditional" social organization and contemporary politics, only this kind of blessing—bestowed on him by his people at a feast—would enable Rahim to become publicly recognized as a known yet young and politically active patron. Seeking to express internal desire and hope for the future, people made the patron the target of their attention. In this regard, gifts were given to him and *kaaloo tilek* were made to celebrate and secure his health, wealth, and success. This was obvious from the symbolic gifts that were presented and whose meaning was explained in the giving, such as high-crowned cap (*Bakai kalpak*) and coat (*chapan*).

Those who blessed Rahim asked him to be strong, attentive, and careful, and stressed his importance for the Chüi people. By praising and honoring Rahim,

Figure 7.6. The gift giving.
Photo: A. Ismailbekova.

they wanted to be assured that he was strong enough to cope with southern politicians and able to help them in the future. Apart from hints regarding future help, people asked him to support their younger brothers, which immediately imposed on him an obligation to support future children. People relied heavily on the support of Rahim's patrilineal ancestors, Ak Jol-Nurmanbet (Suu Murun), by saying, "May your ancestors support you" (*ata-babalaryng koldosun*) (see Figure 7.6).

In their speeches, the guests revealed real and imagined ancestral connections. These justified the barely concealed demands that each speaker made on the victorious Rahim. By praising him people wanted to secure their own wellbeing. The stressed belonging, reciprocity, and aid; they offered favors, including bureaucratic support; and they made their own requests of Rahim. Both exchanges were rendered legitimate through the idioms of shared regional belonging and kinship.

These guests all said nice things about the province and concentrated on how they would deal with the dangers of corruption, greed, competition, and treachery. Some of the guests were sincere supporters of Rahim. For example, Tuigunaly, who was an equally strong politician as Rahim, had decided to support Rahim's bid for parliament because Rahim was his representative son, but also because he respected new ideas and considered him to represent the young generation of politicians. Many guests, however, were jealous and competitive. As elsewhere in the world, a powerful man's guests are also dangerous, and their gifts may be "poison" (Herzfeld 1987; Shryock 2012).

The feast provided the patron, and also his guests, with the opportunity to build networks. The invited state officials had a chance to meet their counterparts from across Chüi Province. Ideally such acquaintances would help Rahim, as their common patron, in his efforts to cultivate networks of loyalists and to forge alliances with the heads of provincial administration across northern Kyrgyzstan. The government officials were important to Rahim because they could help him control and mobilize key state resources to his advantage. As Rahim's success increased, the officials could expect return benefits: their speeches indicate that they hoped that they were promising their loyalties to a future president. During the feast, the *tamada* controlled the appearance of interests in conflict with Rahim's own, but the event still revealed the host's vulnerability. The feast generally served to generate a loyal following, but even as the speeches proclaim this loyalty they also reveal that Rahim has been badly set up to shoulder the responsibility of others' "corruption" if and when it becomes publicly known.

The Political Uses of Segmentary Lineage

In addition to the particular purposes of celebrating Rahim's victory and building the networks of support he would urgently need as a new member of parliament, the feast also contributed to the wider processes of turning kinship to political purposes. Evans-Pritchard (1940) demonstrated that the Nuer used their segmentary lineage system to successfully build demographic and military pressure. In a similar way, Kyrgyzstan's post-socialist politicians appear to be using the population's branching systems of kinship in their favor, turning lineage segments into cohesive groups united behind particular political leaders. By structuring political loyalty along kinship lines, they have alternative routes to accessing power and resources than are provided for in the formal structure of electoral politics or in the organization of the state's administrative apparatus.

Rahim's feast brought together various officials, politicians, village elders, and representatives of important professions, as might be expected at any political gathering. These individuals were also selected, however, as representatives of geographically scattered descent groups that could all be united within one genealogical line. Guests and host alike knew this, and they identified themselves in their speeches as the descendants of common Solto and Nurmanbet (Suu Murun) ancestors. A major segment (Solto) represent northern Kyrgyzstan, while a similarly constituted descent group (Ichkilik or Kipchak) represent southern Kyrgyzstan. In their speeches, they equated their common ancestry with common political interest: they had gathered, they said, because they belonged to the same kin group, and because they shared the same territory, and because they were all members of the SDP. Through various rhetorical devices, they underlined the importance of common kinship: speakers referred to guests according to their specific lineage belongingness, and as in-laws (*kudalar*); they rephrased regional coresidence as shared descent.

In this respect, drawing on identities and principles of obligation and reciprocity, which contrasted with their more formal obligations in relation to state activities and their professional identities, the patron hoped to shape their future activities. Furthermore, through drawing on these informal personal networks, the patron could wield enormous power, allowing him to evade formal rules while protecting his own interests and those of his followers.

By stressing the shared affiliation among all guests with the lineage system, Rahim might have hoped to overcome the reluctance of many officials to help him. As employees of the state, many local officials were duty bound to support the current administration. Rahim hoped to shift the loyalty of these individuals away from the state (which was under Ak-Jol control) and to himself, both personally and as an SDP member. By stressing their shared Solto and Nurmanbet (Suu Murun) lineages, Rahim could also hope that the state officials would invite him to their own feasts as a kinsman, which would enable the development of a personal relationship that might be turned to political purposes.

In the moment of the feast, the realignment of individual loyalties to support Rahim as a fellow kinsman above all other loyalties remained only a potential. Speakers promised their loyalty but made it conditional. It is doubtful that all the guests became truly loyal to Rahim, but certainly the feast helps to show how quickly segmentary lineage can be mobilized to build political solidarity from local levels to the regional, or even national, arena.

In Rahim's case, political success depended on the combination of lineage with patronage. If Rahim had not already made wide use of lineage to build himself as a powerful patron in the region, he may not have been successful in politics. The structure of the system of patronage is parallel to the organization of the government, which is a hierarchically based one. Kyrgyzstan's political organization was the result of the Soviet systems (duality of party and state) and the post-Soviet systems (duality of kinship and state). Thus, the alliance between state officials and the patron was neither fixed nor stable because, depending on the context, this alliance could change.

As Powell (1977) suggests, it is important to present a careful account of how patron-client relations were established and developed into large-scale systems of political patronage. The patron took advantage of loyalists at all levels of the Chüi provincial government: as a result, he stood to gain control over the main administrative departments, such as education and public health. The patron had autonomy within the larger governmental system and connections with state officials, and he could creatively use these connections with ease within an often constraining administrative framework. Thus, the political party was organized along segmentary kinship lines, with the aim of supporting the patron as the SDP leader and strengthening the power of the party. In return, the state officials expected compensation—such as stability in their office and other advantages.

The Conventions of the Feast

In this chapter I argue that the victory feast deviated significantly from the conventions of the feast (*toi*). Neither close kinsmen nor friends were invited as such. Nor were people expected to make cash contributions as is normal. Rather, the feast was carefully tailored to fit the composition of the guests, meat distribution politics, and the table arrangements. Thus the feast facilitated political discourse in a nonpolitical setting. As a result, special guests were united and made loyal through hospitality and social solidarity. The principles of reciprocity and obligation inherent to hospitality also indebted the guests to Rahim.

I would argue that this feast was not only in the interests of the patron but also in the interest of the guests. Common interests and goals bound people together in a way that strengthened their social relations and extended their plans. In other words, the feast was a performative arena that served wider political aims through creating networks, strengthening provincialism, and maintaining provincial alliances. The feast was a vehicle through which SDP members could criticize the Ak-Jol Party and thereby reinforce their own party's unity. Thus party patronage as exhibited at this feast reveals something of the nature of democracy and the system of party building based on solidarity, hospitality, and gift exchange. Thus, social norms and values were integrated into the rules and principles of the party.

Notes

1. The word *kut* has several meanings: spirit, courage, heart, grace, success; stroke of luck, good fortune.
2. Administrative-territorial division is divided according to oblast, rayon, and village municipalities (*aiyl ökmöty*). Kyrgyzstan has seven provinces (Chüi, Naryn, Batken, Osh, Jalal-Abad, Issyk-Kul, Talas). Each province consists of five to nine rayons, and each rayon consists of several village municipalities.
3. I use an emic notion of high status, which mostly refers to the state officials (*chong*).
4. *Yrysky* means holiness, but in this case it also meant prosperity and luck. It is generally considered that an individual's luckiness can be transmitted to others through sharing food and drink and also leftovers.

5. *Uraa* (R.) was used during parades as an expression of happiness and unity during the Soviet Union. It is always placed at the end of the sentence.

6. For a long time, Tuigunaly was in parliament. But following the coming of southerners to power, he was not reelected; he supported Rahim.

7. *Chüi* is sometimes used to refer to all of northern Kyrgyzstan. *Sary Özön Chüi* is translated as "Golden Province," and when used emphasizes the beauty, richness, and importance of the land for survival. The main hymn of Chüi Province is also called "Sary Özön," and describes the beauties of the land.

8. *Kalygyl* is a poet and knowledgeable person.

9. Formal and polite "you," as in French *Vous* or Russian *Vy.*

Concluding Words

Native Son, Democratization, and Poetics of Patronage

The Collapse of a Patronage Empire

From the case of Kanybek and his relationship to his boss, Rahim, this book opened its pages. Kanybek was obliged to support Rahim during his election campaign and to carry out certain tasks for him. But Kanybek described the relationship slightly differently: he was loyal to his boss, who in return would protect him. Rahim was a protector and guarantor of Kanybek's security and well-being. Rahim had supported Kanybek for many years; for example, he had bought Kanybek some land on which to build a house in the capital, helped him erect a stall at the Nurmanbet Bazaar, and promised to educate Kanybek's young children. Kanybek told me that Rahim was like a father to him. Kanybek's story and the others detailed in this book reveal important aspects of Kyrgyz life, particularly kinship and its relationships to patronage networks.

When I returned to Kyrgyzstan in summer 2009, I met Kanybek. He told me that the region no longer had its own native son. I had been surprised to find the villagers of Bulak feeling completely lost and uncertain about their future. Many had even left the village. The figure that I have described in these chapters—that of the native son who brought hope and aspiration—had disappeared. Only the memory remained of Rahim as their native son and the way in which he had been their leader.

What had happened? In 2008 Rahim had been reported by the media as missing. The police assumed that Rahim had been kidnapped. One year later, after a long police investigation, his remains were found in Alamedin, eighteen kilometers from Bishkek. He had been shot with a Makarov pistol. The police report concluded that he had been killed because of his commercial connections in Kazakhstan and because he was in debt to his Kazakh partners. However, his kinsmen in Bulak Village were convinced that his murder had been a politically motivated contract killing (*politicheski zakaz*). He was an ambitious man, they reminded me, a member of the oppositional SDP who had openly challenged the president in public.

Many kinsmen, friends, and supporters expressed their dissatisfaction during the course of the police investigation. At one point, Rahim's fellow villagers had blocked the road between Bishkek and Torugart, demanding an intensification of the police investigation. The investigative group consisting of the Ministry of Interior and the National Security Committee had been reporting their progress with the investigation, but only behind closed doors. The killers were found, members of an organized criminal group, but those who had contracted the assassination were not found. The Head Investigation Department of the Ministry of Interior reported only that the crime leader, Jumabek Zikirbaev, said that the murder of the deputy was the responsibility of some Kazakh criminal organizations. The Kazakh criminals had asked their Kyrgyz "colleagues" to arrange a meeting with Rahim to recover debts of some $300,000. During fighting with the Kazakh colleague, Rahim was killed.

However, when I went to the village in 2009 there was a rumor circulating that President Bakiyev and his brothers had killed Rahim, or at least had contracted the main assassination. The villagers opined that Rahim did not have enemies apart from the president's brothers. I was astonished to hear that there was only one version of the rumor. In other similar assassinations, there had been several variations. The rumor that I heard from people went as follows: Rahim had a big piece of land on the Shore of Issyk-Kul Lake but one of Bakiyev's brothers demanded that Rahim share this land. When Rahim did not hand over a piece of land to Bakiyev's family, they decided to kill him, because he was young, wealthy, and politically influential.

The people in the village had been sorely afflicted by the loss of Rahim. People felt they had to work especially hard because they had no one to support them as Rahim had done. But also people found they had little to discuss with one another. Before people could talk about their native son and other political matters for hours. Once what people had most respected had been taken from them, there was little to do except satisfy basic needs by cultivating land and breeding cattle.

Those who had worked for Rahim on his private farm were totally lost and without any hope for the future when I met them in 2009. The farm had been bought by another businessman, who told the workers that Rahim owed him a lot of money. Subsequently, many farmworkers had lost their jobs on the farm, and, as a consequence, everything appeared to be uncertain. As in Bulak, the losses were greater than the work. Rahim's clients were also emotionally attached to him. One of his clients asked me: "What shall I do now?" The man was very sad and had been sick for many days as a result of Rahim's passing. Another client told me that her son lost his place at school following Rahim's death. Those most affected by these shifts were the families who had lived on the farm itself; they had been asked to leave. Yet these families had no close kin to help them, no appropriate documents to apply for government benefits. Rahim had provided them with their only means of survival.

Following his disappearance, Rahim's business ceased to function and was taken over by strangers. Rahim's kinsmen from the private farm complained that many of his distant kin also had simply disappeared when Rahim was discovered dead. People who previously sought to be supported by him no longer visited the village after his death, nor did they offer basic support to his family. As one of my informants told me, once Rahim had been appointed a member of parliament and had become wealthy and influential, his small number of kinsmen had increased from two to two thousand. But after Rahim died, these thousands of kinsmen no longer sought to emphasize their attachment to him or his nuclear family. It was as if they had never been related to his family and had never formed part of his patronage network.

Rahim was young, and he had built his network in some ten years only. It was a hierarchical network, with few lateral relationships of mutual dependency. Once the leader was killed, the whole structure disintegrated. Although people had been hopeful, the circumstances of Rahim's power were uncertain and changed quickly.

Throughout most of this book, I demonstrated how the appearance of Rahim's patronage network can be understood in relation to the contemporary hardships of economic life and the particularities of post-Soviet politics in Kyrgyzstan. These particularities involve kinship politics, corruption, big business, political patronage, criminal networks, and social stratification.

Rise and Fall of Patronage Networks

The rise and fall of Rahim's patronage network is also an example of the evolution of increasingly business-oriented politicians with criminal backups and connections. Jumabek Zikirbaev and his criminal organization were also held responsible for the murders of the son of the deputy from the SDP of Kyrgyzstan, Zhusup Jeenbekov, and other important business leaders in Kyrgyzstan. Previously, Jumabek Zikirbaev had been a master of sports in wrestling. He had been arrested several times for robbery and illegal possession of firearms.

Rahim's political career, high social status, and economic advancement rose within a short period of time from being the local doctor in Bishkek to the businessman and famous politician. Rahim's election ensured parliamentary immunity for his business ties, interests, and needs in milk export and farming. But even before his election, his businesses were under the protection of the "shadow networks" (Holzlehner 2014) that were a necessary precondition for business in unpredictable political environment.

Rahim's success in politics and business was spectacular but not stable. He experienced struggle over the control of business, constant threat, public criticism, and business competition. In the end, these resulted in his death and the subsequent collapse of his business, political career, and extensive patronage network. The rapid rise and fall of leaders seems to be only a step apart in the rapidly changing political and economic environment of Kyrgyzstan.

Under the former President Bakiyev's tenure, criminal networks had been incorporated into the state structures as protection of political power and business. Thus, scholars of Kyrgyzstan's politics observe the patronage networks, big business, and criminal networks became inseparable and symbiotically coexistent (McGlinchey 2011; Radnitz 2010; Reeves 2014). The fall and rise of important businessmen-turned-political leaders in Kyrgyzstan accompanied the struggle to control lucrative business and political resources. In a similar vein, Holzlehner (2014) argues that criminal networks in the Russian Far East have penetrated the formal political and economic structures and stepped into legal business. The emergence of shadow networks is not due only to the weak power of the state and passive action of state institutions but the actions taken by the existing states have also an effect on those networks. This overlap of business, politics, and criminal networks highlights the result of transformation processes in the post-socialist countries (Humphrey 2012). The specificity of post-Soviet patronage networks have been adapting to different sociopolitical environments throughout the history of Kyrgyzstan.

Transformation of Patronage

In the 1960s and 1970s social scientists predicted that patronage systems would disappear with increasing modernization (Eisenstadt and Roniger 1980; Foster 1963; Gellner and Waterbury 1977; Schmidt et al. 1977; Weingrod 1968). Contrary to their expectations, patronage has been intermeshed with and absorbed into current demands and expectations of new social realities, revealing itself to be omnipresent and adaptable (Roniger and Güneş-Ayata 1994). This description also applies to Central Asia and in particular to Kyrgyzstan, where patronage has persisted throughout history. Patronage relations survived the socialist era and have taken new forms in the transition to democracy and a liberal market economy during the post-Soviet period. The new forms of patronage are characterized by the use of kinship terms to recruit patrons and clients and to regulate patronage relations. They are also characterized by the building of vertical and horizontal bases of loyalty that enable successful businessmen to become powerful politicians. Although patronage is normally considered undemocratic, the patronage networks of Kyrgyzstan are facilitating the institutionalization of electoral party politics.

Not all patrons are as clever, ambitious, or successful as Rahim. I was fortuitous in my choice of field site to encounter a patron whose network expanded beyond a single village or business niche in an urban area. Such limited circles of patronage are by far more common. Rahim's network was truly spectacular: involving his native village of Bulak and its neighboring villages, business networks in Bishkek, transnational business operations in Kazakhstan, and (very nearly) the whole of northern Kyrgyzstan—it provided an opportunity to see how democracy and patronage intersect in all these domains simultaneously.

One of the most salient features of post-Soviet patronage is the degree of economic protection it affords clients. After the collapse of the Soviet Union, Kyrgyz citizens were faced with massive economic crisis and uncertainty. Patrons who could offer security and protection in economic terms, by providing jobs, houses, cash, and animals for ritual needs and higher educational opportunities, were particularly valued and successful. Interestingly, because patronage had existed in the Soviet period, the new relations often emerged from the preexisting ones. The new patrons were the old ones—that is, people with connections to the state as party members or bureaucrats—as well as new businessmen; the state remained the goal of leverage and ultimate resource. Thus, the transition to democracy has been led by the "new" patrons, whose political interests are barely distinguishable from economic interests; both are pursued in tandem with a bid to gain the support of increasing numbers of clients. Post-Soviet patron-client relations are self-interested, but they are built from ritualized expressions of kinship and thus also involve moral sentiments.

Kinship and Patronage

In many studies, irrespective of social scientific discipline, patronage and kinship are interpreted strictly as involving mutually exclusive relationships (Blok 1974; Gellner and Waterbury 1977). However, this model of patron-client relationship does not seem to be dominant in today's rural Kyrgyzstan. What I have found instead is that there is a pronounced tendency of an overlapping of patronage and kinship. This trend reflects the organization of kinship based Kyrgyz society. The Kyrgyz have a well-developed segmentary lineage system. Kyrgyz identity is defined by descent affiliations. Patronage exists within a framework of kinship and serves to extend the system through people's use of kin terms, lineage identification, and manipulation of the genealogies for various strategic purposes. While genealogies and kinship relations may be manipulated to some degree, they still remain a reality as categorical ascriptions. The clients are usually recruited from among kin, and kinship is stretched and manipulated to legitimate and reinforce the patronage. However, other aspects of kinship do not constitute patronage.

Imagined genealogy and space both play a crucial role in manipulating various behaviors and the practices of social actors. Discussion of genealogies both in private and public life is a matter of dealing with present-day concerns. Actors use genealogies in the establishment of patron-client relations, and kinship provides them with space to satisfy their political, social, and economic needs. Schlee's (2007, 2008) theoretical model of processes of identification provides an appropriate perspective for the analysis of the way in which the affiliation of descent groups of different sizes is used to legitimate claims of patronage.

Social Poetics of Patronage

Patronage is grounded in cultural practices and local concepts, and expressed through performance. Seen as social poetics (Herzfeld 2005), patronage becomes a relation of ongoing rhetorical persuasion. The patron is not detached from his community, but shares the community's vision of the world. He knows what people want from him, he takes into account the expectations of others, and he frames his own interest as the interest of the client or of the collective. When he is successful, the patron imposes on people without their knowing, or with their full consent and willing subordination.

Importantly, the patron cannot do without poetics. Although patronage is valued for the economic security it provides, it is not merely an economic transaction. It is not enough for a patron to give jobs or money to clients. This would not secure their loyalty to the degree needed by the patron who must deploy the same labor force to support his interests across multiple domains, even when the clients might have other cross-cutting or conflicting interests. Instead, the patron must convince clients to accept less than they want or need: low and delayed salaries, substandard housing, overwork, confiscated documents. The patron persuades others to cooperate with his plans. He appeals to and legitimates his ideas with the clients' own values—most important, those related to kinship.

Critique of Western Idea of Democracy

Kyrgyzstan's publicly proclaimed "revolutions" that produced a change of leadership at the uppermost levels of government have been viewed skeptically by most political observers.

Juraev (2008, 262) and Lewis (2008, 265) have both concluded that the revolutions were organized by elites and that people were paid to take to the streets. For such authors, the lack of spontaneous revolt by citizens is one more sign of a stalled democratization process.

In this book, I have instead argued that electoral party politics are developing not only in the midst of but because of processes that are "corrupt" from a theoretical perspective. The patronage system and electoral party politics and its norms are intermeshed in Kyrgyzstan. They are complimentary and each is a prerequisite to the other. Rather, the situation in rural Kyrgyzstan involves the localization of electoral party politics as people are emotionally engaged in building "democracy."

Instead of considering democratic political processes and kinship as separate domains or unreflexively criticizing patronage in Kyrgyzstan (Juraev 2008; Khamidov 2006a, 2006b; Pétric 2005; Radnitz 2006), it is vital to consider ethnographic findings. The mobilization of kinship and patronage in the political arena may not threaten democracy quite as has been assumed. One has to look at electoral party politics in their localized form. Here, patronage increases people's participation during elections and mobilizes people in the interests of the parties. Democracy and the free market economy are primarily conceptual categories; in local contexts they are intertwined with other social institutions, beliefs, values, and practices.

Through their participation in political activities (such as elections) that may well be organized and directed by powerful patrons, people also learn about changes in the constitution, the parliamentary election process, and the policy of the party system. They learn the "rules," as well as the ways in which the rules can be bent, adjusted, and broken. People participate actively in rallies and meetings, and they are genuine supporters of democratic reform. They also have high hopes of something changing, and that electoral party politics might improve their lives.

Conventional analyses of Kyrgyz politics are correct to note that much grassroots political activity is "paid" in various ways. But their analysis of the role of "elites," presumed to be urban based, wealthy, and politically powerful, misses the dynamics visible to ethnographic analysis in the countryside. Villagers in Bulak and Orlovka understood well the constraints and risks of political patronage. Orlovka's villagers were determined that their votes for Ak-Jol not be tampered with by Rahim or his supporters through any number of ruses on the road, and safeguarded them all the way to the final counting station in the capital.

In contrast, the villagers of Bulak were proud that they were able to influence and challenge the state through a series of creative maneuvers that guaranteed SDP's local victory and Rahim's nomination to parliament. Moreover, Bulak's villagers worked together to define the boundaries of acceptable manipulation: local consensus was that all the procedural irregularities had supported a "democratic" outcome.

It is important to note that the people who were most likely to have divergent political views (that is, recently married women) were the ones who were silenced during elections. Patronage in electoral politics also serves the community's need to self-reproduce its own patterns of authority and power.

188 | *Blood Ties and the Native Son*

Native Sons and Corrupt State Officials

The rise of native sons in Kyrgyzstan's post-Soviet political domain is a particularly interesting development. Moving beyond a discussion of the "corruption" signaled by their presence and success, native sons reveal how electoral party politics and social institutions are mutually constitutive. On the one hand, native sons are popular because of their perceived capacity to represent localized electorates. At the same time, the election of native sons reinforces local institutions and practices based on social roles, hierarchy, and status.

As elsewhere in the former Soviet Union, Kyrgyzstan's early post-Soviet politics were marked by the desire to create a rupture with Soviet political ideology. In the post-Soviet context, this has generally meant the triumph of nationalism and related identity politics over other ideological programs (for example, class-based interests). In Kyrgyzstan specifically, the widespread desire to "recover" traditional forms of Kyrgyz social and political life has provided particularly favorable ground for kinship-based patronage, and with it the native son has proved a particularly appealing figure for representing localized groups in national political life. The concept of the native son fits into existing forms of social organization and is linked to historical memory. The figure also provides a model in which personalized politics and collective identity are not contradictory.

As an ideal, the native son is subordinate to the community's desires, needs, and wishes, particularly as they are expressed by elder males. In the preceding chapters, I have demonstrated how Bulak villagers enacted this relationship. Senior villagers, in particular, asked Rahim for support and favors on behalf of the community, and he granted them. They also repeatedly exhorted him to observe more traditions: attend and financially support more life cycle events, read the Qur'an more often, pray more often for his own father and his village "fathers." Rahim gained villagers' support as a politician particularly by following this advice. Thus, beyond his role as a patron who dispenses gifts and favors, the native son learns how to conduct the village's affairs from the elders. In politics writ large, villagers continue to believe at some level that it is they who have taught their native sons how to conduct politics; namely, they expect that the native son will habitually act in deference to the community's wishes and needs. The native son is an ideal political representative. Not least because his "care" for villagers vouches for his personal honor in a domain (that is, the state) known to be deeply corrupt.

Paradoxes of Patronage

Both the economic and political sides of patronage in Kyrgyzstan, however, present a paradox. Clients accept and even pursue patronage with the idea that the relation is in their own interest. They believe that they exert some control over the patron, and, particularly, that the patron is bound to act in the client's interest because the client is always free to choose another patron. But is this really so? In the post-Soviet context, economic forms of patronage seem to have rapidly developed because people desperately needed access to resources; forms of access that had existed in the Soviet period were cut with the union's dissolution. People were prepared to accept the manipulative behavior of patronage because they felt they had few other options to secure their own social, economic and political well-being. As my description of the dependent workers on Orlovka's privatized farm shows, patronage is easy to get into but difficult to escape.

Patronage presents itself as a relationship of equal loyalty and support in the midst of an unequal balance of power and resources. The patron is expected to lose credibility and legitimacy if he breaks promises. An untrustworthy patron should lose his capacity to mobilize people. At the time of my research, Rahim had succeeded in maintaining his clients' trust. But, as many informants' stories revealed, much of the support he promised was to be delivered in the future. His clients worked on faith, incurring substantial hardships in the present for the promise of future rewards. Would he have delivered to his clients' satisfaction had he lived? Probably not—attentive villagers in Orlovka already doubted his promises to build a mosque in exchange for the one whose construction he vetoed.

Nor are all patron-client relations structured with a similar balance of power. Access to Rahim's patronage was normally restricted to those who could claim kinship. Moreover, some types of classificatory kin received more favorable treatment than other types.

While nearly everyone in rural Kyrgyzstan during my research seemed to be involved in some relations of patronage, individual patrons received differential judgments of their moral character from clients and others. Clients always used common conventions to legitimize that patronage by a particular individual was morally just and communally legitimate. These people would not judge the patron based on his actual behaviors vis-à-vis legal norms. Instead they would evaluate his moral and ethical worth, and legitimize his behavior within the framework of the native son. In contrast, those excluded from a patronage network judged a (political) patron based on the policy and obligation of state officials to be neutral and protect the rights of the citizens.

Clients themselves help sustain patronage in its various forms by publicly expressing claims to the legitimacy and fairness of patronage. In post-Soviet Kyrgyzstan, legitimacy is framed in a language infused with the expectations, norms, obligations, and emotions of kinship. People find ways to justify their actions through social networks of reciprocity and out of obligation and loyalty to a "son" whether their own, that of their lineage, or that of their community. This language suggests it is the patron who is bound to the client and not vice versa. But is this so? Or is it just a clever disguise?

Glossary of Local Terms

aga	respectful address of an older brother
agaiym tuugandar	dear kinsmen
aial kishi barbait	women do not go
aiyl	village
aiyl ökmötü	local self-governance unit; also name for the mayor
ak joldun ystynon basaly	we should walk on the Ak-Jol party
ak söök	white bone
akim	head of rayon or governor
aksakal	lit. "whitebeard," male elder
aksakaldar sotu	court of elders
alys	distant
apa	grandmother or mother
arky ata	distant father
ash	memorial ritual conducted one year after a death
ashar	community shared labor
ata	father
atalash ini	younger brother from the patrilineal side
atalash tuugandar	kinsmen from patrilineal side
ata babalarybyz bir	we share the same ancestor
ata-babalaryng koldosun	may your ancestors support you
attyy bashtyy kishilerdi	the most important people
baatyr	hero
bai	rich (person)
baike	older brother
bala	child
baldardy butuna turguzuu	support one's own children
bash	head
bata	blessing
bata bereli balabizga	let us bless our son
batya	R. father
bek	see *bai*
berki ata	that father
besh-barmak	lit. "five fingers," traditional Kyrgyz food served during celebrations, consisting of boiled meat and self-made noodles
beshik toi	celebration of the birth of child
besplatnyi dom	house for free
bii	see *bai*; judge during tsarist times
biilik	power
bir atanyn baldary	children of one father

bir kol menen	common hands or one hand
birikme	sedentary work unit
bizdiki	ours
bizdin bala jardam	
berbegende kim beret	if not our son, who else can help us
blat	R. "access of favor" to public resources
bogohylnik	R. people-blasphemous
borsok	fried bread
boz üi	yurt
brigadir	R. head of a working unit in the kolkhoz; head of a group of men digging the grave
buhayut kak loshadi	R. drink like horses
bülöö	member
chapan	embroidered coat for men
chong-apa	grandmother
chong-ata	grandfather
chongdor	big men
Chüilyktor	people from Chüi Province
dejurnyi chal	kyrg./R. "old man on duty"; derogative for an elder engaging in political affairs
dom kultura	R. name for the former "House of Culture"
eje	older sister
ekiatbol	be careful
el	people
el menen bolyy	to be with people
eldik bala	people's son
eldik kishi	people's man
eng uluu aksakal	the oldest *aksakal* of a descent line (*uruu*)
erezhe	customary law
etnograf	R. ethnographer
geshik	bag filled with food and meat given back to a guest at a ritual
gosregistr	state register
gubernator	oblast governor
gulash	fried meat with rice
ini	younger brother
internatsionalnye	R. heterogeneous
jailoo	mountain pasture
jambash	fatty tail
janaza namaz	last death ritual

jakyn	close
jazait	to make
jeen	sister's son
jeen el bolboit	the sister's son would never be his "own" or take our side
jek jaat	former school friends, colleagues, and other male acquaintances
jeti ata	seven fathers; one's ancestors
jezde	husband of an older sister
jigitering	followers
jyzybyz jarygyrak	our faces are open
jumush	work
kaaloo tilek	wishes
kaaloobyz bir	we have the same intentions
kabyl alyy	to accept or to be accepted.
kainaga	elder brother in-law
kainini	younger brother in-law
kalpak	white felt hat worn by *aksakal*
kalyng	bride price
kamok	R. a small shop
karyny syilait	to respect elders
karysy bardyn yrysy bar	to have elderly people in the homes is equal to possess wisdom at home
kedei	poor
kelin	daughter-in-law
kengesh	council or advisers
kesme	noodle
khan	Chinese/Manchu *han*; sovereign, military ruler; see *bai*
kolkhoz	collective farm during Soviet times
konok	guest
konok koidon joosh	guests must sit like lamb
konok üidün kutu	a guest brings good fortune
korenisatsia	R. indigenization
koshumcha	money brought by the former school friends, colleagues, and other male acquaintances to a "good" or a "bad feast"
köngülübüz tüz	we understand each other
köz jumup koidu	close one's eyes
krug doverie	R. circle of trust
kuda	affines
kuda jak	people belonging to the affines
kuda ming jyldyk	affines for thousand years
küiöö bala	younger sister's husband
kul	coll. "slave"; a person without a lineage affiliation
kuran okup turganing jakshy	it is always good to honor one's ancestors
kuran okuu	to read the Koran, praying

kurultai	large political gathering
kyiyit	lit. "cloth/clothes"; gifts and/or money brought by relatives of a deceased during memorial rituals
kyz	girl
kyz aluuchu jak	wife-takers' side
kyz beruuchu jak	wife-givers' side
kyz konok	guest daughter
kyzdy kyrk üidön tyiuu	a girl can be disciplined by forty households
kyrgyzcha or kyrgyzchilik	"in a Kyrgyz way," also "Kyrgyz language"
madrasah	school
mairamingar menen	happy holidays
malai	slave
malchy	horse breeder
manap	sovereign ruler, see *bai*
marshrutka	a mini bus
moldo	arab. *mulla*
molarno	R. morally
myndai bolush kerek	this should be like this
namaz	prayer
narod	R. people
natsia	R. nation
natsionalnost	R. nationality
ob'ektivnyi	R. objective or neutral
oblast	province or district
ofitsialno	R. officially
ökül bala	representative son
ökül apa	representative mother
ökül ata	representative father
ökül kyz	representative daughter
oomiyn	amen
orgplan	R. general plan
öskön jerdi topzragi altin	birthplace's soil is golden
öz bala kyiot	the native son cares about his own community
öz jak	own side
öz kolyna algan	take the elders into one's hands
öz kökürök küchügübüz	own foal
öz mildetin atkaruu	to do one's duty
plemya	R. "tribe"
podderjivat	R. to support
politicheski zakaz	R. political request
priezjie	R. newcomers
prikaz	R. order or request

raiono	he district-level administration
razporojenie	R. direction
reshenie	R. decision
rod	R. "clan"
rodovoi obshina	patrimonial communities
saanchi	milker
sanjyra	Kyrgyz genealogy
sanjyrachy	teller of genealogy
sary özön Chüi	the golden Chüi province
selsovet (selskyi konsul)	village council
sep	dowry
shakirt	teacher
shorpo	soup
siz	the polite way of addressing "you"
smejnye granitsy	R. borders are adjacent
soglasovanno	R. in coordination
som	Kyrgyz Currency
soveshanie	meeting
sovkhoz	collective farm
söök jangyrtuu	to renew bones
svoi	R. own
syilap koi	to honor
synok	R. son
taeke	mother's brother
tamada	toastmaster
tamak	food
tamak ichip koi	please eat food
tartip	order (in the disciplining sense)
tartiptüü adam	a disciplined person
tatyyktyy jigit	charismatic leader
tergeit	to give nickname
tigi düiynö	the other world
tilegibiz ak	our intentions are positive
toi	feast
tokol	a second wife or lover
topy	hat
tördö	place in a room or a yurt facing the door
törkün jak	mother's relative side
traibalizm	R. form of corruption expressed through provincial and kinship ties
tup ata	the ancestor
turmushka chyguu	to get married (for women)
tuugandar	kinsmen or relatives

uchilishe	a technical school
üi bülöö	family
üi	house
üi toi	celebration of the new house
ülöönüü	to get married (for man)
uruu	descent line; major descent line
ustukan	a bone with meat presented to guests
uruk	sublineage
univermag	R. shop
yntymak	unity
yrym	as a sign of success
yrym-zhyrym	customary law
yrysky	success or luck

Bibliography

Abashin, Sergei. 1999. "O Samooznanii narodov Srednei Asii (kak Aleksander Igorevich posporil s Johnom)." *Vostok* 4:207–220.

———. 2015. *Sovetskyi Kishlak. Mejdu Kolonialismom and modernizatsiei.* Moscow: Novoe Literaturnoe Obozrenia.

Abramzon, Saul Matveevich. 1960. *Etnicheskii sostav kirgizskogo naseleniia Severnoi Kirgizii.* Trudy Kirgizskoi arkheologo-etnograficheskoi ekspeditsii Frunze: Izd-vo AN Kirgizskoi SSR.

———. 1971. *Kirgizy i ich etnogeneticeskie i istoriko-kul'turnye svjazi.* Leningrad: Nauka.

Aitbaev, M. T. 1957. *Istoriko-kulturnye svyazi kirgizskogo i russkogo narodov: po materialam Issyk-Kulskoi oblasti Kirgizskoi SSR.* Frunze: AN Kyrgyz SSR.

Akiner, Shirin. 1997a. "Between Tradition and Modernity: The Dilemma Facing Contemporary Central Asian Women." In *Post-Soviet Women: From the Baltic to Central Asia,* edited by M. Buckley, 261–304. Cambridge: Cambridge University Press.

———. 1997b. "Melting Pot, Salad Bowl—Cauldron? Manipulation and Mobilization of Ethnic and Religious Identities in Central Asia." *Ethnic and Racial Studies* 20 (2): 362–398.

———. 1998. "Social and Political Reorganisation in Central Asia: Transition from Pre-Colonial to Post-Colonial Society." In *Post-Soviet Central Asia,* edited by Touraj Atabaki and John O'Kane, 1–34. London: Tauris Academic Press.

"ALA-LC Romanization Tables." 2011. *Library of Congress and the American Library Association.* Retrieved January 28, 2011, from http://www.loc.gov/catdir/cpso /romanization/russian.pdf.

Anderson, Benedict. 1999. *Imagined Communities: Reflections on the Origin and Spread of Nationalism.* London: Verso.

Anderson, John. 1999. *Kyrgyzstan: Central Asia's Island of Democracy?* Amsterdam: Harwood Academic Publication.

Argynbaev, Khadel A. 1984. "The Kinship System and Customs Connected with the Ban on Pronouncing the Personal Names of Elder Relatives among the Kazakh." In *Kinship and Marriage in the Soviet Union: Field Studies,* edited by T. Dragadze, 40–59. London: Routledge and Kegan Paul.

Arutjunov, Sergei.1974. "Modernization in Non-European Urbicultures." In Soviet Ethnology and Anthropology Today, edited by Yu. Bromley, 195–200. The Hague: Mouton.

Bacon, Elizabeth. 1966. *Central Asians under Russian Rule: A Study in Culture Change.* Ithaca, NY: Cornell University Press.

Bailey, Frederick George. 1969. *Stratagems and Spoils: A Social Anthropology of Politics.* Oxford: Westview.

———. 2001. *Treasons, Stratagems, and Spoils: How Leaders Make Practical Use of Values and Beliefs.* Boulder, CO: Westview.

Barth, Fredrik. 1967. "On the Study of Social Change." *American Anthropologist* 69:661–669.

———. 1998. "Pathan Identity and Its Maintenance." In *Ethnic Groups and Boundaries*, edited by Fredrik Barth, 117–134. Long Grove, IL: Waveland.

Baştuğ, Sharon. 1998. "The Segmentary Lineage System. A Reappraisal." In *Changing Nomads in a Changing World*, edited by Anatoly M. Khazanov and Joseph Ginat, 94–123. Brighton: Sussex Academic Press.

Benda-Beckmann, Keebet von, and Franz von Benda-Beckmann. 2007. "Where Structures Merge: State and Off-State Involvement in Rural Social Security on Ambon, Indonesia." In *Social Security between Past and Future: Ambonese Networks of Care and Support*, edited by Keebet von Benda-Beckmann and Franz von Benda-Beckmann, 205–234. Münster: LIT.

Beyer, Judith. 2010. "Authority as Accomplishment. Intergenerational Dynamics in Talas, Northern Kyrgyzstan." In *Eurasian Perspectives: In Search of Alternatives*, edited by Anita Sengupta and Suchandana Chatterjee, 78–92. New Delhi: Shipra.

———. 2016. *The Force of Custom: Law and the Ordering of Everyday Life in Kyrgyzstan.* Pittsburgh: University of Pittsburgh Press.

Bilinski, Yaroslav. 1967. "The Rulers and Ruled." *Problems of Communism* 16 (5): 22–24.

Bloch, Maurice and Dan Sperber. 2006. "Kinship and Evolved Psychological Dispositions: The Mother's Brother Controversy Reconsidered." In *Technology, Literacy and the Evolution of Society*, edited by D. Olson and M. Cole, 115–140. Mahwah, NJ: Lawrence Erlbaum.

Blok, Anton.1974. *The Mafia of a Sicilian Village, 1860–1960. A Study of Violent Peasant Entrepreneurs.* Prospect Heights, IL: Waveland.

Bohannan, Laura. 1952. "A Genealogical Charter." *Africa: Journal of the International African Institute* 22 (4): 301–315.

Boissevain, Jeremy. 1966. "Patronage in Sicily." *Man* 1 (1): 18–33.

Borbieva, Noor. 2008. "Development in the Kyrgyz Republic: Exchange, Communal Networks, and the Foreign Presence." PhD dissertation, Harvard University.

———. 2012. "Kidnapping Women: Function, Symbol, and Power in Central Asian Marriage." *Anthropological Quarterly* 85 (1): 141–169.

Bromley, Julian.1983. *Očerki teorii* ètnosa. Moskva: Nauka.

Broz, Ludek. 2005. "'I Told You, He Is Not My Brother, He Is My Brother . . .' On Altai Kin Terminology and Its Interpretations." Presented at the Forty-Eighth Permanent International Altaistic Conference, July 10–15, Moscow.

Campbell, John Kennedy. 1974. *Honour, Family and Patronage. A Study of Institutions and Moral Values in a Greek Mountain Community.* Oxford: Oxford University Press.

Cash, Jennifer. 2012. *Villages on Stage: Folklore and Nationalism in the Republic of Moldova.* Münster: LIT.

Caton, Steven C. 1987. "Power, Persuasion, and Language: A Critique of the Segmentary Model in the Middle East." *International Journal of Middle East Studies* 19:77–101.

Chatwin, Mary Allen. 2001. "Tamadoba: Drinking Social Cohesion at the Georgian Table." In *Drinking: Anthropological Approaches*, edited by I. Garine and V. Garine, 181–190. Oxford: Berghahn Books.

Chotaeva, Cholpon. 2005. *Etnokulturlnye Faktory v Istorii Gosudarstvennogo Stroitelstva Kyrgyzstana (Ethnocultural Factors in the History of State Building of Kyrgyzstan).* Bishkek: International University of Kyrgyzstan.

Chuloshnikov, Alexander. 1924. *Ocherki po isstorii kazak-kirgizskogo naroda v svyazi s obshimi istoricheskimi sudbami drugih turkskih plemen.* Frunze: Kirgizkoe Izdatelstvo.

Clapham, Christopher.1982. *Private Patronage and Public Power. Political Clientelism in the Modern State.* London: Frances Pinter.

Cohen, Abner. 1974. *Two-Dimensional Man: An Essay on the Anthropology of Power and Symbolism in Complex Society.* London: Routledge and Kegan Paul.

Collins, Kathleen. 2002. "Clan, Pacts, and Politics in Central Asia." *Journal of Democracy* 13 (3): 137–152.

———. 2004. "The Logic of Clan Politics: Evidence from the Central Asian Trajectories." *World Politics* 56 (2): 224–261.

Coles, Kimberley A. 2004. "Election Day: The Construction of Democracy through Technique." *Cultural Anthropology* 19 (4): 551–580.

Comaroff, John L., and Jean Comaroff. 1997. "Postcolonial Politics and Discourses of Democracy in Southern Africa: An Anthropological Reflection on African Political Modernities." *Journal of Anthropological Research* 53 (2): 123–146.

Cook, Karen, and Robin Cooper. 2003. "Experimental Studies of Cooperation, Trust and Social Exchange." In *Trust and Reciprocity,* edited by E. A. W. Ostrom, 209–244. New York: Sage.

Di Cosmo, Nicola. 1993. *Reports from the Northwest: A Selection of Manchu Memorials from Kashgar (1806–1807).* Bloomington: Indiana University Research Institute for Inner Asian Studies.

Diemberger, Hildegard. 2006. "Faith, Nation and Gender Politics: Three Women Rulers in the Mongolian-Tibetan Borderlands." In *States of Mind: Power, Place and the Subject in Inner Asia,* edited by David Sneath, 151–165. Bellingham: Western Washington University, Center of East Asian Studies.

Djamgerchinov, B.D. 1946. *Iz geneologii Kirgizov.* Frunze: Kirigizskiy Filial Akademii Nauk SSSR.

Donahoe, Brian. 2004. "A Line in the Sayans: History and Divergent Perception of Property among the Tozhu and Tofa of South Siberia." PhD dissertation, Indiana University.

Dragadze, Tamara. 1984. *Kinship and Marriage in the Soviet Union: Field Studies.* London: Routledge and Kegan Paul.

———. 2001. *Rural Families in Soviet Georgia: A Case Study in Ratcha Province.* London: Routledge.

Dresch, Paul. 1986. "The Significance of the Course Events Take in Segmentary Systems." *American Ethnologist* 13 (2): 309–324.

Dubuisson, Eva-Marie. 2017. *Living Language in Kazakhstan: The Dialogic Emergence of an Ancestral Worldview.* Pittsburgh: Pittsburgh University Press.

Dudwick, Nora, and Kathleen R. Kuehnast. 2002. "Better a Hundred Friends Than a Hundred Rubles? Social Networks in Transition." *World Bank Economists' Forum: The Kyrgyz Republic* 2:51–88.

Dzhunushaliev, Dzhenish, and Vladimir Ploskikh. 2000. "Tribalism and Nation Build-
ing in Kyrgyzstan." *Central Asia and the Caucasus* 3:115–123.
Eisenstadt, Shmuel Noah, and Luis Roniger. 1980. "Patron-Client Relations as a Model of
Structuring Social Change." *Comparative Studies in Society and History* 22 (1): 43–78.
———. 1984. *Patrons, Clients and Friends. Interpersonal Relations and the Structure of
Trust in Society.* Cambridge: Cambridge University Press.
Ensminger, Jean. 1992. *Making a Market. The Institutional Transformation in an African
Society.* New York: Cambridge University Press.
———. 2001. "Reputations, Trust, and the Principal Agent Problem." In *Trust in Society,*
edited by K. S. Cook, 185–201. New York: Sage.
Evans-Pritchard, Edward Evan. 1940. *The Nuer: A Description of the Modes of Livelihood
and Political Institutions of a Nilotic People.* Oxford: Oxford University Press.
Finke, Peter. 2002. "Wandel sozialer Strukturen im ländlichen Mittelasien." In *Zentral-
asien und Islam/Central Asia and Islam,* edited by Andrea Strasser, Siegfried Haas,
Gerhard Mangott, and Valeria Heuberger, 137–149. Hamburg: Deutsches Orient-
Institut.
———. 2004. *Nomaden im Transformationsprozess: Kasachen in der post-sozialistischen
Mongolei.* Münster: LIT.
———. 2014. *Variations on Uzbek Identity: Concepts, Constraints and Local Configura-
tions.* Oxford: Berghahn Books.
Finke, Peter, and Meltem Sancak. 2012. "To Be an Uzbek or Not to Be a Tajik: Ethnicity
and Locality in the Bukhara Oasis." *Zeitschrift für Ethnologie* 137:47–70.
Foster, George M. 1961. "The Dyadic Contract: A Model for the Social Structure of a
Mexican Peasant Village." *American Anthropologist* 63 (6): 1173–1192.
———. 1963. "The Dyadic Contract in Tzintzuntzan, II: Patron-Client Relationship."
American Anthropologist 65 (6): 1280–1294.
Geiss, Paul Georg. 2004. *Pre-Tsarist and Tsarist Central Asia: Communal Commitment
and Political Order in Change.* Abingdon: Routledge
Gellner, Ernest. 1977. "Patrons and Clients." in *Patrons and Clients in Mediterranean
Societies,* edited by E. Gellner and J. Waterbury, 1–7. London: Duckworth.
Gellner, Ernest, and John Waterbury. 1977. *Patrons and Clients in Mediterranean Societ-
ies.* London: Duckworth.
Giovarelli, R. 1998. *Land Reform and Farm Reorganization in the Kyrgyz Republic.* RDI
Reports on Foreign Aid and Development (No. 96).
Gleason, Gregory. 1991. "Fealty and Loyalty: Informal Authority Structures in Soviet
Asia." *Soviet Studies* 43 (4): 613–628.
Goffman, Erving. 1959. *The Presentation of Self in Everyday Life.* New York: Anchor
Books.
Goldstein, Darra. 1999. *The Georgian Feast: The Vibrant Culture and Savory Food of the
Republic of Georgia.* Berkeley: University of California Press.
Gouldner, Alvin. 1977. "The Norm of Reciprocity: A Preliminary Statement." In *Friends,
Followers, and Factions: A Reader in Political Clientelism,* edited by J. C. S. Stef-
fen, W. Schmidt, Carle Lande, and Laura Guasti, 28–42. Berkeley: University of
California Press.
Grodekov, Nikolai. 1889. *Kirgizy i Karakirgizy Syr-Dariinskoi Oblasti. (Tom pervyi.
Yuridicheskii byt.)* Tashkent: S. I. Lakhtin.

Gudeman, Stephen. 1975. "Spiritual Relationships and Selecting a Godparent." *Man* 10 (2): 221–237.

Gullette, David. 2006. "Kinship, State, and 'Tribalism': The Genealogical Construction of the Kyrgyz Republic." PhD dissertation, Cambridge University.

———. 2008. "A State of Passion: The Use of Ethnogenesis in Kyrgyzstan." *Inner Asia* 10 (2): 261–279.

———. 2010. *The Genealogical Construction of the Kyrgyz Republic: Kinship, State, and "Tribalism."* Kent: Global Oriental.

Gupta, Akhil. 1995. "Blurred Boundaries: The Discourse of Corruption, the Culture of Politics, and the Imagined State." *American Ethnologist* 22 (2): 375–402.

Handrahan, L. 2004. "Hunting for Women: Bride-Kidnapping in Kyrgyzstan." *International Feminist Journal of Politics* 6 (2): 207–233.

Hann, Chris, Caroline Humphrey, and Katherine Verdery. 2002. "Introduction: Postsocialism as a Topic of Anthropological Investigation." In *Postsocialism. Ideals, Ideologies, and Practices in Eurasia*, edited by Chris Hann, 1–29. London: Routledge.

Hardenberg, Roland. 2009. "Reconsidering 'Tribe,' 'Clan' and 'Relatedness': A Comparison of Social Categorisation in Central and South Asia." *Scrutiny: A Journal of International and Pakistan Studies* 1 (1): 37–62.

———. 2010. "The Efficacy of Funeral Rituals in Kyrgyzstan." *Journal of Ritual Studies* 24 (1): 29–43.

Herzfeld, Michael. 1985. *The Poetics of Manhood: Contest and Identity in a Cretan Mountain Village*. Princeton, NJ: Princeton University Press.

———. 1987. "'As in Your Own House': Hospitality, Ethnography, and the Stereotype of Mediterranean Society." In *Honor and Shame and the Unity of the Mediterranean*, edited by D. D. Gilmore, 75–89. Washington, DC: American Anthropological Association.

———. 1992. *The Social Production of Indifference: Exploring the Symbolic Roots of Western Bureaucracy*. Oxford: Berg.

———. 2005. *Cultural Intimacy: Social Poetics in the Nation-State*. New York: Routledge.

Hiro, Dilip. 2009. "Kyrgyzstan's Tulip Revolution Wilts." *Guardian*, July 24, 2009. Retrieved August 17, 2009, from http://www.guardian.co.uk/commentisfree/2009/jul/24/kyrgyzstan-election-tulip-democracy.

"History of Hizb-ut-Tahrir." *The Official Website of Hizb-ut-Tahrir*. Retrieved January 22, 2010, from http://www.hizb-ut-tahrir.org/EN/.

Holzlehner, Tobias. 2014. *Shadow Networks: Border Economies, Informal Markets and Organized Crime in the Russian Far East*. Berlin: LIT.

Hudson, Alfred Emmons. 1964. *Kazak Social Structure*. New Haven, CT: Human Relations Area Files.

Human Rights Watch. 2009. *World Report 2009. Kyrgyzstan: Events of 2008*. Retrieved September 17, 2012, from http://www.hrw.org/world-report/2009/Kyrgyzstan.

Humphrey, Caroline. 1979. "The Uses of Genealogy. A Historical Study of the Nomadic and Sedentarised Buryat." In *Pastoral Production and Society*, edited by Maison des Sciences de l'Homme, Paris, Equipe Ecologie et Anthropologie des Sociétés Pastorales, 235–260. Cambridge: Cambridge University Press.

———. 1998. *Marx Went Away—but Karl Stayed Behind*. Ann Arbor: University of Michigan Press.

————. 2002. *The Unmaking of Soviet Life: Everyday Economies after Socialism*. Ithaca, NY: Cornell University Press.

Huskey, Eugene. 1997a. "The Fate of Political Liberalization in Kyrgyzstan." In *Conflict, Cleavage, and Change in Central Asia and the Caucasus*, edited by K. Dawisha and B. Parrott, 242–271. Cambridge: Cambridge University Press.

————. 1997b. "Kyrgyzstan: A Case Study for Conflict Potential." *Soviet and Post-Soviet Review* 24 (3): 229–249.

————. 2008. "Foreign Policy in a Vulnerable State: Kyrgyzstan as Military Entrepot between the Great Powers." *China and Eurasia Forum Quarterly* 6 (4): 5–18.

Isakov, Baktybek, and John Schoeberlein. 2014. "Animals, Kinship and the State: Kyrgyz Chabans Rebuilding Herds and Reorienting Belonging after the Soviet Collapse." In *Ethnographies of Belonging and the Future in Kyrgyzstan*, edited by Jeanne Féaux de la Croix and Aksana Ismailbekova, 33–48. Bloomington, IN: Anthropology of East Europe Review.

Ismailbekova, Aksana. 2013a. "Circle of Trust: Functions and Mechanism of Patron-Client Relations in the Private Farm." In *Politics, Identity and Education in Central Asia*, edited by Pinar Akçali and Cennet Engin-Demir, 71–98. London: Routledge.

————. 2013b. "Coping Strategies: Public Avoidance, Migration, and Marriage in the Aftermath of the Osh Conflict, Fergana Valley." *Nationalities Papers: The Journal of Nationalism and Ethnicity* 41 (1): 109–127.

————. 2014a. "Migration and Patrilineal Descent: The Role of Women in Kyrgyzstan." *Central Asian Survey* 33 (3): 375–389.

————. 2014b. "Performing Democracy: State-Making through Patronage in Kyrgyzstan." In *Performing Politics: Ethnographies of the state in Central Asia*, edited by Reeves M, J. Rasanayagam and B. Beyer, 78–98. Bloomington: Indiana University Press.

Israilova-Khar'ekhuzen, Ch. R. 1999. *Traditsionnoe obshchestvo kyrgyzov v period russkoi kolonizatsii vo vtoroi polovine XIX—nachale XX v. i sistema ikh rodstva*. Bishkek: Ilim.

Jacquesson, Svetlana. 2010a. *Pastoréalismes: anthropologie historique des processus d'intégration chez les Kirghiz du Tian Shan*. Wiesbaden: Dr. Ludwig Reichert.

————. 2010b. "Power Play among the Kyrgyz: State versus Descent." In *Representing Power in Modern Inner Asia: Conventions, Alternatives and Oppositions. Studies on East Asia*, edited by Isabelle Charleux, 221–244. Bellingham, WA: Center for East Asian Studies.

————. 2010c. "Reforming Pastoral Land Use in Kyrgyzstan: From Clan and Custom to Self-Government and Tradition." *Central Asian Survey* 29 (1): 103–118.

Juraev, Shairbek. 2008. "Kyrgyz Democracy? The Tulip Revolution and Beyond." *Central Asian Survey* 27 (3): 253–264.

Kandiyoti, Deniz. 1996. "Modernization without the Market? The Case of the 'Soviet East.'" *Economy and Society* 25 (4): 529–542.

————. 2003. "Pathways of Farm Restructuring in Uzbekistan: Pressures and Outcomes." In *Transition, Institutions and the Rural Sector*, edited by M. Spoor, 143–162. Lexington, MA: Lexington Books.

Kaufman, Robert. 1974. "The Patron-Client Concept and Macro-Politics." *Comparative Studies I Society and History* 16 (3): 284–308.

Khamidov, Alisher. 2006a. "Kyrgyzstan: Kinship and Patronage Networks Emerge as a Potent Political Force." *A EurasiaNet Commentary*, November 20, 2006. Retrieved March 9, 2010, from http://www.eurasianet.org/departments/insight/articles /eav112106a.shtml.

———. 2006b. "Kyrgyzstan's Unfinished Revolution." *China and Eurasia Forum Quarterly* 4 (4): 39–43. Retrieved March 9, 2010, from http://www.silkroadstudies.org /new/docs/CEF/Quarterly/November_2006/Khamidov.pdf.

Khazanov, Anatoly M. 1984. *Nomads and the Outside World*. Cambridge: Cambridge University Press.

"Kirgizskyu bandu priznali vinovnoi v gromkih ubyistavh." *LentaRu*, August 24, 2010. Retrieved October 10, 2015, from http://lenta.ru/news/2010/08/24/jail/.

Kleinbach, Russell, Mehrigiul Ablezova, and Medina Aitieva. 2005. "Kidnapping for Marriage (*ala kachuu*) in a Kyrgyz Village." *Central Asian Survey* 24 (2): 191–202.

Knight, J. 1992. *Institutions and Social Conflict*. Cambridge: Cambridge University Press.

Köllner, Tobias. 2012. *Practising without Belonging? Entrepreneurship, Religion and Morality in Contemporary Russia*. Berlin: LIT.

Koroteyeva, Victoria, and Ekaterina Makarova. 1998. "Money and Social Connections in the Soviet and post-Soviet Uzbek City." *Central Asian Survey* 17 (4): 579–596.

Krader, Lawrence. 1955. "Principles and Structures in the Organization of Asiatic Steppe-Pastoralists." *Southwestern Journal of Anthropology* 11 (2): 67–92.

———. [1963] 1997. *Social Organization of the Mongol-Turkic Pastoral Nomads*. The Hague: Mouton.

Kuchumkulova, Elmira. 2007. "Kyrgyz Nomadic Customs and the Impact of Re-Islamization after Independence." PhD dissertation. Washington: University of Washington.

Kuehnast, Kathleen R. 2003. "Kyrgyz." In *Encyclopedia of Sex and Gender: Men and Women in the World's Cultures Topics and Cultures A-K*, edited by C. R. Ember and M. Ember, 592–600. New York: Springer.

Kuper, Adam. 1982. "Lineage Theory: A Critical Retrospect." *Annual Review of Anthropology* 11:71–95.

Kushner, P. P. 1929. *Gornaya Kirgizia (Sotsiologicheskaya razvedka)*. Moskva: Izdanie Kommunisticheskogo Universiteta Trudyashihsya Vostoka imeni I. V. Stalina.

———. 1952. "Ob etnographicheskom izuchenii kolkhoznogo krestyanstva." *Sovetskaya etnographia* 1:135–141.

"Kyrgyzstan: Crackdown Follows New Religion Law." *Forum 18 News Service*, May 28, 2009. Retrieved February 2, 2010, from http://www.forum18.org/Archive .php?article_id=1302.

"Kyrgyzstan: Human Rights Activists Condemn New Religion Law." *Eurasia Insights*, January 16, 2009. Retrieved January 22, 2010, from http://www.eurasianet.org /departments/insightb/articles/eav011609c.shtml.

Ledeneva, Alena. 1998. *Russia's Economy of Favours: Blat, Networking and Informal Exchange*. Cambridge: Cambridge University Press.

———. 2006. *How Russia Really Works: Informal Practices in the 1990s*. Ithaca, NY: Cornell University Press.

Lemarchand, René. 1977. "Political Clientelism and Ethnicity in Tropical Africa (Competing Solidarities in Nation Building)." In *Friends, Followers, and Factions:*

A Reader in Political Clientelism, edited by S. Steffen Schmidt, Carl Lande, and Laura Guasti, 100–122. Berkeley: University of California Press.

———. 1981. "Comparative Political Clientelism: Structure, Process and Optic." In *Political Clientelism, Patronage and Development*, edited by S. Eisenstadt and R. Lemarchand, 7–32. Beverly Hills: Sage.

Lewis, David. 2008. "The Dynamics of Regime Change: Domestic and International Factors in the Tulip Revolution." *Central Asian Survey* 27 (3): 265–277.

Light, Nathan. 2011. "Genealogy, History, Nation." *Nationalities Papers* 39 (1): 33–53.

———. 2015. "Animals in the Kyrgyz Ritual Economy. Symbolic and Moral Dimensions of Economic Embedding." In *Economy and Ritual. Studies of Postsocialist Transformations*, edited by Stephen Gudeman and Chris Hann, 52–79. Oxford: Berghahn Books.

Lindholm, Charles. 1986. "Kinship Structure and Political Authority: The Middle East and Central Asia." *Comparative Study of Society and History* 28:334–355.

Lindner, Peter, and Aleksandr M. Nikulin. 2004. "'Everything around Here Belongs to the Kolkhoz, Everything around Here Is Mine': Collectivism and Egalitarianism: A Red Thread through Russian History?" *Europe Provincial* 12:32–41.

Luong, Pauline J. 2002. *Institutional Change and Political Continuity in Post-Soviet Central Asia: Power, Perceptions, and Pacts.* Cambridge: Cambridge University Press.

Marat, Erica. 2006. "Kyrgyz Government Unable to Produce New National Ideology." *Central Asia-Caucasus Institute Analyst*, February 22, 2006. Retrieved May 17, 2010, from http://www.cacianalyst.org/?q=node/126/print.

———. 2008a. "National Ideology and State-building in Kyrgyzstan and Tajikistan." The Central Asia-Caucasus Institute & Silk Road Studies Program. *Silk Road Papers Series*. Retrieved May 17, 2010, from www.isdp.eu/images/stories/isdp-main -pdf/2008_marat_national-ideology-and-state-building.pdf.

———. 2008b. "The Tulip Revolution; Three Years After: Kyrgyzstan's Pyrrhic Victory." *Central Asia-Caucasus Analyst*, February 4, 2008. Retrieved August 17, 2009, from www.cacianalyst.org/?q=node/4833.

Mauss, Marcel. 2000. *The Gift: the Form and Reason for Exchange in Archaic Societies.* New York: W. W. Norton.

McBrien, Julie. 2008. "The Fruit of Devotion: Islam and Modernity in Kyrgyzstan." PhD dissertation, Martin Luther University Halle-Wittenberg.

McBrien, Julie, and Mathijs Pelkmans. 2008. "Turning Marx on His Head: Missionaries, 'Extremists,' and Archaic Secularists in Post-Soviet Kyrgyzstan." *Critique of Anthropology* 28 (1): 87–103.

McGlinchey, Eric. 2011. *Chaos, Violence, Dynasty: Politics and Islam in Central Asia.* Pittsburgh: University of Pittsburgh Press

Michaels, Paula A. 2007. "An Ethnohistorical Journey through Kazakh Hospitality." In *Everyday Life in Central Asia: Past and Present*, edited by J. Sahadeo and R. Zanca, 145–159. Bloomington: Indiana University Press.

Mühlfried, Florian. 2005. "Banquets, Grant-Eaters and the Red Intelligentsia in Post-Soviet Georgia." *Central Asian Studies Review* 4 (1): 16–19.

———. 2006. *Postsowjetische Feiern. Das Georgische Bankett im Wandel.* Stuttgart: Ibidem.

"National Land Fund (FPS)." *Land Reform in Kyrgyzstan*. Retrieved February 12, 2009, from http://www.gosreg.kg/index.php?option=com_content&view=article&id=89

Nikulin, Aleksandr M. 2003. "Kuban *kolkhoz* between a Holding and a Hacienda: Contradictions of Post-Soviet Rural Development." *Focaal—European Journal of Anthropology* 14:137–152.

North, D. C. 1990. *Institutions, Institutional Change and Economic Performance*. Cambridge: Cambridge University Press.

Olcott, Martha Brill. 1987. *The Kazakhs*. Stanford, CA: Hoover Institution Press.

Olivier, Bernard V. 1990. "Korenizatsiia." *Central Asian Survey* 9 (3): 77–98.

Olivier de Sardan, Jean-Pierre. 1999. "A Moral Economy of Corruption in Africa?" *Journal of Modern African Studies* 37 (1): 25–52.

"OSCE's Office for Democratic Institutions and Human Rights Report." Retrieved May 14, 2010, from http://www.osce.org/odihr/.

Paley, Julia. 2002. "Toward An Anthropology of Democracy." *Annual Review of Anthropology* 31:469–496.

Pétric, Boris-Mathieu. 2005. "Post-Soviet Kyrgyzstan or Birth of a Globalized Protectorate." *Central Asian Survey* 24 (3): 319–332.

Piattoni, Simona. 2001. "Clientelism in Historical and Comparative Perspective." In *Clientelism, Interests, and Democratic Representation: The European Experience in Historical and Comparative Perspective*, edited by S. Piattoni, 1–31. Cambridge: Cambridge University Press.

Pitt-Rivers, Julian Alfred.1968. "The Stranger, the Guest and the Hostile Host: Introduction to the Study of the Laws of Hospitality." In *Contributions to Mediterranean Sociology*, edited by J. G. Peristiany, 13–31. The Hague: Mouton.

Pogorelskyi, P., and B. Batrakov. 1930. *Ekonomika Kochevogo Aula Kirgizstana*. Moscow: Izdanie Sovnarkom K.A.S: SR.

Poliakov, S. 1992. *Everyday Islam: Religion and Tradition in Rural Central Asia*. New York: M. E. Sharpe.

Powell, John Duncan. 1977. "Peasant Society and Clientelist Politics." In *Friends, Followers, and Factions: A Reader in Political Clientelism*, edited by Steffen W. Schmidt, 147–161. Berkeley: University of California Press.

Prior, Daniel. 2000. *Patron, Party, Patrimony: Notes on the Cultural History of the Kirghiz Epic Tradition*. Bloomington: Indiana University, Research Institute for Inner Asian Studies.

———. 2006. "Heroes, Chieftains, and the Roots of Kirghiz Nationalism." *Studies in Ethnicity and Nationalism* 6 (2): 71–88.

"Pryamaya Linia Interview with Toigonbek Kalmatov." *Vechernyi Bishkek*, October 5, 2007. Retrieved October 5, 2007, from www.vb.kg/.

Pulleyblank, E. G. 1990. "The Name of the Kirghiz." *Central Asiatic Journal* 34 (1–2): 98–108.

Putnam, Robert D. 1993. *Making Democracy Work, Civic Traditions in Modern Italy*. Princeton, NJ: Princeton University Press.

Radnitz, Scott. 2005. "Networks, Localism and Mobilization in Aksy, Kyrgyzstan." *Central Asian Survey* 24 (4): 405–424.

———. 2006. "What Really Happened in Kyrgyzstan?" *Journal of Democracy* 17 (2): 132–146.

———. 2007a. "Review of Clan Politics and Regime Transition in Central Asia by Kathleen Collins." *Review of Politics* 69:497–500.

———. 2007b. "Review of Modern Clan Politics: The Power of 'Blood' in Kazakhstan and Beyond by Edward Schatz." *Nationalities Papers* 34 (4): 383–406.

———. 2010. *Weapons of the Wealthy: Predatory Regimes and Elite-led Protests in Central Asia*. Ithaca, NY: Cornell University Press.

Rasanayagam, Johan. 2002a. "The Moral Construction of the State in Uzbekistan: Its Construction within Concepts of Community and Interaction at the Local Level." PhD dissertation, University of Cambridge.

———. 2002b. "Spheres of Communal Participation: Placing the State within Local Modes of Interaction in Rural Uzbekistan." *Central Asian Survey* 21 (1): 55–70.

———. 2011. "Informal Economy, Informal State: The Case of Uzbekistan." *International Journal of Sociology and Social Policy* 31 (11–12): 681–696.

"Realnaya Politika Kyrgyzstan: sorodichi reshaut vse." *Delo*, February 4, 2010. Retrieved February 10, 2010, from http://delo.kg/index.php?option=com_content&task=view&id=666&Itemid=60.

Reeves, Madeleine. 2014. *Border Work: Spatial Lives of the State in Rural Central Asia*. Ithaca, NY: Cornell University Press.

Roniger, Luis. 1994a. "Civil Society, Patronage and Democracy." *International Journal of Comparative Sociology* 35 (3–4): 207–220.

———. 1994b. "Conclusions: The Transformation of Clientelism and Civil Society." In *Democracy, Clientelism, and Civil Society*, edited by Luis Roniger and Ayşe Güneş-Ayata, 207–215. Boulder, CO: Rienner.

Roniger, Luis, and Ayşe Güneş-Ayata. 1994. *Democracy, Clientelism, and Civil Society*. Boulder: Rienner.

Roy, Oliver. 1999. "Kolkhoz and Civil Society in the Independent States of Central Asia." In *Civil Society in Central Asia*, ed. H. Ruffin and D. Waugh, 109–121. Seattle: University of Washington Press.

———. 2000. *The New Central Asia: The Creation of Nations*. London: Tauris.

Ruget, Vanessa. 2007. "Social Rights and Citizenship in Kyrgyzstan: A Communitarian Perspective." In *Theorising Social Change in Post-Soviet Countries: Critical Approaches*, edited by B. Sanghera, 61–85. Oxford: Lang.

Schatz, Edward. 2000. "The Politics of Multiple Identities: Lineage and Ethnicity in Kazakhstan." *Europe-Asia Studies* 52 (3): 489–506.

———. 2004. *Modern Clan Politics: The Power of "Blood" in Kazakhstan and Beyond*. London: University of Washington Press.

———. 2005. "Reconceptualizing Clans: Kinship Networks and Statehood in Kazakhstan." *Nationalities Papers* 33 (2): 231–254.

Schlee, Günther. 2007. "Brothers of the Boran Once Again: On the Fading Popularity of Certain Somali Identities in Northern Kenya." *Journal of Eastern African Studies* 1 (3): 417–435.

———. 2008. *How Enemies Are Made: Towards a Theory of Ethnic and Religious Conflicts*. Oxford: Berghahn Books.

———. 2009. "Descent and Descent Ideologies. The Blue Nile Area (Sudan) and Northern Kenya Compared." In *Changing Identifications and Alliances in North-East Africa*, edited by G. Schlee and E.E. Watson, 2:117–135. Oxford: Berghahn Books.

———. 2010. "Choice and Identity." *Report Max Planck Institute for Social Anthropology 2008/2009* 1:9–28.

Schlee, Günther, and Karabo Sahado. 2003. *Rendille Proverbs in Their Social and Legal Context*. Cologne: Rüdiger Köppe.

Schmidt, Steffen W., James Scott, Carl Lande, and Laura Guasti. 1977. *Friends, Followers and Factions: A Reader in Political Clientelism*. Berkeley: University of California Press.

Schneider, David. 1984. *A Critique of the Study of Kinship*. Ann Arbor, MI: University of Michigan Press.

Scott, James C. 1972a. "The Erosion of Patron-Client Bonds and Social Change in Rural Southeast Asia." *Journal of Asian Studies* 32 (1): 5–37.

———. 1972b. "Patron-Client Politics and Political Change in Southeast Asia." *American Political Science Review* 66:91–113.

———. 1977a. "Patronage or Exploitation?" In *Patrons and Clients in Mediterranean Societies*, edited by E. Gellner and J. Waterbury, 21–40. London: Duckworth.

———1977b. Political Clientelism: A bibliographical essay. In *Friends, Followers and Factions: A Reader in Political Clientelism*, edited by Schmidt, Steffen W., James Scott, Carl Lande, and Laura Guasti, 483–505. Berkeley: University of California Press.

Selwyn, Tom. 2002. "An Anthropology of Hospitality." In *Search of Hospitality: Theoretical Perspectives and Debates*, edited by C. Lashley and A. Morrison, 18–37. Oxford: Butterworth-Heinemann.

Shahrani, Nazif. 1979. *The Kirghiz and Wakhi of Afghanistan: Adaptation to Closed Frontiers*. Seattle: University of Washington Press.

———. 1986. "The Kirghiz Khans: Styles and Substance of Traditional Local Leadership in Central Asia." *Central Asian Survey* 5 (3–4): 255–271.

Silverman, Sydells F. 1977. 'Patronage as Myth in Patrons and Clients in Mediterranean Societies,' in E. Gellner and J. Waterbury (eds), *Patrons and Clients in Mediterranean Societies*. London: Duckworth, 7–19.

Shryock, Andrew. 1997. *Nationalism and the Genealogical Imagination: Oral History and Textual Authority in Tribal Jordan*. Berkeley: University of California Press.

———. 2012. "Breaking Hospitality Apart: Bad Hosts, Bad Guests, and the Problem of Sovereignty." *Journal of the Royal Anthropological Institute* 18 (1): 20–33.

Sjoberg, Frederik. 2011. *Competitive Elections in Authoritarian States*. Uppsala: Uppsala University.

Smith, Daniel Jordan. 2001. "Kinship and Corruption Contemporary Nigeria." *Ethnos* 66 (3): 344–364.

———. 2008. *A Culture of Corruption: Everyday Deception and Popular Discontent in Nigeria*. Princeton, NJ: Princeton University Press.

Sneath, David. 2007. *The Headless State: Aristocratic Orders, Kinship Society and Misrepresentations of Nomadic Inner Asia*. New York: Columbia University Press.

Snesarev, G. P. 1974. "On Some Causes of the Persistence of Religio-Customary Survivals among the Khorezm Uzbeks." In *Introduction to Soviet Ethnography*, edited by S.P. Dunn and E. Dunn. Berkeley: Highgate Road Social Science Research Station.

Spencer, Jonathan. 2007. *Anthropology, Politics, and the State: Democracy and Violence in South Asia*. Cambridge: Cambridge University Press.

Tarkowski, Jacek. 1981. "Poland: Patrons and Clients in a Planned Economy." In *Political Clientelism, Patronage and Development*, edited by S. Eisenstadt and R. Lemarchand, 173–188. Beverly Hills: Sage.

———. 1983. "Patronage in a Centralized, Socialist System: The Case of Poland." *International Political Science Review/Revue internationale de science politique* 14(4): 495–518.

The Archival Book of the Village Bulak—"The History of Kolkhoz 'Trud.'" 1937. Yssyk-Ata Rayon, Chüi Oblast, Kyrgyzstan: Bulak Main Library.

Tishkov, Valery A. 1997. *Ethnicity, Nationalism and Conflict in and after the Soviet Union: The Mind Aflame.* London: Sage.

Tolmacheva, Marina. 2005. "Writing Kyrgyz History: Historiography in the Year of Kyrgyz Statehood." *Newsletter of the Danish Society for Central Asia* 1 (2): 22–28.

Trevisani, Tommaso. 2007. "After the Kolkhoz: Rural Elites in Competition." *Central Asian Survey* 26 (1): 85–104.

"UCLA Language Material Projects (Kyrgyz Language Section)." 2004. Retrieved January 28, 2011, from http://www.lmp.ucla.edu/profile.aspx?langid=62&menu=004.

UN High Commissioner for Refugees (UNHCR). 2012. *Freedom in the World 2012: Kyrgyzstan.* Retrieved September 17, 2012, from http://www.unhcr.org/refworld/topic, 4565c22538,4565c25f455,4ff542d928,0,,,.html. Valikhanov, Chokan Ch. [1861] 1961a. "O sostoianii Altyshara ili shesti vostochnykh gorodov Kitaiskoi provintsii Nan-lu (Maloi Bukharii) v 1858-9 godakh." In *Sobranie Sochineni v pyati tomah*, edited by A. Margulan, 81–89. Alma-Ata: Izdatelstvo Akademii Nauk Kazakhskoi SSR.

———. 1961b. "Zapiski o kirgizah." In *Sobranie Sochineni v pyati tomah*, edited by A. Margulan, 41–44. Alma-Ata: Izdatelstvo Akademii Nauk Kazakhskoi SSR.

———. 1985. *Sobranie Sochineni v pyati tomah.* Glavnaya Redaktsia Kazakskoi Sovetskoi Entsiklopedii: Tom 5 Alma-Ata: Izdatelstvo Akademii Nauk Kazakhskoi SSR

Van der Heide, Nienke. 2008. "Spirited Performance: The Manas Epic and Society in Kyrgyzstan." PhD dissertation, University of Amsterdam.

Verdery, Katherine. 1996. *What Was Socialism and What Comes Next?* Princeton, NJ: Princeton University Press.

———. 2003. *The Vanishing Hectare: Property and Value in Postsocialist Transylvania.* Ithaca, NY: Cornell University Press.

Village Census. 2000. *Report on Orlovka Village Statistics.* Yssyk-Ata Rayon, Chüi Oblast, Kyrgyzstan: Orlovka Main Library.

Village Census. 2005. *Report on Bulak Village Statistics.* Yssyk-Ata Rayon, Chüi Oblast, Kyrgyzstan: Bulak Main Library.

Vinnikov, Y. R. 1956. "Rodo-plemennoi sostav i rasselenie kirgizov na territorii yuzhnoi kirgizii." In *Trudy kirgizskoi arkheologo-etnograficheskoi ekspeditsii*, edited by G. F. Debets, 136–181. Moscow: Izdatel'stvo akademii nauk SSSR.

Walker, Barbara B. 2002. "*Kruzhok* Culture and the Meaning of Patronage in the Early Soviet Literary World." *Contemporary European History* 2 (1): 107–123.

Weingrod, Alex.1968. "Patrons, Patronage and Political Parties." *Comparative Studies in Society and History* 10 (4): 377–400.

Werner, Cynthia Ann. 1997. "Household Networks, Ritual Exchange and Economic Change in Rural Kazakhstan." PhD dissertation, Indiana University.

———. 2002. "Gifts, Bribes, and Development in Post-Soviet Kazakhstan." In *Economic Development: An Anthropological Approach*, edited by J. Cohen and N. Dannhaeuser, 183–208. Walnut Creek, CA: AltaMira.

———. 2004. "Women, Marriage, and the Nation-State: The Rise of Non-Consensual Bride Kidnapping in Post-Soviet Kazakhstan." In *Transformations of Central Asian States: From Soviet Rule to Independence*, edited by Pauline Jones Luong, 59–89. Ithaca, NY: Cornell University Press.

Willerton, John P. 1992. *Patronage and Politics in USSR*. Cambridge: Cambridge University Press.

Wolf, Eric R. 1966. "Kinship, Friendship, and Patron-Client Relations in Complex Societies." In *The Social Anthropology of Complex Societies*, edited by M. P. Banton, 1–22. London: Tavistock.

Yoshida, Setsuko. 2005. "Ethnographic study of privatization in a Kyrgyz village: Patrilineal kin and independent farmers." *Inner Asia* 7 (2): 215–247.

Zanca, Russell. 2000. *Kolkhozes into Shirkats: A Local Label for Managed Pastoralism in Uzbekistan*. Washington, DC: National Council for Eurasian and East European Research.

———. 2007. "Fat and All That: Good Eating the Uzbek Way." In *Everyday Life in Central Asia: Past and Present*, edited by J. Sahadeo and R. Zanca, 178–198. Bloomington: Indiana University Press.

Index

Abashin, Sergei, 30, 31
Abramzon, Saul Matveevich, 13, 24, 26, 30, 47, 66, 79
adaptability of patronage, 10–11, 184
Adyl (village historian), 54–55, 78
affective ties, 87, 103–104
affinal relations, 19, 21, 25, 46, 70, 76, 78; marriage and, 82–87
Afghanistan, 23, 26, 35, 116; Kyrgyz pastoralists, 26
age distinctions, 70
agnatic kin groups, 19, 26, 33, 70, 83, 113; kinship terminology, 46, 67, 69, 70
Ainura (client), 138–139, 141, 143, 153
Aitmatov, Chingiz, 41n4
aiyl administrative units, 30
Akayev, Askar, 37, 38, 39, 41n4, 142
Ak Jol lineage, 1, 40, 45, 46, 51, 55–59, 62, 166–167; obligations, 81; Orlovka workers, 93
Ak-Jol Party, 1, 134, 136, 139, 141–142, 166–167
aksakal court of elders (*aksakal sotu*), 52–53, 145
Alamedyn rayon, 59, 60
alcoholism, 115
Altai terminology, 70
alys (distant kinsmen), 46, 57, 63, 65, 83
Anar (mullah), 114–124, 127, 130, 132
ancestors, 13, 1–25, 37, 46–59, 70, 80, 81, 144, 146, 157, 173, 177–178
Anderson, Benedict, 163
animal sacrifices, 80
apa (mother, wives of the elder, and younger brothers of the father), 68–69, 71, 72, 74
ata (father), 2, 21n2, 67–68, 70–75
atalash ini (younger brother), 5, 59, 66n10

bai (rich), 23, 26, 44, 55, 59, 162
baike (elder brother), 2, 13, 63, 70–72, 74, 86, 87, 191
Baikonok lineage. *See* Shaibek (Baikonok) lineage
Bailey, F. G., 12, 15–16
Baiymbet (Rahim's great grandfather), 55–57, 62, 64
Bakiyev, Kurmanbek, 38, 39, 134, 182, 184

Balta (ancestor), 47, 50, 53, 56
bargaining power, 6, 17–18
Batrakov, B., 25
Bedouins, 53, 161
bek or *baatyr* (hero), 26, 28
belongingness, 37, 178
bey (leaders), 31
Beyer, Judith, 52–53, 66n9
"beyond the salary" (*ailyktan syrtkary*), 97–98
"big men" (*chongdor*), vii, 4, 11, 26, 58, 59, 158, 192
bii (judge), 24, 26–28
biological closeness, 13, 65, 78, 80
birthplace, importance of, 146, 194
Bishkek (city), 43, 181–185
"black bones" (*kara söök*), 27
blat "to be someone's man," 32, 21n4, 32, 41n3, 192
blessings, 68, 157, 164, 168, 171, 174–176, 191
Boissevain, Jeremy, 103
brothers: elder brother (*baike*), 2, 5, 19, 36, 45, 51, 52, 54, 57, 60, 63, 65; mother's brother (*taeke*), 71, 72, 75, 77–78; obligations; of, 65; "we are all brothers," 36; wife's elder brother (*kainaga*), 73, 75, 75–77; younger brother (*atalash ini*), 5, 59, 66n10
Buchuk (ancestor), 49–51, 53, 63, 64
bugu lineage, 24, 38, 47–48
Bulak (village), 1–3, 19, 42–44, 43, 49, 51–60, 63; Ak Jol lineage, 55–58; election of 2007 in, 135–144; five lineages; of Nurmanbet (Suu Murun), 51–53, 52; kinship in, 44–46, 46; kinship in practice, 67–69
place described through kinship terminologies, 78–80. *See also* mosque proposal
Burut (nomadic tribesmen), 28–29
Buryatia, 33
business aspirations, 1–2, 4–5, 11, 38

Campbell, John, 10
caste system, 27
Central Asia: lineage system, 9–10, 12–13; nation building, 19, 22, 36–37, 40; Russian imperial rule, 27, 29–30, 41n2
chong uruk (big lineage), 26

Chopa (villager), 60–61, *62, 94*
Chüi Province (*Chüilüktör*), 47, 51; in toasts, 161, 166, 169–174, 180n7
Chüi Valley, 5, 42–44, 47, 48, 106, 143, 174
Chuloshnikov, Alexander, 24–25
circle culture (*kruzhok*), 32
"circle of trust" (*krug doverie*), 19, 20, 89–90, 98; checks and balances, 106, 108–109; irony of, 105–110. *See also* Emgek farm (Orlovka village)
clan politics, 8–9, 12
class relations, 27, 30, 34
clientelism, 11
clients, 3, 6–10; naming of ancestors, 59–60; obligations of, 27–28. *See also* patron-client relationships
close (*jakyn*) kinship, 54, 60, 65, 79–80, 150, 156, 179, 182
Coles, Kimberley A., 139
collective farms (*kolkhoz*), 10, 19, 30–31; decollectivization, 89–92, 95–96, 98–100; Nurmanbet descent groups, 50–51; organizational continuity in post-Soviet era, 110–111; post-Soviet reorganization, 34–35. *See also* Emgek farm
collectivization, 26, 30–31, 60, 79, 89–90
color terms, 25–26
Comaroff, Jean, 135, 152
Comaroff, John L., 135, 152
Communist Party, 7, 10, 22, 31, 32, 38, 40, 166
compadrazgo relation, 84
constitutional referendum, 134
corporate groups, 12–13, 24
corruption, 11, 16, 20; blurred boundaries, 131–132, 148; elections and, 138–139; laws and, 128–130; local perspective, 152–153; as mode of political action, 147; native sons and, 58–60, 147–149; native sons and state officials, 188; privatization period, 35
cousins, 9, 19, 45, 57, 63, 71–72, 82
co-wives (*tokol*), 13
criminal networks, 11, 182–184
cross-cousin terms (*taike* or *taieje*), 71–72
customary law, 29

"daughter of the village," 61
decollectivization, 89–90, 95–96, 98–100
Delo (newspaper), 38–39
democracy, 4–5, 10, 112; critique of Western idea, 186–187; local idioms of, 147–149; localized,

20, 135, 152–153; performative and rhetorical aspects, 19–20; relevance of patronage to, 7–8; show of hands voting, 121, 124–126
democratization, 6–8, 15, 36, 181, 184
development studies, 6
Di Cosmo, Nicola, 28–29
distant kinsmen (*alys tuugan*), 46, 57, 63, 65, 83
Djamgerchinov (historian), 24–25
Dolon (ancestor), 23, *47–48*
donations (*yntymak*), 81, 123, 145
dowries, 27, 28, 76, 104
Dresch, Paul, 12
dual allegiance, 32
Dulas (ancestor), 27
Dzhunushaliev, Dzhenish, 34

economics, 7, 16–18, 23, 28, 44; loans, 28, 38, 145. *See also* Emgek farm (Orlovka village)
Eid al-Adha (*Kurban ait*), 80
elders (*aksakal*), 27, 52–53, 57–58, 66n9, 67, 69, 75, 80, 81–84, 108, 119, 124, 131, 135–137, 139–140, 144–145, 149–150, 157, 159, 161, 169–171, 174, 177, 188 ; aksakal court (*aksakal sotu*), 52–53, 66n9, 145
election of 2005, 39, 142
elections, 5, 20, 134–153; facilitated by patronage, 186–187; pre-Soviet period, 27
elections of 2007, 1–2, 5, 11, 18, 20, 27, 39, 86, 91, 97, 127, 132–133, 134–154; allocation of unused ballots, 139, 141; in Bulak village, 135–144; commission members, 136–137; democracy, education about, 139–140; independent observers, 136, 141–142, 147; international organizations and, 136, 142, 147; kinship and, 137–139; Parliamentary Election Day (December 16, 2007), x–xi, 136; party-list voting procedure, 134; Rahim's pre-election contributions, 144–147
Emgek farm (Orlovka village), 89–111, *94–95*; individual benefits of cooperative action, 93–97; internal dynamics, 101–103; old collective farmworkers and, 91–93; Rahim's death and, 182–183; salary and pay of private farmworkers, 97–101; shared community labor (*ashar*), 108; specialist workers, 96, 102. *See also* "circle of trust" (*krug doverie*)
emic terms, 6, 8, 46, 158, 179n3
Ensminger, Jean, 17
ethnic identity, 36, 123; hospitality and tradition, 157, 161

ethnicity, privileging of, 36–37
ethnography, 8–9
Evans-Pritchard, E. E., 12, 25, 50, 177
exchange, 6, 11, 17, 33, 41, 44–45, 67, 81, 88–89, 99, 102–105, 109–111n5, 123, 145, 147–148, 150, 152–153, 155–157, 163–164, 176, 179, 189
exclusion, 51, 130–132

families, 44, 57, 59, 84, 86, 98–99, 102–103, 138, 182, ideals of, 67–69, 81, 87–88. *See also* kinship terminology
father (*ata*), 2, 21n2, 67–68, 70–75
father, representative (*ökül ata*), 2, 5, 21n1, 2, 75, 84–86
female members of lineages, 54
festivities, public, 20, 36–37, 41, 59, 81; elections and, 144, 155; family-related, 67–68; hospitality as exchange and acceptance, 156–158; local, ethnic, and national levels, 157, 161; loyalty cultivated, 174–177; Rahim's victory feast, 20, 153, 155–180, *160, 162*; sacred food, 162; *tamada* ("toastmaster"), 155, 156, 159, 161, 163, 164–174; toasts, 166, 169–174; traditional conventions, 156, 161, 169, 179. *See also* life cycle events
feudalism, 22, 33–34
fission, generational, 26, 50, 52
friendship, 85; overlap with patronage, 10
"front stage" and "backstage" behaviors, 113
Fund for Entrepreneurship Development and Crediting, 5
future behavior, 3, 17, 52, 57

Gellner, Ernest, 11
genealogies, 2, 3, 7, 19, 21, 24, *47;* boys' education, 53–55; identity, construction of, 11–15, 42, 45; nation building and, 36–37; official vs. oral, 54–55, 57, 65n1, 66n6; as social constructs, 13–14, 53–54, 185–186; Solto, *48. See also* Nurmanbet (Suu Murun) (ancestor)
generational differences, 12, 26, 51, 70–71, 79
geographic units of administration, 30
gift exchange, 33, 41, 81, 86, 88, 138, 145, 155–159, 161–165, 168–171
Gleason, Gregory, 32
Goffman, Erving, 113, 128
grandparents , 73, 78, 170
Grodekov, Lieutenant General, 27
Gullette, David, 8–9, 22, 36–37

Hardenberg, Roland, 8–9, 13, 80–81
hereditary distinctions, 27–28
Herzfeld, Michael, 18, 112, 127, 129, 157, 169, 177, 186
hierarchies, 10–11, 13, 20, 23, 28–30, 40, 52, 69, 73, 77, 87, 88n1, 93, 97, 134, 147, 150, 170, 178, 183, 188
Hizb-ut-Tahrir, 116, 118, 120, 133n2
Holzlehner, Tobias, 183, 184
hospitality, 7, 41, 101, 149–150, 156–158; of native sons, 161–164, 170, 179
households, gerontocratic, 22, 25, 29, 42–46, 51, 60, 65, 67, 79, 92, 110, 147
Hudson, Alfred Emmons, 25, 28
Humphrey, Caroline, 4, 14, 33, 90, 110, 128, 149, 184

ichkilik 'internal' lineage, 24, 38–39, 177
ideals of family, 67–69, 87–88
identification, 14, 88, 137, 174, 185–186; strategies of, 9, 55–58
identity, 3– 4, 11–12, 17, 36–37, 41–42, 54–55, 58, 61, 63–65, 69, 79, 117–118, 123–125, 134, 143, 146, 157, 167–168, 185; documentation of, 137, 147–148; genealogical construction of, 11–15, 26
identity politics, 155–156, 188; loyalty cultivated, 174–177
identity work, 14
imaginative constructs, 12, 17
imagined political community, 163
India, 147
indigenization (*korenizatsia*), 30, 31–32
informal economy, 33
inheritance, 42, 45, 67, 68
instrumental ties, 10, 31, 103–104, 150
intelligentsia, Russian, 32
interdependence, 17, 21n4, 23, 102, 109
International Center InterBilim, 136, 142, 147, 154n2
investment metaphor, 20
Islam/Muslims, 10, 23, 114–116, 120, 123–124, 133n1, 2
Israilova-Khar'ekhuzen, Ch. R., 23, 26, 29, 34, 88n1
Issyk-Ata rayon, 43, 49, 51, 59, 65n2, 3, 76, 171–172, 174

Jalal-Abad, 37–38
Jeenbekov, Zhusup, 183

jezde (elder husbands), *71, 72, 73, 75*, 76
Juraev, Shairbek, 8, 38, 153, 186–187

Kalmatov, Toygonbek, 113, 130
Kanybek (Rahim's friend), 1–3, 21n2, *63–64*, 181
Karachal (ancestor), 60, *62, 64*
Karachor, descendants of, 23, *47, 56*
Kara-Kyrgyz ("black Kyrgyz"), 25–26
Karasakal (son of Nurmanbet) lineage, 45, 49–53, 56, 95, 138
Kazakhs, 5, 13, 19, 23, 25–26, 28
Kazakhstan, 5, 29, 36, 106, 145, 147, 157; Rahim's businesses in, 77–78, 181–182
Kazak terminology, 70
Kengesh (client), 63, *64*
khan (leaders), 27, 31
Khazanov, Anatoly M., 12
kichi uruk (small lineage), 26
kinship, vii, 2–3, 8, 18–19; as biological closeness, 65; in Bulak village, 44–46, *46*; categories and practices, 87–88; democratization and, 6; domestic level, 22; electoral process and, 137–139; extending and localizing, 78–80; kidnapping of brides, 76, 82–83; Kyrgyz historical context, 22–41; "masses," 131–132; normative model, 16, 45, 63, 79; north and south division, 25–27, 37–38; overlap with patronage, 7, 10; patrilineal descent, 7, 13, 24, 42–43, 70–71; patronage and, 6–7, 9, 14, 181, 185–186; political level, 9, 12, 22; politics, scholarship on, 33–34; post-Soviet period, 34–35; practical aspects, 45; in practice, 67–69; pre-Soviet period, 22–25; rhetoric of, 36–37; Soviet era, 32–33; stretched, 8, 11–12, 14–15, 45–46, 48, 65, 88, 185. *See also* legitimation; lineage system
kinship terminology, 2, 6–7, 11, 67, *71, 72,* 74–75; classificatory *vs.* descriptive, 71, 78; cousins, 71–72, *72*; as idiom of respect, 72–73; "new names for the men," 45, 54, 55; social relations and, 70–71; use of, 75–78
"Klara Tsetkin" kolkhoz (Orlovka), 90
Kokand Khan, 29
kul (slaves), 26, 46, 66n5
Kulov, Felix, 39
Kuper, Adam, 12
Kyrgyz, 3, 6–7, 9, 13, 15–16, 18–21n1; in Afghanistan, 26; as ethnic group, 23; historical context of kinship and patronage, 22–41; neighbors, 25–26; nomadic, 29; outside Kyrgyzstan, 25. *See also* patrilineal descent

Kyrgyz language, 2, 6–7, *71*
Kyrgyz Province, 27
Kyrgyzstan; geographical separation, 37–38; independence, 4 ; map, *35*; Russian-speaking people in, 29–30

laws, 29, 112–114, 119, 121, 123, 125–127, 137, 154n2; corruption and, 128–132
leaders, 5, 27, 31–32, 37–39, 58–59, 108, 116, 126, 131, 143, 152, 172–173, 177, 183–184, 186; generational transition, 3–4
left wing lineage. *See sol kanat* "left wing" lineage
legitimation, 3, 9, 14, 46, 57–58, 102, 104, 112; acceptance of "illegal" actions, 127–128, 131; of election process, 143; festivities and, 164; mosque proposal, 115–116
Lewis, David, 152, 186
life cycle events, 13, 20, 23, 34, 45, 51, 54, 67, 68, 78, 86, 135, 164, 188; collective farm and, 97–98; before election, 135, 146, 156; funerals, 80–81. *See also* festivities, public
Light, Nathan, 156
lineage system, 7; across Kyrgyzstan, 46–48, *48*; Central Asian, 12–13; deviations from, 51–53; fluid relationships, 2, 42, 45, 58, 63, 80, 87–88; maximal, major, minor, and minimal, 12, 45–47, *47,* 50; maximal lineages, 12, *47,* 47–49; political parties and, 39–40; segmentary, 7, 9, 12, 44–45, 69, 177–179; seniority, 13, 20, 54–55; splits in, 50–51; territory and, 48–49, *49*; ultimogeniture (house, land, animals), 67, 68; unilateral descent, 12
loans, 28, 38, 145
"lost generation," 4
loyalty, 2, 8–9, 21, 65, 87, 89, 174–177; circles of trust, 98, 104–106, *108,* 110; elections and, 131, 135–136, 139, 141, 145, 147–148, 152–153, 155, 174, 177–178, 184, 186, 189

malchy (loan of a horse), 28
manap (*uruk* leader), 24, 26–29, 55
Manas (hero of Kyrgyzstan), 41n4, 170, 173
Manas epic (*manaschi*-Sagynbaj Orozbakov), 24, 37
Manchu Memorial from Kashgar, 28–29
manipulation, 3, 5, 7–11; of identity, 11–15, 42, 55, 58, 65, 69, 75, 110–111; of legal system, 128–130; strategies, 9, 15–16, 19–20
Maratov (farm worker), 98, 99–101
Maria (villager), 61, 63

market economy, 10, 19, 34–35, 184, 187
marriage, 15, 19; affinal distance, respect, and support, 82–87; exogamous, 67, 79, 82; kidnapping of brides, 76, 82–83; to renew kinship bonds, 85
Marxism, 30
matrilateral relationships, 70, 73, 77–178
maximal lineages, 12, 47, 47–50, 63
McBrien, Julie, 113, 117
middle class (*orto*), 44
minimal lineages, 12, 45–46, 49–50, 63, 104, 110
modernization paradigm, 6, 7, 10, 184
moral systems, 10–11, 16, 80–81
mosque proposal, 112–133; debate around influence of Islam, 123–124; Islam, emphasis on, 114–116; public order approach, 118–119; show of hands, 122, 124–128; speeches, 120–123; supporters of Rahim, 116–118
mother (*apa, apai*), 5, 9, 43, 57, 70, 77–78, 119; representative mother (*ökül apa*), 84, 138; wives of the elder, and younger brothers of the father, 68–69, 71, 72, 74
mother's brother (*taeke*), 71, 72, 75, 77–78
Muradil (client), 85–86
murders, 3–4, 181–183
"Mutakalim," 113
mythologies, 2, 12, 57; at festivities, 170, 176; Kyrgyz, 13; Nuer, 12; Nurmanbet, 49; origins of the duality of Kyrgyz *uruu*, 23–24

naming of lineages, strategic, 40, 55, 59–61
nationality categories, 30–31
nationalization, 30
National Security Service (NSS), 123
nation building rhetoric, 36–37, 152
native sons, 1–3; birthplace, importance of, 146; corruption and, 58–60, 147–149; corrupt state officials and, 188; as elected officials, 149–151; election process and, 134; father-son tie, 150, 152; as framework, 16; hospitality of, 163–164; post-Soviet period, 58–59; as protectors, 131–132, 134, 149–151, 181. See *also* Rahim (patron)
neighboring villages, 10, 19, 44, 46, 51, 76, 78–80, 115, 140, 185
neighbors, 25–26, 45, 61, 69, 79
New Institutional Economics (NIE), 16–18
"new names for the men," 45, 54, 55
Nigeria, 147
noble lineages, 19, 55, 57
normative model, 16, 45, 63, 79, 149

Nuer, 12, 177
Nur Ata Café (Tokmok), 158, 159
Nurmanbet (company), 1–2
Nurmanbet (Suu Murun) (ancestor), 1–2, 42–43, 47–48, 174, 176, 178; descendant lines, 45, 46, 49; five lineages in Bulak, 51–53, 52; genealogical chart, 50, 53; joint kolkhoz of descent groups, 50–51; segmentation of, 48–51
Nurmanbet (village). See Bulak (village)

oblasts, 30, 31, 38, 47
obligations, 2–3, 41, 65, 97, 108, 153; of "brothers," 65; of clients, 27–29, 61; of elected officials, 150; funerals, 80–81, 84; gift exchange, 138–139, 155, 157; local, ethnic, and national levels, 157
officials, 38, 58–59, 128–130, 188; as guests of feast, 158–161, 160, 163–164, 166; native sons as, 147, 149, 150, 152; subordination of, 131; toasts by, 171–174
ökül ata (representative father), 2, 5, 21n2, 84–86
Olivier, Bernard V., 31
Omaha-type kinship terminology, 67, 70
ong kanat 'right wing' lineage, 24, 39, 47
oral genealogies (*sanjyra*), 14–15, 19, 23–24, 52, 57, 65n1, 66n6; female roles in, 54, 55
Organization for Security and Cooperation in Europe, 147
Orlovka (village), 19, 43, 43, 89–111, 136, 187, 189; elections of 2007, 140–141
Oroz (client), 106–107, 137–138, 141
Osh Uzbeks, 82
Otunbayeva, Roza, 39
öz bala ("own son"), 57–58, 135, 148

Pamir Province, 26
parents, representative. See representative parents
parliamentary elections. See elections of 2007
patrilineal descent, 7, 13, 24, 42, 45, 48–49, 51, 54, 65, 150; kinship terminology, 70–71; Nurmanbet (Suu Murun), 42–43
patronage: adaptability, 10–11; continuity and transformation, 40–41; defined, 6; electoral party politics facilitated by, 184, 186–187; kinship and, 6–7, 185–186; myth of, 151–152; overlap with friendship, 10; paradoxes of, 188–189; performative and rhetorical aspects, 19–20; socially acceptable, 127–128; in Soviet era, 32–33; state structures and, 112–113; study of, 9–11; transformation of,

patronage (*continued*)
184–185. *See also* patronage networks; patron-client relationships; Rahim (patron)
patronage networks: between community and bureaucracy, 128–130; kinship terminology and, 69; post-Soviet, 38–40; rise and fall of, 183–184; variety of, 5–6
patron-client relationships, 3; analysis of descent and affinity as frames for, 63–65; balance of affective and instrumental ties, 103–104; balance of voluntarism and coercion, 104–105; cultural legitimacy, 87–88; economic, 28; Kazak, 28; kinship categories and, 76–77, 84–85; local clients and dependent clients, 101, *102,* 103–104; loyalties, 178–179; moral systems, 10–11, 16; pre-Soviet, 26–29; resource base, 103; as substitute for kinship, 6; use of kin terms, 75–78; variations of, 103–105
Pelkmans, Mathijs, 117
"people power," 39
performative and rhetorical aspects of patronage, 19–20
Pétric, Boris-Mathieu, 151, 153, 187
Piattoni, Simona, 11
Ploskikh, Vladimir, 34
poetics of democracy, 112–133. *See also* social poetics
Pogorelskyi, P., 25
political aspirations, 1–3, 15
political domain, 33, 135, 188
political parties, 1, 15, 133n2, 149, 174, 179; province of origin and, 39–40. *See also* Ak-Jol Party; Social Democratic Party (SDP)
politics, patronage, and kinship, 6–8
politics, 16, 138–139, 148–149, 152–153, 155–156, 164, 167–168; scholarship on, 33–34
poor (*kedei),* 35, 44, 59, 65, 84–85, 131, 145, 151; obligations of, 27–29, 31
post-Soviet period, 3, 19, 22, 24, 34–35, 37, 40–41n3, 43, 184, 188; kinship networks, importance of, 15, 87; native sons, 58–59; patronage networks, 38–40
Powell, John Duncan, 102, 178
pragmatic rules, 16
pre-Soviet period, 40, 57; kinship, 22–25; patron-client relationships, 26–29
privatization, 35, 38, 88, 90–92
proverbs, 2, 3, 77–78, 88n3, 148, 152, 156, 168, 174
public order, 118–119, 122–124

public property, 113–114, 132
Putnam, Robert D., 106

quasi-kin or kinlike relationships, 70

Rahim (patron), 1–6, 7–8, 31; affinal relatives, 75–76; Ak-Jol lineage, 55–59, *62,* 155; ancestors, 42–43; biography of, 3–6; "circle of trust" terminology, 105; clients, 59–63, 84; collapse of patronage empire, 181–183; community norms and, 132–133; Emgek farm ownership, 89–111; as entrepreneur, 5, 112, 123, 125–126, 128–130; kinship terminology used by, 69, 75–76; levels and scales of kinship, 42, 61; manipulative strategies, 9, 15–16, 19–20, 42, 55, 58; murder of, 3, 20, 181–182; Orlovka kolkhoz and, 89, 91–93; as parliamentarian, 149–151; parliamentary elections and, 20, 91, 134–154; patronage networks, 4–5; pre-election contributions to village, 144–147; as representative parent, 84–87; respect, models for, 69; self-interest, 125–126; speech about mosque, 120–121; stretching kin relations, 45; supporters in mosque proposal, 116–118; victory feast, 20, 153, 155–180, *160, 171, 175;* weak kin ties, 19, 43, 45, 54, 57
Rasanayagam, Johan, 148
reciprocity, 6, 33, 148, 157, 163–164, 176, 178–179, 189
religion, 23, 88, 112, 114–116, 119, 123–124, 130. *See also* mosque proposal
"renewing the bones" (*söök jangyrtuu),* 84–87
representation, 13, 16, 36, 103, 108, 147–148
representative mother (*ökül apa),* 84
representative parents (*ökül-ata-ene),* 67, *75,* 83–84
republics, 22, 30–34, 36, 38, 119, 126, 166
residence patterns, 13, 33, 45, 67, 79, 178
respect, 11, 52–54, 58, 67–69, 104, 105, 113, 126, 131, 150, 152, 156–157, 161, 164, 166, 170, 172–173, 177, 182; electoral process and, 136–137, 141, 145; kinship terminology and, 71–73, 76; marriage and, 83; relations of, 70, 80–84, 86–87
"responsible person" (*joopkerchiliktuu),* 1–3, 58, 69, 76, 80, 85, 93, 101, 107, 119
right wing lineage. *See ong kanat* "right wing" lineage
rod (corporate grouping), 24–25
Rose Revolution, 39
ru and *zhuz* (lineage-based) identities, 36

rule breaking, 18, 112, 187
Russian businessmen, 123
Russian imperial rule, 27, 29–30
Russian Orthodox Church, 123

saanchi (loan of a dairy cow), 28
Sagyndyk lineage, 51, 61, 63, *64*
slaves (*kul*), 26, 30, 46, 66n5, 99
sanjyrachi (expert in genealogy), 14, 15, 19, 23
San Sabirovich (farm worker), 100–101
Sarakatsani shepherds, 10
Sardan, Olivier de, 148
sarybagysh lineage, 38–39
Schlee, Günther, 3, 14, 61, 65, 186
Scott, James C., 11, 89, 103
security and stability, rhetoric of, 16, 87
segmentary lineage system, 7, 9, 12, 69; markers when meeting new acquaintants, 44–45; political uses of, 177–179
self-interest, 10, 16, 123, 125, 151, 185
seniority, 13, 20, 54–55
shadow networks, 183
Shahrani, Nazif, 26, 149
Shaibek (Baikonok) lineage, 51, *53*, 55, *56*, 59
show of hands, 20, 121–122, 124–128, 132
Shryock, Andrew, 14, 53, 57–58, 157, 161, 177
siblings, 57, 70–71. *See also* brothers; sisters
signifying practice, 139
Silverman, Sydells F., 152
sister's husband (*küiöö bala*), *71, 73, 73*, 75–77
sister's son (*jeen*), 70, *71, 72–73, 74*, 75, 77–78
slaves (*kul*), 26, 30, 46, 66n5, 99
Sneath, David, 34
social conventions, 169
Social Democratic Party (SDP), 1, 4, 134–136, 141–143; victory feast and, 155–156
socialism, 7, 33
Socialist Party, 141
social organization, 3, 8–13, 18–19, 28, 31, 33, 87, 175, 188
social poetics, 9, 18, 112, 127, 156, 186. *See also* poetics of democracy
solidarity, 13–14, 19–21, 31, 45, 71, 80, 87, 104–105, 112
elections and, 131, 138, 147, 151
postelection, 155, 178–179
solidarity group, 13, 80
sol kanat 'left wing' lineage, 24, 39, 47
Solto (ancestor), 24, 47–48, 59, 66n4, 5, 174, 177, 178

Soviet period, 22, 40, 45; collectivization processes, 26; kinship and patronage in, 32–33
Soviet Union, 30–34, 113, 180n5; collapse of, 4, 7, 34, 38, 40–41n3, 80, 96, 155, 185, 188
sovkhoz farms, 31
space, kinship terminologies and, 78–80, 83
Spencer, Jonathan, 135, 153
Sri Lanka, 135, 153
state structures, 17, 112–113, 129, 184
Stratagems and Spoils (Bailey), 16
"support," 2–4, 7, 10, 12, 15, 19–22, 28, 34, 37–40, 45, 57–59, 65–66, 69–70, 78–89, 92–93, 98–100
Suu Murun. *See* Nurmanbet (Suu Murun) (ancestor)
symbolic resources, 3, 4, 6, 9, 54, 58, 91, 97–98, 129, 149, 151, 157, 164, 175

Tagai (ancestor), 47
tamada ("toastmaster"), 144, 155, 156, 159, 161, 163, 164–169; as neutral, 168–169; toasts, 166, 169–174; territory, 48–49, *49*, 51; levels, 46; Russian-speaking people in Kyrgyz, 29–30
titular nationalities, 30–31
toasts (*kaaloo tilek*), 144, 159, 164, 169–174
Toguzak (ancestor), 57
Toktogul Dam, 44
Toktogul Province, 37–38
Toktonaliev, Sultan, 59
Tolbashiev lineage, 63
"transition," 3–4, 11, 34, 38, 125, 184–185
treason, 16
Treason, Stratagems, and Spoils (Bailey), 16
tribalism, 8
trust, 6, 11, 17, 19–20d, 89–90, 104–111, 124, 126, 148, 167, 189. *See also* "circle of trust" (*krug doverie*)
tsarist administration (1876–1917), 25–26
Tuigunaly (official), 167, 170–173, 176–177, 180n6
Tulip Revolution, 39
Turdu (client), 59–60
Turkestan, 29

ultimogeniture (house, land, animals), 67, 68
uncertainty, 6, 17, 97–99, 102–103, 110, 181–182
uruk (sublineage), 8–9, 23, 25, 31, 45–46, 63, 81; *chong uruk* (big lineage), 26; *kichi uruk* (small lineage), 26; *uruu* (lineage), 9, 13, 23, 25, 26, 45–46, 81

Uzbek, 27, 82

Uzbekistan, 23, 29, 33, 148, 157, 111n7, 133n2

Valikhanov, Chokan, 23–24, 27–28

Verdery, Katherine, 32, 33, 91, 110

village headman (*aiyl ökmöt*), 114, 119–122, 132, 133n5, 138, 154n2

villagers, 31, 34–35, 42, 44, 54, 58–61, 69, 76, 79–80, 88–93, 98, 107–108, 113–116, 119, 122, 124–125, 130–133, 134–139, 143–146, 148–153, 161, 167, 173, 181–182, 187–189

Vinnikov, Y. R., 24

voting: show of hands, 122, 124–128, 132. *See also* elections of 2007

Wakhi pastoralists, 26

Walker, Barbara B., 32

"we are all brothers," 36

Werner, Cynthia, 70, 83, 147, 157

"white bones" (*ak söök*), 27, 57

wife's elder brother (*kainaga*), 73, 75, 75–77

wife taking and wife giving, 72–73, 76–77, 79

Wolf, Eric, 10

Yemenite, 12

yurt (*boz üi*), 26, 81, 135, 145, 159

Zikirbaev, Jumabek, 182, 183

AKSANA ISMAILBEKOVA is lead researcher for Kyrgyzstan in the project "Informal Governance and Corruption—Transcending the Principal Agent and Collective Action Paradigms," which is funded by the British Academy (BA)—DFID Anti-Corruption Evidence Programme (ACE) and led by the Basel Institute on Governance (2016–2017). She conducted her doctoral research at the Max Planck Institute for Social Anthropology in Halle/Saale, Germany (2006–2012) and was research fellow at the Zentrum Moderner Orient (ZMO) (Center for the Modern Orient) in Berlin (2011–2015). At ZMO Ismailbekova was a member of the competence network "Crossroads Asia."

CPSIA information can be obtained
at www.ICGtesting.com
Printed in the USA
LVOW13s1349170618
580993LV00014B/87/P